The
South
Atlantic
Quarterly

Spring 1998
Volume 97
Number 2

The *South Atlantic Quarterly* (ISSN 0038-2876) is published quarterly, at $92.00 for libraries and institutions and $30.00 for individuals, by Duke University Press, 905 W. Main St., 18-B, Durham, NC 27701. Periodicals postage paid at Durham, NC. POSTMASTER: Send address changes to *South Atlantic Quarterly*, Box 90660, Duke University, Durham, NC 27708-0660.

Library exchanges and orders for them should be sent to Duke University Library, Gift and Exchange Department, Durham, NC 27708.

The *South Atlantic Quarterly* is indexed in *Abstracts of English Studies, Academic Abstracts, Academic Index, America: History and Life, American Bibliography of Slavic & East European Studies, American Humanities Index, Arts & Humanities Citation Index, Book Review Index, CERDIC, Children's Book Review Index (1965–), Current Contents, Historical Abstracts, Humanities Index, Index to Book Reviews in the Humanities, LCR, Middle East: Abstract & Index, MLA Bibliography, PAIS,* and *Social Science Source*. This journal is a member of the Council of Editors of Learned Journals.

ISSN 0038-2876

ISBN for this issue: 0-8223-6460-3

Psycho-Marxism: Marxism and Psychoanalysis Late in the Twentieth Century

SPECIAL ISSUE EDITOR: ROBERT MIKLITSCH

The South Atlantic Quarterly
Spring 1998
Volume 97
Number 2

Robert Miklitsch

Introduction

Only since Freud have we begun to suspect what listening, and hence what speaking (and keeping silent), *means* (*veut dire*); that this "*meaning*" (*vouloir dire*) of speaking and listening reveals beneath the innocence of speech and hearing the culpable depth of a second, *quite different* discourse, the discourse of the unconscious. . . . Only since Marx have we had to begin to suspect what, in theory at least, *reading* and hence writing *means* (*veut dire*).
—Louis Althusser, *Reading "Capital,"* 1968

It is not terribly difficult to say what is meant by the Real in Lacan. It is simply History itself; and if for psychoanalysis the history in question here is obviously enough the history of the subject, the resonance of the word suggests that a confrontation between this particular materialism and the historical materialism of Marx can no longer be postponed.
—Fredric Jameson, "Imaginary and Symbolic in Lacan: Marxism, Psychoanalytic Criticism, and the Problem of the Subject," 1977

***P**sycho-Marxism: Marxism and Psychoanalysis Late in the Twentieth Century* examines the recent theoretical convergence between Marxism and psychoanalysis, although, given that these two "master" discourses have enjoyed a rich and

The *South Atlantic Quarterly* 97:2, Spring 1998.

complex discursive relationship, it might be more appropriate to say that this collection explores the *re*articulation of Marxism and psychoanalysis.

While the first phase of articulation comprised important interventions by a number of major figures from a number of different philosophical schools (among them Adorno, Fromm, Marcuse, Reich, Sartre, and Fanon), the second phase arguably coalesced in a single theoretician: Althusser. The discursive space of psycho-Marxism could, of course, be demarcated otherwise (one thinks immediately of that anti-Oedipal duo, Deleuze and Guattari); however, Althusser's contributions—especially "Freud and Lacan" (written in 1964, before the revolution and in an institutional atmosphere decidedly hostile to psychoanalysis, i.e., the French Communist Party)—seem particularly originary in retrospect. Indeed, Althusser's return to Marx, influenced as it was by Lacan's return to Freud, was a return to Freud as well. The still resourceful concept of overdetermination is just one, albeit paradigmatic, consequence of this "writerly" return.

Yet, if it is difficult to underestimate Althusser's general and particular influence on, say, post-Marxism and screen theory, respectively, *Althusserianism* has been subject over the years to a devastating critique (by Althusser himself, among others) that has reduced it to something less than a theoretical half-life—until, that is, the advent of Slavoj Žižek. Although it would probably be too much to say that Žižek's *Sublime Object of Ideology* (1989) resurrected Althusser (an impossible and no doubt unnecessary task today), it did effectively reopen the seemingly moribund question of Freudo-Marxism.

This said, it is important to note that the "subject" presupposed by psycho-Marxism is by no means the same as the Freudo-Marxist or even the Althusserianist subject, since in the latter school Lacan's split subject somehow gets lost in the translation into the interpellative language of recognition and misrecognition, identification and subjectivation. That is, if anything unifies the very different *récits* of Marxism and psychoanalysis, it is the signifier or hyphen that divides them. Still another, more grammatological way of putting this would be to say that psycho-Marxism takes seriously that division or separation which is original to the discourse of psychoanalysis.

One contemporary model for this hybridic relation is *postmodernism*, as shorthand for the "liquidizing" of the modernist distinction between "high" and "low" culture. A locus classicus of sorts here—one that comes, appropriately enough, not from literature but from cinema, *Hitchcockian* cinema—is the seminal slasher film *Psycho* (1960). As Žižek puts it in *Everything You Always Wanted to Know about Lacan (But Were Afraid to Ask Hitchcock)*: "*Psycho* is . . . a kind of hybrid of two heterogeneous parts: it is easy to imagine two 'rounded off' stories, quite consistent in themselves, glued together . . . to form a monstrous whole." Similarly, this particular collection seeks less to define *the* articulation between the properly heterogeneous discourses of Marxism and psychoanalysis—*much* less to suggest some "bad," orthopsychic sublation—than to repose, once again, the *question* of their relation. In just this sense, the "psycho" in psycho-Marxism is the sign of a certain pathology, call it "wild Marxism."

At the same time, if the main title mirrors the "monstrous," mutually denaturalizing totality extravagantly on display like some psychotic taxidermist's dream, the subtitle—*Marxism and Psychoanalysis Late in the Twentieth Century*—suggests that the current coincidence of Marxism and psychoanalysis cannot be thought outside its concrete, political-economic conditions of possibility. In other words, for all its discursive surplus, the problematic of psycho-Marxism is not without a very real material stake, and this stake is not simply postmodernity but late or transnational capitalism.

In fact, yet another synonym of psycho-Marxism may well be *political psychoanalysis*, where—and this particular determination is crucial—the political is understood not so much as the predestined and merely superstructural result of the economic laws of motion (as in "vulgar" Marxism) as the incalculable, though by no means inaudible or illegible, effects of social antagonism—aftereffects that can be audited and enunciated, rendered and reinscribed, and, in the final analysis (most importantly), *endorsed.*

Revisiting Alain Badiou's 1988 *L'être et l'événement* (in hindsight, an important moment in the history of post-Althusserian French Marxism), Slavoj Žižek interrogates Badiou's critique of psychoanalysis and, in particular, his version of post-Marxism in "Psychoanalysis in Post-Marxism." Žižek points out not only how Badiou's *génériques* uncannily mirror Althusser's four fundamental modalities of subjectivity but, more importantly, how Badiou's and Althusser's projects fail to grasp that eventful "being" which is subjectivity (for Žižek, both product *and* process, subject *and* subjectivation). Given this stereoscopic focus, he also returns in his essay (in the strong, Montaignean sense) to the topic of the "two deaths," although the real heart of the piece (at least for this reader) is the deliciously textual moment when Žižek cites Lacan citing St. Paul. This meta-recitation (Lacan's ventriloquism an act of postmodern travesty par excellence) yields another, equally extraordinary moment of textuality when Žižek, punning on the French *plus*, discloses "the elementary matrix of subjectivity." It is in just such moments that "Psychoanalysis in Post-Marxism" analyzes even as it dramatizes the discursive antinomies that constitute psycho-Marxism. For if, as Žižek suggests, any reading of Marxism that conceives of psychoanalysis as its "psychic" Other or repressed desire merely confirms the law of Marxism (and thereby condemns it to the dead orthodoxies of the letter), then Badiou's post-Marxist critique of psychoanalysis, for all its conjunctural interest and engagement, produces the same fatal effect. In short, since neither approach "sins" with real gusto, neither can access that intimately foreign space which is "beyond the law." Psycho-Marxism, on the other hand, endeavors (as in *essayer*) to traverse this space and enact this difficult passage: to submit the "being" of Freudo-Marxism to the vicissitudes of the death drive and then, and only then, see what—in the "event"—*materializes.*

Eugene Victor Wolfenstein's "Michel Foucault and Psychoanalytic-Marxism" stages a double session: a close, critical reading of the first (1976) volume of the *History of Sexuality*—Foucault's counter-discourse to the Reichian/Marcusean critique of capitalist culture and its "sexual discontents"—together with a lively defense of a properly "psychoanalytic-marxism" distinct from those Freudo-Marxian theories that are the object of Foucault's critique. The key, for Wolfenstein, is Nietzsche, not least because *La volonté de savoir* is explicitly indebted, as Foucault's title indicates, to the Nietzschean will to power. Wolfenstein's *Phaedo*-esque strategy is not so much to refute Foucault's argument—which, he readily acknowledges, lays bare the economism and sexual fetishism of classical left Freudianism—as to provide a set of anthropological presuppositions that can effectively address the Foucaldian analytics of *pouvoir/savoir.*

In "Why the Time Is Out of Joint," Teresa Brennan invokes the letter of Derrida—here, his own spirited invocation of *Hamlet* in *Specters of Marx*—as a pretext to *re*read and consequently *re*formulate Marx. Brennan's ambitious task is to see what happens when Marx's value-theory is stripped of its subjectivist emphasis (hence her subtitle: "Marx's Political Economy without the Subject"). The interest of this revised value-theory is that it unconceals the positive, energetic connections between human nature and nature as such, the latter of which, for Marx, was merely an object to be exploited. The critical *differend*, according to Brennan, is the difference between real value, as measured by the time of natural reproduction, and the classical economic notion of price, as measured by speed. The net material consequences of this difference, at once human and ecological, are enormous, as Brennan makes clear in this powerful reformulation of an argument from *History After Lacan* (1993).

Catherine Liu's "Conspiracy (Theories)" commences with some critical remarks on recent institutional attempts to envision a new coincidence of psychoanalysis and social change. This caveat registered (one can only imagine what Marx would have made of the various Lacanian Marxisms!), Liu then turns to the conspiratorial figure of JFK for popular-cultural signs of theoretical production. Drawing, like Brennan, on the Derrida of *Specters of Marx*, Liu argues for the continuing critical use-value of the *Eighteenth Brumaire* (in the process, marking her distance from cultural-populist versions of critical theory); she also argues, after the Benjamin of the *Trauerspiel*, that the relation between theater and history, acting and authenticity, is profoundly, even scandalously, indeterminate. Liu's final coup—one-part Brecht, one-part Benjamin—is to show that *revolutionary gestures* emerge only out of just such convulsively performative moments.

Like Liu, Stathis Gourgouris reflects, in "A Lucid Drunkenness," on the inherent theatricality of revolutionary discourse. For Gourgouris, revolutionary inspiration in the latter half of the twentieth century must be sought, beyond both Marxism and psychoanalysis, in "poetic cognition," which he derives from the Castoriadian concept of "society's radical imagination." This imaginary (not to be confused with the "early," Lacanian mirror stage) is readily apparent in the late Jean Genet of the posthumous *Captif amoureux* (1986). In this text of *jouissance*, which arguably delivered its author not from prison (as his early work did) but from another, more literal death-in-life, Genet chronicles his extraordinary experiences in the early 1970s with both Palestinian fedayeen and the Black Panthers. Gourgouris's intricate reading of Genet's description of being impersonated by a Black Sudanese officer in the Palestinian corps (itself a complex replay of an earlier moment when Genet espied the man dancing to the Rolling Stones in the middle of the Jordanian desert) encapsulates the spirit of "A Lucid Drunkenness": a lucid and poetic essay on both the "performative politics of revolutionizing identity" and that politically incorrect couple, art and revolution.

Abdul-Karim Mustapha's "Meta-Prolegomena for a Study of Psychoanalysis and Imperialism" sets out to elucidate the "absent" interrogative conditions that structure the relationship between psychoanalysis and imperialism, where imperialism serves as the other or outside against which psychoanalysis constructs its objects, however large or small, primal or petty. For Mustapha, it is especially critical at this particular, neopragmatic moment to resume the task of reading—*philosophical* reading—that Althusser initiated when he decided to reread *Capital*. Indeed, any answer to the relational question of psychoanalysis and imperialism must eventually engage the *question of form*, since if history is epistemology (as Althusser argued in "Freud and Lacan"), it is virtually impossible to write—not to say, *read*—the history of psychoanalysis and imperialism without coming to terms with this originary question. Mustapha's brief and dense but rewarding essay, informed as it is by what Hegel called the "work of the negative," assumes the daunting task of rethinking the study of psychoanalysis and imperialism and, in so doing, opens up a new space for the radical reconfiguration of their relationship.

In "Intimate Enemies," Elizabeth Jane Bellamy makes a case for reconsidering the matrix of psycho-Marxism, on the one hand, and the aftermath of this discursive constellation in the context of postcolonialist theory, on the other. Although Bellamy underscores the Eurocentric presuppositions of the classic "master narratives" of Marxism and psychoanalysis, she is equally intent on exploring—on teasing out and disentangling—the play of affect in postcolonialist discourse. In fact, for Bellamy, affect is a radically charged site (as in the work of Homi Bhabha and of Gayatri Spivak) for investigating the complicated discursive negotiations currently being played out between psycho-Marxism and postcolonialism. Accordingly, affect is less the province of a quintessentially modern Western discourse such as psychoanalysis than a category, as Bellamy insists, with real critical potential for articulating subaltern experience and, a fortiori, postcolonialist critique itself.

Rosaria Champagne's "Queering the Unconscious" dissects the (un)-

happy marriage between (anti-)queer Marxism and gay conservatism (strange bedfellows these!). In addition to showing how these seemingly antithetical discourses share a common program (a profoundly dialectical strategy), Champagne proposes a notion of the unconscious as always already queer, albeit a queerness that is a function neither of need (as in [anti-]queer Marxism) nor of self-policing rules of conduct (as in gay conservatism). While Champagne rightly warns that "you cannot buy queer theory at Wal-Mart," her essay eloquently proposes that an activist, accessible version of queer theory can in fact be found—and that the rich, overdetermined contradiction between Marxism and psychoanalysis is one place to look for it.

In "Giving Up the Ghost of a Fetish," Laurence Rickels returns, like Brennan and Liu, to the Derrida of *Specters of Marx* and, more generally, to a coupling of Marxism and psychoanalysis perhaps best symbolized by that most uncanny and undecidable concept *commodity fetishism*. Rickels's opening commentary on the current state of psycho-Marxism is a prelude to his provocative discussion of "Nazi psychoanalysis" and the techno-fetishism, or "gadget love," cultivated by the German air force during the Second World War. Indeed, in Rickels's wide-ranging and fascinating essay, the fetish goes to war, a world-historical event that propels his meditation on trauma, on loss and castration, "mourning and melancholia." The result is not only a nuanced, historically informed understanding of the military psychology that the Germans fashioned to map the stress points of intrapsychic space in wartime, but a fresh conception of fetishism itself, that "gadget love" which effectively bound pilot to plane or—worst-case scenario—left him high and dry: in a word, *un*bound.

Kathleen McHugh's "Women in Traffic" crosses Laura Mulvey's celebrated 1975 essay on the gaze and visual pleasure, arguably the founding text of feminist psychoanalytic film criticism, with Gayle Rubin's contemporaneous and almost equally seminal essay on the "traffic in women." One aim of this suggestive rhetorical gambit is to disclose the sort of class-based distinctions that subtend Mulvey's analyses of individual films. In fact, one need only think of Hitchcock's *Vertigo* (1958) and the mesmerizing sequences in which Madeleine cruises aimlessly through the hilly streets of San Francisco in her sedan—with Scottie, in POV close-up, right behind—to recognize the originality of McHugh's premise. (Needless to say, Madeleine's alter ego, Judy, the *working* woman, does not drive.)

Appropriately enough, McHugh's more general argument is that the cinematic representation of female automobility is a trope for women's agency, autonomy, and social mobility. Reading a number of representative films, including *The Terminator* (1984), *Thelma and Louise* (1991), *Safe* (1995), and *Set It Off* (1996), "Women in Traffic" persuasively shows that, while women still remain spectacular objects on the big screen, they are also increasingly seen, like Thelma and Louise, behind the wheel.

My own contribution, "Going through the Fantasy," comes full circle back to Žižek to determine whether, as his work promises, there really is something to the recent renascence of Freudo-Marxian or Marxo-Lacanian cultural criticism. While the first part situates Žižekian critical theory within its own, quite specific geopolitical and philosophical conditions of possibility (the Balkans and poststructuralism, respectively), the second, more general part offers an overview of that theory in order to excavate its conceptual deep structure—what might be called, after Žižek himself, its *traumatic kernel*. Since his work is clearly central to current debates about capital and subjectivity, among other things, the point of the overview is to punctuate Žižek's complex relation to classical Marxism and Lacanian psychoanalysis. Last but by no means least, "Going through the Fantasy," in concluding this special issue of *SAQ*, sketches some of the political implications of Žižek's work and, rather more pointedly, of psycho-Marxism itself.

Acknowledgments. I would like to thank Fredric Jameson for graciously offering to sponsor an issue on this topic, with special thanks going to Candice Ward, rock/confidante and virtual coeditor, for her critical acumen and editorial contribution.

Slavoj Žižek

Psychoanalysis in Post-Marxism: The Case of Alain Badiou

In the history of Marxism, the reference to psychoanalysis played a precise strategic role: psychoanalysis was expected to "close the gap" by explaining why, despite the presence of "objective" conditions for the revolutionary transformation, individuals willingly persisted in their enslavement to the ruling ideology (i.e., why they *desired their subordination* and even found a perverse satisfaction in it). Why did the masses prefer the Fascist temptation to the Communist revolution in the 1930s? Why did they let themselves be lured into dull satisfaction by the Sirens of the late-capitalist "society of consumption" in the 1960s? In short, psychoanalysis functioned as an ambiguous (necessary but dangerous) *pharmakon* invoked in order to supplement the inherent insufficiency of the Marxist theoretic edifice.

Today, however, with the apparent demise of Marxism, the entire situation has changed: the emerging post-Marxist "radical" political philosophy as a rule insists that psychoanalysis cannot provide access to the specific dimension of the political; useful as it is in clarifying the libidinal foundation of a multitude of "regressive" phenomena (from ethnic violence to the

The *South Atlantic Quarterly* 97:2, Spring 1998.

"apolitical" passivity of the postmodern subject), psychoanalysis cannot account for the miraculous emergence of an egalitarian democratic enthusiasm—of an unconditional demand for what Etienne Balibar called *égaliberté*. For that reason, the political use of psychoanalysis has always wound up in a justification of failure, in an explanation of why things had to go wrong.

The author who has provided the ultimate formulation of this critique of psychoanalysis is Alain Badiou. He deserves special attention insofar as his "post-Marxism" has nothing whatsoever to do with the fashionable deconstructionist dismissal of the alleged Marxist "essentialism"; on the contrary, he is unique in radically rejecting the deconstructionist *doxa* as a new form of pseudo-thought, as a contemporary version of sophism. Since Badiou is not yet well-known in Anglo-American academia, the basic outlines of his philosophy will be rehearsed here prior to offering a Lacanian response to his depiction of the limits of psychoanalysis.

The axis of Badiou's theoretic edifice is, as the title of his main work indicates, the gap between *Being* and *Event*.[1] "Being" stands for the positive ontological order accessible to *Knowledge*, for the infinite multitude of that which presents itself in our experience, categorized by genus and species in terms of its properties. At bottom, as it were, lies the pure multiple, the not yet symbolically structured multitude of experience, that which is given; this multitude is not a multitude of Ones, since the counting has not yet taken place. What Badiou calls a "situation" is any particular consistent multitude (e.g., French society, modern art): a situation is structured, and it is its structure which allows us to "count" it "as One." Here, however, the first cracks in the ontological edifice of Being appear: in order for us to "count" it "as One," the *reduplicatio* proper to symbolization (symbolic inscription) of a situation must be at work, that is, in order for a situation to be "counted as One," its structure must always already involve a metastructure which designates it as One. (The signified structure of the situation must be redoubled in the symbolic network of signifiers.) When a situation is thus "counted as One," identified by its symbolic structure, we have the "state of the situation." (Badiou plays here on the ambiguity of the term *state*—"state of things" versus "State" in the political sense; there is no "state of society" without a "State" in which the structure of society is re-presented/redoubled.) This symbolic *reduplicatio* already involves the minimal dialectic of *Void* and *Excess*. The pure multiple of Being is not yet a multitude of Ones, since, as we have just seen, to have One the pure multiple must be "counted as One"; from the standpoint of the state of a situation, the preceding multiple can only appear as *nothing*, so nothing is the "proper name of Being as Being" prior to its symbolization. "Void" has been the central category of ontology from Democritean atomism onward: "atoms" are nothing but the configurations of Void. The "Excess" correlative to this Void takes two forms. On the one hand, each state of things involves at least one excessive element which, though clearly belonging to the situation, is not "counted" by it, properly included in it (e.g., the "non-integrated" rabble in a societal situation): this element is *presented*, but not *re-presented*. On the other hand, there is an *excess* of *re-presentation* over *presentation*: the agency which brings about the passage from situation to its state (State in society) is always in excess relative to what it structures. In contrast to the impossible liberal dream of a State reduced to a service of civil society, State power is necessarily "excessive," that is, it never simply and transparently re-presents society, but acts as a violent intervention in what it re-presents.

This, then, is the structure of Being. From time to time, however, in a wholly contingent, unpredictable way, out of reach for the Knowledge of Being, an Event takes place which belongs to a wholly different dimension—that, precisely, of non-Being. Take, for example, French society in the late eighteenth century: what is accessible to Knowledge is the state of society—its strata, economic, political, and ideological fights, and so on; no Knowledge, however, enables us to predict or account for the properly unaccountable Event which consists in the so-called French Revolution. In this precise sense, an Event emerges ex nihilo. But the fact that it cannot be accounted for in the terms of the situation does not mean that it is simply an intervention from Outside or Beyond: it attaches itself, precisely, to the Void of every situation—to its inherent inconsistency and/or its Excess. The Event is the Truth of the situation, that which renders visible/readable what the "official" state of the situation had to "repress," but it is also always localized, that is, the Truth is always the Truth *of* a specific situation. The French Revolution is the Event that renders visible/readable the excesses and inconsistencies, the "lie," of the ancien régime; and it is the truth *of* the ancien régime situation—what is localized, or attaches to it.

An Event thus involves its own series of determinations: the Event itself; its denomination ("French Revolution" not being an objective-categorizing designation but part of the Event itself, the way its participants or adherents perceived and symbolized their activity); its ultimate Goal (the society of fully realized emancipation, of freedom–equality–fraternity); its "operator" (the political movements struggling for the Revolution); and, last but not least, its *subject* (the agent who, on behalf of the Truth-Event, intervenes in the historical multiple of the situation and discerns/identifies in it the signs–effects of the Event). What defines the subject is his *fidelity* to the Event: coming *after* the Event, the subject persists in discerning its traces within the situation. "Subject," for Badiou, is thus a finite contingent emergence: not only is Truth not "subjective" in the sense of being subordinated to the subject's whims, but the subject himself is "serving the Truth" which transcends him; since he is never fully adequate to the infinite order of Truth, the subject always has to operate within a finite multiple of a situation in which he discerns the signs of Truth. Take, for example, Christianity (perhaps *the* example of the Truth-Event): the Event is Christ's advent and death; its ultimate Goal is the Last Judgment (the Redemption); its "operator" in the multiple of the historical situation is the Church; and its "subject" is the corps of believers who intervene in their situation on behalf of the Truth-Event, searching for the signs of God in it.

When Badiou speaks of "cette torsion symptomale de l'être qu'est une vérité dans le tissu toujours total des savoirs" (this symptomal torsion of being which is a truth in the always total texture of knowledges),[2] every term bears weight here. The texture of Knowledge is always by definition total, that is, for the Knowledge of Being, there is no excess (a situation's excess or lack being visible only from the standpoint of the Event). From within the standpoint of the knowing servants of the State, of course, "problems" can be seen, but they are automatically reduced to local "difficulties" or contingent "errors": what Truth does is to render visible that (what Knowledge misperceives as) marginal malfunctionings and points of failure are a structural necessity. With regard to the ancien régime, for example, what the Truth-Event of the Revolution renders visible is that injustices are not marginal malfunctionings but effects of the very structure of the system, which is *essentially* "corrupt." Such an effect, when misperceived by the system as a local "abnormality," condenses the global "abnormality" of the system as such, in its entirety (what, in the Freudo-Marxian tradition, is called *symptom*). In psychoanalytic terms, lapses, dreams, compulsive formations and acts, and so forth, are "symptomal torsions" that render the Truth of the given individual inaccessible to Knowledge, which sees them as mere malfunctionings; in Marxist terms, an economic crisis is such a "symptomal torsion."

Today, when even the most radical intellectual readily succumbs to the compulsion to distance himself from communism, it seems appropriate to reassert the October Revolution as a Truth-Event defined against the opportunistic leftist "fools" and conservative "knaves." That revolution also allows us to clearly identify three ways to betray the event of Truth: (1) a simple *disavowal*, with a corresponding attempt to follow old patterns as if nothing had happened, as if it were just a minor disturbance (the reaction of the "utilitarian" liberal democracy); (2) the false *imitation* of the event of Truth (the Fascist staging of the conservative revolution as a pseudo-event); and (3) a direct *ontologization* of the event of Truth, with its reduction to a new positive order of Being (Stalinism).[3] One can clearly grasp here the gap that separates Badiou's "Truth" from the deconstructionist notion of the "multitude of truths" (or, rather, "truth-effects"); for Badiou, truth is contingent, hinging as it does on a concrete historical situation—*of which* it is the truth. Nevertheless, in every concrete and contingent historical situation, there is *one and only one* Truth, which, once articulated, functions as the index of itself and of the falsity of the field subverted by it.

One of Badiou's main theses is that the pure multiple lacks the dignity of the proper object of thought: from Stalin to Derrida, the philosophical common sense has always insisted on infinite complexity (everything is interconnected, reality is so complex that it is accessible to us only in approximations, etc.); deconstruction is the latest version of this commonsense motif of "infinite complexity." Advocates of "anti-essentialist" identity politics, for example, tend to stress that there is no "woman in general," only White middle-class women, Black single mothers, lesbians, and so on and so forth, but such "insights" should be rejected as banalities unworthy of being considered objects of thought. The problem for philosophical thought resides precisely in how the universality of "woman" emerges from this "infinite" multitude, a problem that also enables one to rehabilitate the Hegelian distinction between bad ("spurious") and true infinity: the first refers to the commonsense infinite complexity, while the second concerns the infinity of an Event which transcends, precisely, the "infinite complexity" of its context. A homologous distinction can be drawn between historicism and historicity proper: historicism refers to the set of circumstances (economic, political, cultural, etc.) whose complex interactions allow us to account for a given event, while historicity proper involves the specific temporality of the Event and its aftermath, the span between the Event and its ultimate End (between Christ's death and the Last Judgment, between the October Revolution and communism, between falling in love and the accomplished bliss of living together).

Badiou is clearly and radically opposed to the postmodern anti-Platonic thrust whose basic dogma is that the era when it was still possible to ground a political movement in a direct reference to some eternal metaphysical or transcendental truth is definitely over, and, the experience of our century having proved that such a reference to some metaphysical a priori leads to catastrophic "totalitarian" social consequences, the only solution is to accept that we live in a new era deprived of metaphysical certainties, an era of contingency and conjectures, and in a "society of risks" that renders politics a matter of *phronesis*, of strategic judgments and dialogue, not of applying fundamental cognitive insights. What Badiou is aiming for, against this postmodern *doxa*, is precisely the resuscitation of the *politics of (universal) Truth* in today's conditions of global contingency. He would thus rehabilitate, in the current conditions of multiplicity and contingency, not only philosophy but the properly *meta-physical* dimension: the infinite Truth is "eternal" and *meta* relative to the temporal process of Being; it is a flash of Another Dimension which transcends the positivity of Being.

However, an Event does not entail any ontological guarantee: its status is radically undecidable; it cannot be reduced to (nor deduced or generated from) a (previous) situation, since it emerges "out of Nothing" (the Nothing that was the ontological truth of this previous situation). On that account, there is no neutral gaze of Knowledge which could discern the Event in its effects. A *Decision* for the Event is always already here (i.e., one can discern the signs of an Event in the situation only from a previous Decision for Truth), just as in Jansenist theology divine miracles are readable as such only to those who have already opted for Faith. A neutral historicist gaze will never see in the French Revolution a series of traces of the Event called "French Revolution," but merely a multitude of occurrences caught in the network of social determinations (and to an external gaze, Love is only a succession of psychical and physiological states).[4] The engaged observer perceives positive historical occurrences as parts of the Event of the French Revolution only insofar as he observes them from the uniquely engaged standpoint of the Revolution. In Badiou's terms, an Event is self-referential in that it includes *its own designation*: the symbolic designation "French Revolution" is part of the designated content itself, since, if we subtract this designation, that content turns into a multitude of positive occurrences available to Knowledge. It is in this precise sense that an Event involves subjectivity: the engaged "subjective perspective" on the Event is part of the Event itself.

The Marxist thesis that the entire hitherto history is the history of class struggle already presupposes such an engaged subjectivity, for it is only from its partial point of view that the entire hitherto history appears as such—only from this "interested" perspective can traces of the class struggle be discerned in the entire social edifice, up to the highest cultural products. The answer to the obvious counterargument (that this very fact proves we are dealing with a distorted view, not with the true state of things) is that the allegedly "objective," "impartial" gaze is not neutral, but rather is the partial gaze of the winners, of the ruling classes. (No wonder the rhetoric of right-wing historical revisionists includes so many constructions like "let's approach the topic of the Holocaust in a cool objective way," "let's put it in context," and "let's look at the facts.") A theorist of the Communist revolution is not the one who, after establishing on the basis of objective study that the future belongs to the working class, decides to take its side and place his bets on the winner; the engaged view permeates his theory from the very outset. Within the Marxist tradition, this notion that partiality is not a *positive* condition of Truth was most clearly articulated by Georg Lukács in *History and Class Consciousness*, as well as in a more messianic or proto-religious mode by Walter Benjamin in "Theses on the Philosophy of History." The "truth," for them, emerges when a victim, from his catastrophic position in the present, gains a sudden insight into the entire past as a series of catastrophes leading up to the victim's current predicament. So, when we read a text of Truth, we should be careful not to confuse the level of Knowledge with the level of Truth. In Marx himself, although he mainly used "proletariat" as a synonym for "the working class," one can nevertheless discern a clear tendency to conceive "the working class" as a descriptive term belonging to the domain of Knowledge (e.g., that class as the object of "neutral" sociological study, as a social stratum subdivided into components, etc.), whereas "proletariat" designates the operator of Truth, namely, the engaged agent of the revolutionary struggle.

An Event is thus circular in the sense that its identification is possible only from the standpoint of what Badiou calls "an *interpreting intervention*," meaning the perspective of those who accept the "wager" that such an Event exists. An *intervention* is any "procedure by means of which a multiple is recognized as Event." Moreover, "it would remain forever doubtful if there had been any Event at all, except for the intervening one [*l'intervenant*], who determined his belonging to the situation."[5] Fidelity to the Event consists of continually attempting to traverse the field of Knowledge from the standpoint of Event, of intervening in it and searching for the signs of Truth. Thus the difference between Event and its denomination: Event is the traumatic encounter with the Real (Christ's death, the historic shock of a revolution, etc.), while its denomination is its inscription into language (Christian doctrine, revolutionary consciousness, etc.). In Lacanese, Event is *objet a*, while denomination is the new signifier that establishes what Rimbaud called the New Order—for Badiou, the new readability of the situation on the basis of Decision.

Badiou calls the language in which the Truth-Event is purportedly denominated the "subject-language [*langue-sujet*]." This language is meaningless from the standpoint of Knowledge, which judges propositions according to their referents within the domain of positive Being (or according to the proper functioning of speech within the established symbolic order). When confronted with the subject-language of Christian redemption, revolutionary emancipation, or love, for example, Knowledge dismisses it all as empty phrases lacking any proper reference (i.e., as "political-messianic jargon," "poetic hermeticism," etc.). Imagine a man in love describing the features of his beloved to a friend who, not being himself in love with that particular person, will simply find this enthusiastic description meaningless—he will not get "the point" of it. In short, subject-language involves the logic of shibboleth, of a difference which is visible only from within. This, however, in no way means that a given subject-language involves another, "deeper" reference to a hidden, true referent; it is rather that subject-language "derails" or "unsettles" the standard use of language on the basis of its established meanings and leaves the reference "empty," but with a "wager" that this Void will be filled when the Goal is reached, that is, when Truth actualizes itself as a new situation (the reign of God on Earth, the emancipated society, etc.). The denomination of the Truth-Event is thus "empty" precisely insofar as it refers to the "fullness" yet to come.

From this brief description, one can already get a presentiment of what one may be tempted to term, in all naiveté, the intuitive power of Badiou's notion of the subject, which effectively describes the experience each of us has when fully engaged, subjectively, in some Cause that is "our own." Isn't that when, in those precious moments, I *fully am a subject*? And doesn't this very feature make it *ideological*? That is to say, the first thing that strikes anyone versed in the history of French Marxism is how uncannily close Badiou's notion of Truth-Event comes to Althusser's notion of (ideological) interpellation. Is the process Badiou describes as Truth-Event not that of an individual interpellated into a subject by a Cause? Is the circular relationship between Event and subject (i.e., the subject serving the Event, which is itself only visible as such to an already engaged subject) not the very circle of ideology? Prior to constraining the notion of subject to ideology, that is, identifying the subject as such as ideological, Althusser briefly entertained the idea of subjectivity as comprising four modalities: the subject of ideology, the subject of art, the subject of the unconscious, and the subject of science. Badiou's four "generics of truth" (love, art, science, and politics) would seem to clearly parallel these four modalities of subjectivity (with love corresponding to the subject of the unconscious—the focus of psychoanalysis—and politics, of course, to the subject of ideology).

Is this identity between Truth-Event and ideology not further confirmed by *futur antérieur* as the specific temporality of generic procedures? Starting with the denomination of the Event (Christ's death, the Revolution), the generic procedure is to search for signs of the Event in the multiple with a view to the ultimate Goal, which will bring about full plenitude (Last Judgment, communism, or, for Mallarmé, *le Livre*). Generic procedures thus involve a temporal loop: fidelity to the Event enables the historic multiple to be judged from the standpoint of the plenitude to come, but the arrival of this plenitude already involves the subjective act of Decision, or the Pascalian "wager." Take, for example, the democratic-egalitarian political Event: its reference to the Democratic Revolution enables history to be read as a continuous democratic struggle aimed at total emancipation, so the present situation is experienced as fundamentally "dislocated" or "out of joint" (the corruption of the ancien régime, the class society, the fallen terrestrial life) relative to the promise of a redeemed future. "Now," in subject-language, is always a time of antagonism, split between the corrupted "state of things" and the promise of Truth.

Badiou defines as "generic" the multiple within a situation that has no particular properties, the referent of which would enable us to classify it as its subspecies; the generic multiple belongs to the situation but is not properly included in it as its subspecies (the "rabble" in Hegel's philosophy of right, for example). Of course, Badiou simultaneously mobilizes the association of "generic" with "generating": this generic element is what enables us to generate the propositions of the subject-language in which Truth resonates. *Generic* is thus a multiple element/part of the situation that doesn't fit into it, that sticks out precisely insofar as it gives body (as it were) to the Being of the situation as such, subverting the situation by directly embodying its universality. With regard to this point, isn't it significant that Badiou's ultimate example of the Event is *religion* (Christianity from Paul to Pascal), as the arch-model of *ideology*, and that this Event, precisely, does *not* fit any of his four *génériques* of truth (love, art, science, and politics[6])? If we take Badiou's thought itself as a "situation" of Being, subdivided into four generics, however, doesn't religious ideology occupy precisely this generic place? Isn't religion itself his "symptomal torsion," the element which belongs to the domain of Truth without being one of its acknowledged parts or subspecies? This would seem to confirm that the Truth-Event consists in the elementary ideological gesture of interpellating individuals (parts of a "situation" of Being) into subjects (bearers/followers of Truth). It is tempting to go one step further, given that Badiou's paradigmatic example of Truth-Event is not religion in general but *Christianity* in particular, the religion centered on the Event of Christ's advent and death. (As was pointed out by Kierkegaard, Christianity inverts the standard metaphysical relationship between eternity and time, with eternity in a sense hinging on a temporal event, Christ.) Perhaps, then, Badiou can also be read as the last great author in the French tradition of Catholic dogmaticists that began with Pascal and Malebranche (suffice it to recall that two of his key references are Pascal and Claudel). The parallel between revolutionary Marxism and messianic Christianity was a commonplace among liberal critics like Bertrand Russell, who dismissed Marxism as a secular messianic ideology; Badiou, by contrast (following a line from the later Engels to Fredric Jameson), fully endorses this homology.

Badiou passionately defends Paul for having articulated the Christian Truth-Event—Christ's Resurrection—as the "universal singular" (a singular event which interpellates individuals into subjects universally, irrespective of their race, sex, social class, etc.), along with the conditions of fidelity to it.[7] Of course, Badiou is well aware that today, in our era of modern science, we are no longer inclined to accept as the form of the Truth-Event the fable of the miraculous Resurrection, although the Truth-Event invariably designates the occurrence of something which, from within the horizon of the predominant order of Knowledge, appears to be impossible (as witness the laughter with which Athenian philosophers greeted Paul's announcement of the Resurrection upon his arrival there). Today, any positing of the Truth-Event at the level of the supernatural or the miraculous necessarily entails a regression to obscurantism, since the Event of Science is irrefutable and cannot be undone. Today, we can accept as Truth-Events (i.e., intrusions of the traumatic Real, which shatters the predominant symbolic texture) only those occurrences that take place in a universe compatible with scientific knowledge, even if they happen at its borders and place its presuppositions in question. The "sites" of the Event are now scientific discovery itself, as well as political act, artistic invention, and psychoanalytic confrontation with Love. Apropos of Paul, Badiou tackles the problem of locating his position relative to the four generics that generate effective truths. His solution is to propose Paul as the antiphilosophical *theoretician of the formal conditions of the truth-procedure*, since he provided the first detailed articulation of how fidelity to a Truth-Event operates in its universal dimension: the excessive (*surnuméraire*) Real of a Truth-Event ("Resurrection"), emerging by means of grace (i.e., it cannot be accounted for in terms of the constituents of the given situation), sets in motion—in those subjects who recognize themselves in its call—the militant "work of Love," or the struggle to propagate, with persistent fidelity, this Truth in its universal scope (i.e., as concerning everyone).

So, although Paul's particular message may no longer be operative for us, the terms in which he formulated the operative mode of Christianity apply to every Truth-Event. Each Truth-Event leads to a kind of "Resurrection," that is, by means of fidelity to it and a labor of love on its behalf, one enters another dimension irreducible to a mere *service des biens* (the smooth running of affairs in the domain of Being)—the dimension of Immortality, of Life not encumbered by death. Nevertheless, the problem remains of how it was possible for the first and still most pertinent description of the operation of fidelity to a Truth-Event to occur apropos of a Truth-Event that was a mere semblance, not an effective Truth. From the Hegelian standpoint, there is a deep necessity to this, confirmed by the fact that the twentieth-century philosopher who provided the definitive description of an *authentic* political act (Heidegger, in *Sein und Zeit*) got seduced by a *fake* political act, that is, one which was not an effective Truth-Event (Nazism). So it is as if rendering the formal structure of fidelity to the Truth-Event means doing so apropos of an Event which is merely its own semblance. Perhaps the lesson in this is more radical than it may appear: What if what Badiou calls Truth-Event is, at its most radical, a purely formal act of decision, not only not grounded in an effective Truth but ultimately *indifferent* to the precise status (effective or fabulous) of the Truth-Event to which it refers? What if we are dealing here with a key component of the Truth-Event, notably, that true fidelity to the Event is "dogmatic" in precisely the sense of unconditional Faith, of an attitude which, not needing any grounds, cannot be refuted by any argument?

Paradoxically, this topic of Pauline Christianity is crucial to Badiou's confrontation with psychoanalysis. In adamantly opposing the Truth-Event to the death drive, to what he repeatedly calls the "morbid obsession with death," he is at his weakest, succumbing to the *temptation of the nonthought*. It is indeed symptomatic that Badiou is compelled to identify the liberal-democratic *service des biens*, the smooth running of things in the positivity of Being where "nothing effectively happens," with the "morbid obsession with death." One can easily see the element of truth in this equation: the mere *service des biens*, deprived of the dimension of Truth and far from able to function as the "healthy" everyday life that is not bothered by "eternal" questions, necessarily regresses to nihilistic morbidity. In Christian terms, there is true Life only in Christ, so life outside the Event of Christ sooner or later turns into its opposite, a morbid decadence; when one's life is dedicated to an excess of pleasures, these very pleasures are sooner or later spoiled. At the same time, it is important to emphasize here what Lacan calls the space or distance *between the two deaths*: in order to be able to open oneself up to the true life of Eternity, one's attachment to "this" life must be suspended for entry into the domain of *ate*, the domain between the two deaths, the domain of the "undead."

This point is worthy of a more detailed examination, since it condenses the gap that separates Badiou from Lacan and psychoanalysis in general. Badiou, of course, is well aware of the two Deaths (and two Lives) entailed by the Pauline opposition of Life and Death (or Spirit/Life vs. Flesh/Death), one that has nothing to do with the biological distinction between life and death as stages of the generation–corruption cycle, or with the standard Platonic opposition of Soul and Body. For Paul, "Life" and "Death," Spirit and Flesh, designate two subjective stances, two ways of living one's life. This leads Badiou to interpret Christianity as *radically dissociating* Death and Resurrection: not only are they not the same, they are not even dialectically interconnected in the sense that the price of Eternal Life is the suffering which redeems our sins. For Badiou, Christ's death on the cross—God's having had to become man and die (to suffer the fate of all flesh) in order to be resurrected—simply signals that Eternal Life is accessible to humanity, to all men qua finite mortal beings, that each of us can be touched by the grace of the Truth-Event and enter the domain of Eternal Life. Badiou is openly anti-Hegelian here: there is no dialectic of Life and Death, no emergence of the Truth-Event of Resurrection as the magic that turns negativity into positivity once we are fully ready to "tarry with the negative," to assume our mortality and suffering in its most radical form. This Truth-Event is simply a radical New Beginning, accompanied by the violent, traumatic, and contingent intrusion of Another Dimension that is not "mediated" by the domain of terrestrial finitude and corruption.

One must accordingly avoid the pitfalls of the morbid masochist morality which perceives suffering as inherently redeeming; this morality, remaining within the confines of the Law (which demands that a price be paid for admission to Eternal Life), has thus not attained the level of properly Christian Love. As Badiou sees it, the Truth-Event is not Christ's death in itself, which just prepares the site for the Event (Resurrection) by asserting the identity of God and Man, that is, if the infinite dimension of Immortal Truth is also accessible to a finite/mortal human being, then what ultimately matters is only the Resurrection of the dead (mortal/human) Christ because it signals that every human being can be redeemed and can participate in the Truth-Event. Therein resides the message of Christianity: the positivity of Being, the Order of Cosmos regulated by its Laws, which is the domain of finitude and mortality, is not "all there is." (From the standpoint of Cosmos, of the totality of positive Being, we are just particular beings determined by our specific place in the global order, with the Law ultimately another name for the Order of Cosmic Justice which allocates to each of us our proper place.) Rather, there is Another Dimension, that of True Life in Love, accessible to all of us through divine grace. Christian Revelation is thus an example (*the* example) of how we, human beings, are not limited to the positivity of Being, since from time to time, in a contingent and unpredictable way, a Truth-Event can occur which opens up the possibility of our participation in Another Life by means of a persistent fidelity to that Event. The interesting thing to note here is how Badiou inverts the standard opposition of universal Law and accidental Grace (or charisma), that is, the idea that we are all subject to divine law, whereas only some of us can be touched by grace and thus redeemed. In Badiou's reading of Paul, it is rather law (however "universal" it may appear to be) that is ultimately "particularist" (a legal order always imposing specific duties and rights on us, as well as always defining a specific community at the expense of excluding members of other communities), while divine grace is truly universal (i.e., nonexclusionary), available to all human beings regardless of race, sex, or social status.

Corresponding to the two lives (the finite biological life and the Eternal Life of participation in the Truth-Event of Resurrection) are two deaths: (biological) death and Death, in the sense of going the "way of the flesh." How does Paul determine this opposition of Life and Death as two opposing subjective, existential attitudes? Here we get to the crux of Badiou's argument, which also pertains to psychoanalysis, for the opposition of Death and Life overlaps with the opposition of Law and Love. For Paul, succumbing to the temptations of the flesh does not simply mean indulging in unbridled worldly pursuits (of pleasure, power, wealth, etc.), heedless of the Law (or moral prohibitions). On the contrary, his central tenet, elaborated in what is probably the (deservedly) most famous passage in his Epistles (Romans 7:7–18), is that there was no Sin prior to or independent of the Law, that what preceded the Law was the simple, innocent prelapsarian life once and forever lost to us mortal human beings. The universe in which we live, *our* "way of the flesh," is one in which Sin and Law, desire and its prohibition, are inextricably twined, and it is the very act of Prohibition that gives rise to the desire for its transgression, or fixes our desire on the prohibited object:

> What then should we say? That the law is sin? By no means! Yet, if it had not been for the law, I would not have known sin. I would not have known what it is to covet if the law had not said, "You shall not covet." But sin, seizing an opportunity in the commandment, produced in me all kinds of covetousness. Apart from the law sin lies dead. I was once alive apart from the law, but when the commandment came, sin revived and I died, and the very commandment that promised life proved to be death to me. For sin, seizing an opportunity in the commandment, deceived me and through it killed me. . . . I do not understand my own actions. For I do not do what I want, but I do the very thing I hate. Now if I do what I do not want, I agree that the law is good. But in fact it is no longer I that do it, but sin that dwells within me. For I know that nothing good dwells within me, that is, in my flesh. I can will what is right, but I cannot do it.

The direct result of the intervention of the Law is thus to *divide* the subject, introducing a morbid confusion between life and death, between the (conscious) obedience of the Law and the (unconscious) desire for its transgression that is *generated by the legal prohibition*. It is not me, the subject, who transgresses the Law but (nonsubjectivized) "Sin" itself, the sinful impulses in which I do not recognize myself and that I even hate. Because of this split, my (conscious) Self is ultimately experienced as "dead," as deprived of living impetus, while "life," the ecstatic affirmation of living energy, can only appear in the guise of "Sin," of a transgression which gives rise to a morbid sense of guilt. My actual life-impulse, my desire, appears to me as an autonomous foreign automatism which insists on and follows its own path regardless of my conscious Will and intentions.

Paul's problem is thus not the standard morbid moralistic one (how to crush my transgressive impulses, how finally to purify myself of sinful impulses) but its exact opposite: *How can I break out of this vicious cycle of Law and desire, of the Prohibition and its transgression, within which I can assert my passion for life only as its opposite, a morbid death drive?* How would it be possible for me to experience my "life drive" not as a foreign automatism, a blind "compulsion to repeat" which compels me to transgress the Law (with the unacknowledged complicity of the Law itself), but as a fully subjectivized, positive *yes!* Here, Paul (like Badiou) seems to fully endorse Hegel's point that there is Evil only in the gaze that perceives it, while it is the Law that not only opens up and sustains the domain of Sin, of sinful impulses to transgress its prohibitions, but also finds a perverse and morbid satisfaction in making us feel guilty for such transgressions. The ultimate results of the Rule of Law are thus all the well-known twists and paradoxes of the superego; since I can enjoy only what I feel guilty about, I can find enjoyment only, in (a self-reflective) turn, *in feeling guilty*, in punishing myself for sinful thoughts, and so on and so forth. When Badiou speaks of the "morbid fascination of the death drive," therefore, he is not resorting to platitudes, but articulating a specific Pauline reading of psychoanalytic notions to do with the *complex entanglement of Law and desire*, this morbid intertwinement of life and death in which the "dead" letter of the Law perverts my very life-enjoyment, turning it into a fascination with death. In this perverted universe the ascetic who whips himself on behalf of the Law enjoys himself more intensely than anyone who takes an innocent pleasure in worldly delights, for it is not only the *illicit* sinful desires (i.e., those that are *against the Law*) which Paul considers "the way of the flesh" (as opposed to "the way of the Spirit"). "Flesh" includes *both* what is against the Law *and* the excessive self-torturing, self-mortifying, morbid fascination with the flesh that is *begotten by the Law*. As Badiou emphasizes, Paul comes unexpectedly close here to his great detractor Nietzsche, whose problem was also that of how we can break out of the vicious cycle of a morbid, self-mortifying denial of Life: the Christian "way of the Spirit" is for Nietzsche precisely the magic rupture, the New Beginning which delivers us from this morbidly debilitating deadlock and enables us to open ourselves to the Eternal Life of Love without Sin (i.e., without the Law and the guilt induced by the Law).

Here we have *two* divisions of the subject, which are not to be confused. On the one hand, the subject of the Law is divided between his conscious ego, which adheres to the letter of the Law, and his decentered desire, which—operating against the subject's conscious will, "automatically"—compels him to "do what he hates," to transgress the Law and indulge in illicit *jouis-*

sance. On the other hand, we have the more radical division between this entire domain of the Law/desire, of the prohibition that generates its own transgression, and a properly Christian Love, the New Beginning of which means breaking out of the deadlock of Law and its transgression.

Where does the Lacanian "divided subject" stand in relation to each of these divisions? At first glance, the answer to this question may appear to be simple and straightforward: psychoanalysis is *the* theory that conceptualizes—brings to light—the paradoxical structure of the first division. Isn't Badiou's description of the intertwinement of Law and desire full of implicit (and even some explicit) references to or paraphrases of Lacan? Isn't the ultimate domain of psychoanalysis the intersection of the (symbolic) Law and desire? Isn't the multitude of perverse satisfactions the form in which that very intersection is realized? Isn't the Lacanian division of the subject one that concerns precisely the subject's relationship to the symbolic Law? Furthermore, isn't that ultimately confirmed by Lacan's *Kant avec Sade*, in which the Sadean universe of morbid perversion is posited as the "truth" of the most radical assertion of the moral weight of symbolic Law in human history (Kantian ethics)?[8] However, the crucial question with regard to psychoanalysis here is whether it remains within the confines of this morbid/masochistic obsession with death, this perverse intermingling of Life and Death that characterizes the dialectics of a prohibitory Law generating a transgressive desire. Perhaps the best way to answer this question is to start with Lacan's own recourse to that same passage from Paul's Epistle to the Romans in elaborating the link between Law and desire, where he refers to the availability of "the Thing" (the impossible object of *jouissance*) via only the prohibitory Law, as its transgression:

> Is the Law the Thing? Certainly not. Yet I can only know of the Thing by means of the Law. In effect, I would not have had the idea to covet it if the Law hadn't said: "Thou shalt not covet it." But the Thing finds a way by producing in me all kinds of covetousness thanks to the commandment, for without the Law the Thing is dead. But even without the Law, I was once alive. But when the commandment appeared, the Thing flared up, returned once again, I met my death. And for me, the commandment that was supposed to lead to life turned out to lead to death, for the Thing found a way and thanks to the commandment seduced me; through it I came to desire death.

> I believe that for a little while now some of you at least have begun to suspect that it is no longer I who have been speaking. In fact, with one small change, namely, "Thing" for "sin," this is the speech of Saint Paul on the subject of the relations between the law and sin in the Epistle to the Romans, Chapter 7, paragraph 7.
>
> . . . .
>
> The relationship between the Thing and the Law could not be better defined than in these terms. . . . The dialectical relationship between desire and the Law causes our desire to flare up only in relation to the Law, through which it becomes the desire for death. It is only because of the Law that sin . . . takes on an excessive, hyperbolic character. Freud's discovery—the ethics of psychoanalysis—does it leave us clinging to that dialectic?[9]

Crucial here is the concluding question, which clearly points toward there being, for Lacan, "a way of rediscovering the relationship to *das Ding* somewhere beyond the Law."[10] The whole point of "the ethics of psychoanalysis" is to formulate the possibility of such a relationship, which would avoid the pitfalls of superegoic culpability and "morbid" enjoyment in sin, while also avoiding what Kant called *Schwärmerei*, the obscurantist claim to give word to (and thus legitimize one's position by reference to) spiritual illumination, or direct insight into the impossible Real Thing. The desire to which Lacan refers in his maxim of psychoanalytic ethics, "ne pas céder sur son désir" (not to compromise, or give way on, one's desire), is no longer transgressive or, consequently, involved in a "morbid" dialectic with the prohibitory Law; it is rather one's own desire, to which one owes fidelity—desire elevated to the level of ethical Duty. Thus "ne pas céder sur son désir" is ultimately another way of saying "do your duty!"[11]

It would thus be tempting to risk a Badiouan/Pauline reading of the end of psychoanalysis—which is to say, a New Beginning or symbolic "rebirth"—with the analysand's subjectivity radically restructured such that the vicious cycle of the superego is suspended, left behind. (Doesn't Lacan himself drop many hints that the end of analysis opens up the domain of *Love beyond Law*, using the same Pauline terms as Badiou?[12]) Nevertheless, Lacan's way is not that of Paul or Badiou: psychoanalysis is not "psychosynthesis"; it does not *posit* a "new harmony," a new Truth-Event, but merely wipes the slate clean for it. This "merely," however, should be put in quotation marks because it is Lacan's contention that, in this negative gesture of "wiping the slate clean," something (a Void) is confronted which is already "sutured" with the arrival of a new Truth-Event. For Lacan, negativity—a negative gesture of withdrawal—precedes any positive gesture of enthusiastic identification with a Cause, functioning as its condition of (im)possibility, that is, laying the ground or opening up the space for it, but simultaneously being obfuscated by it and undermining it. For that reason, Lacan implicitly shifts the balance between Death and Resurrection toward Death, which at its most radical stands for not merely the passing of earthly life but the "night of the world," the self-withdrawal, the absolute contraction of subjectivity in which its very links with "reality" are severed—*this* is "wiping the slate clean," which opens up the domain of the symbolic New Beginning and enables the emergence of the "new harmony" sustained by a newly emerged Master-Signifier.

Here, Lacan parts company with Paul and Badiou: God not only is dead, but was always already dead. After Freud, one could not place one's faith in a Truth-Event, since every such Event ultimately remains a semblance obfuscating a prior Void whose Freudian name is *death drive*. So where Lacan differs from Badiou is in the determination of the exact status of this domain beyond the Rule of Law. Like Badiou, Lacan delineates the contours of a domain beyond the Order of Being, beyond the politics of *service des biens*, beyond the "morbid" superegoic intersection of Law and its transgressive desire. However, for Lacan, the Freudian concept of death drive cannot be accounted for in terms of this intersection; the death drive is *not* the outcome of a morbid confusion of Life and Death caused by the intervention of the symbolic Law. The uncanny domain beyond the Order of Being is what Lacan calls the domain "between the two deaths," the preontological domain of monstrous spectral apparitions, which is "immortal" yet not in Badiou's sense of the immortality of participating in Truth, but rather in the sense of what Lacan calls *lamella*—the monstrous "undead" object-libido. This domain, in which Oedipus (or King Lear, to take another exemplary case) finds himself after the fall, when his symbolic destiny has been fulfilled, is for Lacan "beyond the Law." In his reading of the Oedipus myth, the early Lacan was already focusing on what the standard version of the Oedipus complex leaves out of sight: the first figure of what is "beyond Oedipus," which is *Oedipus himself* after he has fulfilled his destiny to the bitter end: the horrifying figure of Oedipus at Colonus, that embittered old man with his thoroughly uncompromising attitude, cursing everyone around him. Doesn't this figure confront us with the inherent deadlock, the impossibility of *jouissance*, concealed by its Prohibition? Wasn't Oedipus the one who transgressed the Prohibition and paid the price for it in having to assume this impossibility? Lacan exemplifies the status of Oedipus at Colonus by comparison with that of the unfortunate Mr. Valdemar, the famous Poe character who, via hypnosis, is put to death and then, reawakening, implores the observers of this horrible experiment: "*For God's sake!—quick!—quick!—put me to sleep—or, quick!—waken me! quick!—*I SAY TO YOU THAT I AM DEAD!" Upon being awakened, Mr. Valdemar, says Lacan,

> is no more than a disgusting liquefaction, something for which no language has a name, the naked apparition, pure, simple, brutal, of this figure which it is impossible to gaze at face on, which hovers in the background of all the imaginings of human destiny, which is beyond all qualification, and for which the word carrion is completely inadequate, the complete collapse of this species of swelling that is life—the bubble bursts and dissolves down into inanimate putrid liquid.
>
> That is what happens in the case of Oedipus. As everything right from the start of the tragedy goes to show, Oedipus is nothing more than the scum of the earth, the refuse, the residue, a thing empty of any plausible appearance.[13]

The ultimate object of horror is this sudden emergence of the "life beyond death," of the undead-indestructible object, of Life deprived of any support in the symbolic order. This is perhaps not unrelated to today's phenomenon of cyberspace: the more our (experience of) reality is "virtualized"—changed into a "screen phenomenon" or interface encounter—the more the "indivisible remainder," that which resists integration into the interface, appears as the horrifying remainder of the undead Life. No wonder images of such a formless "undead" substance of Life abound in today's science fiction/horror narratives, from *Alien* on. Let us recall the scene from Terry Gilliam's *Brazil* in which a waiter in a high-class restaurant recommends the daily specials to his customers ("Today, our tournedos is really special!"), yet what they get is a dazzling color photo of the meal they've ordered on a stand above the plate, and on the plate itself a loathsome excremental, pastelike lump. This split between the food's image and the real of its formless excremental remainder perfectly exemplifies the disintegration of reality into an interface image, ghostlike and insubstantial, and the raw stuff of the remainder of the Real—our obsession with which is the price we have to pay for the suspension of the paternal Prohibition/Law that sustains and guarantees our access to reality. And, of course, Lacan's point is that, if one exploits to the limit the potentials opened up by our existence as *parlêtres* ("beings of language"), one sooner or later finds oneself in this horrifying in-between state, the threatening possibility of which looms over each of us.

This "indivisible remainder," this formless stain of the "little piece of the real" that "is" Oedipus after the fulfillment of his symbolic Destiny, is the direct embodiment of what Lacan calls *plus-de-jouir*, the "surplus-enjoyment" or excess that cannot be accommodated by any symbolic idealization. In Lacan's use of the term, of course, there is a play upon the French ambiguity of "excess of enjoyment" versus "no longer any enjoyment"; on this model, it is tempting to speak here, apropos of this formless "indivisible remainder" that is Oedipus, of a case of *plus d'homme*: "excessively human," he has lived, to the bitter end, the "human condition," realizing its most fundamental possibility, and, on that very account, he is in a way "no longer human," having turned into an "inhuman monster" bound by no human laws and considerations. As Lacan emphasizes, there are two main ways to cope with this "remainder": on the one hand, traditional humanism disavows it, avoids confronting it, covers it up by means of idealizations (i.e., concealing it with noble images of Humanity); on the other hand, the ruthless and boundless capitalist economy, as it were, puts this excess/remainder to use, manipulating it in order to keep its productive machinery in perpetual motion (as they usually put it—there being no desire, no depravity, too low to exploit for capitalist profiteering). At this point, when Oedipus has been reduced to the "scum of humanity," we again encounter the ambiguous relationship (or, in Hegelese, the speculative identity) between the lowest and the highest, between the excremental scum and the sacred, for now, all of a sudden, messengers from different cities appear and vie for Oedipus's favor, asking him to bless their hometowns with his presence, to which the embittered Oedipus responds with the famous lines:

> Am I to be counted as something
> according to some readings: as a man
> only now, when I am reduced to nothing
> when I am no longer human?

Don't these lines expose the elementary matrix of subjectivity: you become "something" (you are accounted a subject) only after going through the zero-point, after being deprived of all those "pathological" (in the Kantian sense of empirical, contingent) features that support your identity, thus being reduced to "nothing"—"a Nothingness counted as Something," which is the most concise formula for *subject*.[14]

We are now in a position to precisely determine how much of a gap separates Badiou from Lacan. For Badiou, what psychoanalysis provides is *insight* into the morbid intertwining of Life and Death, of Law and desire, insight into the obscenity of the Law itself as the "truth" of the thought and the moral stance which limit themselves to the Order of Being and its discriminatory Laws; as such, psychoanalysis cannot properly render thematic the domain beyond the Law, that is, the mode of operation of fidelity to the Truth-Event. The psychoanalytic subject is the divided subject of the (symbolic) Law, *not* the subject divided between Law (which regulates the Order of Being) and Love (as fidelity to the Truth-Event). (The logical consequence for Badiou is that psychoanalysis remains constrained by the field of Knowledge, unable to approach the properly positive dimension of Truth processes: in the case of love, psychoanalysis reduces it to a sublimated expression of sexuality; in the cases of both science and art, psychoanalysis can only speak to the subjective libidinal conditions of a scientific invention or a work of art—such as that an artist or a scientist was driven by his unresolved Oedipus complex or latent homosexuality, and so on—conditions which are ultimately irrelevant to the work's truth dimension; in the case of politics, psychoanalysis can only conceive of collectivity against the background of a *Totem and Taboo* or *Moses and Monotheism* problematic of primordial crime and guilt, so is unable to think a militant "revolutionary" collective that is *not bound* by parental guilt, but rather *freed* by the positive force of Love.) For Lacan, on the other hand, the Truth-Event operates only against a background of *traumatic encounter with the undead/monstrous Thing*, and what are Badiou's four *génériques* if not four ways of reinscribing the encounter with the Real Thing into the symbolic texture? In *art*, beauty is "the last veil of the Monstrous," while *science*, far from being just another symbolic narrative, endeavors to formulate the structure of the Real beneath the symbolic fiction; *love*, no longer merely the narcissistic screen obfuscating the truth of desire in the later Lacan, is the way to "gentrify" and come to terms with the traumatic drive, while militant *politics* is a means of putting the terrific force of Negativity to use in restructuring our social affairs. So Lacan is not a postmodern cultural relativist with respect to the authenticity of the Truth-Event: there really *is* a difference between an authentic Truth-Event and its semblance, and it can be traced to the fact that in a Truth-Event the Void of the death drive, of a radical negativity that momentarily suspends the Order of Being, continues to resonate.

This difference between Badiou and Lacan turns precisely on the status of the subject: Badiou's main point is that the subject should not be identified with the constitutive Void of the structure, since such an identification already *ontologizes* the subject, though in a purely negative way, turning the subject into an entity that is consubstantial with the structure and thus belongs to the order of the necessary and a priori ("no structure without a subject"). To this Lacanian ontologization of the subject, Badiou opposes its "rarity"—the local-contingent-fragile-transient emergence of subjectivity. When a Truth-Event (contingently, unpredictably) occurs, a subject emerges and exercises fidelity to it by discerning its traces in a Situation the Truth of which is this Event.[15] Lacan, however, introduces a distinction between the subject and the gesture of subjectivization (or what Badiou describes as the *process of subjectivization*, in which the subject's engagement with and fidelity to the Event occurs, versus *subject* as the negative gesture of breaking out of the constraints of Being that opens up the possibility of subjectivization). The subject prior to subjectivization is the pure negativity of death drive prior to its reversal into identification with some new Master-Signifier.

In Lacan, act is a purely *negative* category, which (in Badiou's terms) stands for the gesture of breaking out of the constraints of Being, for the reference to the Void at its core, *prior to the filling in of this Void*. In this precise sense, *act* involves the dimension of death drive which grounds the decision (to exercise fidelity to a Truth), but it cannot be reduced to it. The Lacanian death drive is thus a kind of "vanishing mediator" between Being and Event, a "negative" gesture constitutive of subject that is then obfuscated in "Being" (the established ontological order) and in fidelity to the Event.[16] One should insist here on the irreducibly vicious cycle of subjectivity: "the wound is healed only by the spear which smote it," that is, the subject "is" the very gap filled in by the gesture of subjectivization. In short, the Lacanian answer to the question asked (and answered in the negative) by such different philosophers as Althusser, Derrida, and Badiou—*Can the gap/opening/Void which precedes the gesture of subjectivization still be called "subject"?*—is an emphatic *yes!* The subject is at once the ontological gap (the "night of the world" or madness of radical self-withdrawal) and the gesture of subjectivization that closes, or heals up the wound of, that gap (in Lacanese: the gesture of the Master which establishes a new harmony). *Subjectivity* is a name for this irreducible circularity, for a power that does not fight an external, resisting force (say, the inertia of the given substantial order) but an obstacle that is *absolutely inherent*, which ultimately "is" *the subject itself*.[17] In other words, the subject's very endeavor to fill in the Gap is precisely what both generates and sustains it. "Death drive" is thus the constitutive obverse of every emphatic assertion of Truth irreducible to the positive order of Being, that is, the negative gesture which clears the way for creative sublimation; the fact that sublimation presupposes death drive means that a sublime object by which we are enthusiastically transfixed is effectively a "mask of death," a veil that covers over the primordial ontological Void. (To will this sublime object effectively amounts to willing a Nothingness, as Nietzsche would have put it.) If there is an ethico-political lesson to be learned from psychoanalysis, it consists of the insight that the great calamities of our century (from the Holocaust to the Stalinist *désastre*) resulted not from our succumbing to the morbid attraction of this Void but, on the contrary, from our endeavoring to avoid confronting it and to impose the direct rule of Truth and/or Goodness.

The political consequences of reasserting psychoanalysis in the face of Badiou's critique are the very opposite of the standard psychoanalytic skepticism about the final outcome of the revolutionary process (i.e., the revolutionary process has to go wrong and end up in self-destructive fury because it is unaware of its own libidinal foundations, of the murderous aggressivity which sustains its idealism, etc.). It is tempting to claim instead that Badiou's resistance to psychoanalysis is part of his hidden Kantianism, on account of which he also ultimately opposes the full revolutionary *passage à l'acte*. That is to say, although Badiou is adamantly anti-Kantian and, in his political stances, radically leftist (rejecting not only parliamentary democracy outright, but also multiculturalism or "identity politics"), at a deeper level his distinction between the order of the positive Knowledge of Being and the wholly different Truth-Event remains Kantian. When he emphasizes how, from the standpoint of Knowledge, there simply is no Event (i.e., that its traces can be discerned as signs only by those who are already engaged with the Event), doesn't he thereby echo Kant's notion of signs as announcing the noumenal fact of freedom without positively proving it (e.g., the enthusiasm for the French Revolution)?

What a true Leninist and an authentic political conservative have in common is the fact that they both reject what could be called liberal-leftist "irresponsibility" (advocating grand projects of solidarity, freedom, etc., yet ducking out when their price proves to be concrete and often cruel political measures); an authentic conservative, like a true Leninist, is not, however, afraid to *pass to the act* and bear all the consequences, unpleasant as these may be, of realizing a political project. Kipling, for example (whom Brecht admired very much), despised British Liberals who advocated freedom and justice while silently counting on the Conservatives to do the necessary dirty work for them; the same can be said of the attitude of liberal leftists (or "democratic Socialists") toward Leninist Communists: "democratic Socialists" reject the social-democratic "compromise," wanting a true revolution yet shirking the price to be paid for it; they thus prefer to adopt the attitude of a Beautiful Soul and keep their hands clean. In contrast to this false liberal-leftist position (pro-democracy for the people so long as there are no secret police to fight and no threat to their academic privileges), a Leninist is, like a conservative, *authentic* in the sense of fully assuming the consequences of his politics, of being fully aware of what it actually means *to take power and exert it*. Therein lies the fatal weakness of those who, like Badiou, rely on a proto-Kantian opposition between the positive order of Being (or of the *service des biens*) and the radical, unconditional demand for *égaliberté* that signals the presence of the Truth-Event—an opposition, that is, between the global social order and the dimension of universality proper, which cuts a line of separation into this global order—their unconditional demand for the Truth remains at the level of a hysterical provocation directed at the Master, testing his limits ("Can he reject—or meet—our demands and still maintain the appearance of omnipotence?"). The test of the true revolutionary stance, as opposed to this game of hysterical provocation, is the heroic readiness to endure the subversive undermining of the existing System as it undergoes conversion into the principle of a new positive Order that can *give body* to this negativity—or, in Badiou's terms, the conversion of Truth into Being.

Notes

1 Alain Badiou, *L'être et l'événement* (Paris, 1988).
2 Ibid., 24–25.
3 Another Badiou example of Truth-Event, the atonal revolution in music accomplished by the Second Viennese school (Schoenberg, Berg, Webern), also exemplifies three ways to betray the event of Truth: (1) the traditionalists' dismissal of atonal music as an empty formal experiment, which allowed them to continue to compose in the old ways, as if nothing had happened; (2) the pseudo-modernist fake imitation of atonality; and (3) the tendency to change atonal music into a new positive tradition.
4 Perhaps therein resides the negative achievement which brought such fame to François Furet: the *de-event-ualization* of the French Revolution, that is, adopting an external perspective toward it and thereby turning it into a succession of complex historical facts.
5 Badiou, *L'être et l'événement*, 224, 229.
6 As Badiou perspicuously notes, these four domains of Truth-Event are increasingly displaced in the public discourse of today by their non-evenementential fake doubles. We speak of "culture" instead of "art," of "sex" instead of "love," of "know-how" or "wisdom" instead of "science," of "management" (*gestion*) instead of "politics," and thereby reduce art to an expression/articulation of historically specific culture, and love to an ideologically dated form of sexuality, while science is dismissed as a falsely Western-universalized form of practical knowledge equal to many forms of prescientific wisdom, and politics (with all the passion of struggle that this notion involves) as an immature ideological version or forerunner of the art of social management.
7 See Badiou's unpublished 1995/96 seminar, "Saint Paul: La fondation de l'universalisme."
8 An irony worth noting here is Foucault's conception of psychoanalysis as the last link in the chain beginning with the Christian confessional mode of sexuality, which thereby links it to Law and guilt. However, Paul, the founding figure of Christianity, does exactly the opposite (at least on Badiou's reading) by endeavoring to *break* the morbid chain that links Law and desire.
9 Jacques Lacan, "On the Moral Law" (1959), in *The Ethics of Psychoanalysis 1959–1960*, Bk. 7 of *The Seminar of Jacques Lacan*, ed. Jacques-Alain Miller, trans. Dennis Porter (New York and London, 1992 [1986]), 71–84; quotation from 83–84.
10 Ibid., 84.
11 The status of the reference to Kant here is another matter. Insofar as Kant is conceived as the philosopher of the Law in Badiou's Pauline sense, Lacan's concept of *Kant avec Sade* retains its full validity, that is, the Kantian moral Law retains its status as a superego formation, so its "truth" remains the Sadean universe of morbid perversion. However, there is another way to conceptualize the Kantian moral injunction which delivers it from the superego's constraints; for a Lacanian approach to this "other Kant," see Alenka Zupančič, *Die Ethik des Realen* (Vienna, 1995).
12 For example, the very last sentence of Lacan's *Séminaire XI* speaks of the "signification of a limitless love [which] is outside the limits of the law"; Jacques Lacan, "In You More

than You" (1964), in *The Four Fundamental Concepts of Psycho-Analysis*, ed. Jacques-Alain Miller, trans. Alan Sheridan (New York and London, 1978 [1973]), 263–76; quotation from 276.

13 Jacques Lacan, "Desire, Life and Death" (1955), in *The Ego in Freud's Theory and in the Technique of Psychoanalysis 1954–1955*, Bk. 2 of Miller, ed., *Seminar of Jacques Lacan*, trans. Sylvana Tomaselli (New York and London, 1991 [1978]), 221–34; quotations from 231–32.

14 The other famous quip of the embittered Oedipus is uttered in response to the claim by the Chorus that the greatest boon to mortal man is not to have been born at all; the well-known comic rejoinder, quoted by Freud and referred to by Lacan ("Unfortunately, that happens to scarcely one in a hundred thousand"), has acquired new meaning today amidst the heated debate over abortion: Aren't aborted children in a sense those who *do* succeed in not being born?

15 See Badiou, *L'être et l'événement*, 472–74.

16 This difference between Lacan and Badiou also has certain implications for the appreciation of political events. The disintegration of East European socialism was not, for Badiou, a Truth-Event; apart from giving rise to a brief popular enthusiasm, the dissident fomentation never managed to transform itself into a stable movement of followers consistently engaged in militant fidelity to the Event, but soon disintegrated such that what we have today is either the resurgence of vulgar liberal-parliamentarian capitalism or the rise of racist/ethnic fundamentalism. However, if we accept the Lacanian distinction between the negative gesture of the act (saying *no!*) and its positive aftermath (i.e., locating the key dimension in the primordial negative gesture), then the process of socialism's disintegration can be said to have produced a true *act* nonetheless, in the guise of an enthusiastic mass movement of saying *no!* to the Communist regime for the sake of authentic solidarity—a negative gesture that counted more than its later, failed positivization did.

17 The first and still unsurpassed description of this paradox was perhaps Fichte's notion of *Anstoss*, the "obstacle/impetus" which sets in motion the subject's productive effort to "posit" objective reality; no longer the Kantian Thing-in-itself—an external stimulus affecting the subject from outside—the *Anstoss* is a kernel of contingency which is *extimate*: a foreign body in the very heart of the subject. Subjectivity is thus defined not by a struggle against the inertia of the opposing substantial order but by an absolutely inherent tension.

Teresa Brennan

Why the Time Is Out of Joint: Marx's Political Economy without the Subject

In *Specters of Marx,* Derrida runs together a rereading of Marx with evocations of *Hamlet,* especially Hamlet's understanding that "the time is out of joint." Derrida's general concern is with the logic of haunting (hence *Hamlet* and its untimely ghost), but he also has a particular "haunting obsession" in mind: "At a time when a new world disorder is attempting to install its neo-capitalism and neo-liberalism, no disavowal has managed to rid itself of all of Marx's ghosts."[1] Nor does Derrida think these spirits should be suppressed. *Specters of Marx* is a major, courageous political statement. Marx's stakes have never been lower, but the most influential philosopher of recent times has chosen this point to insist that deconstruction is only an extension of a "certain spirit of Marx." Moreover, Derrida thinks that a reworking of Marxism is the condition for subverting the easy dominance of neocapitalism. But this reworking has to be much more than a rerun. "Marxism remains at once indispensable and structurally insufficient: it is still necessary *but* provided it be transformed and adapted to new conditions and to a new thinking of the ideological, provided it be made to

The *South Atlantic Quarterly* 97:2, Spring 1998.

analyze the new articulation of techno-economic casualties and of religious ghosts, the dependent condition of the juridical at the service of socio-economic powers or States that are themselves never totally independent with regard to capital."[2] But how, as the old question has it, is this to be done? One way of doing it is by theorizing why "the time is out of joint," the refrain that is the centerpiece of *Specters of Marx*. We can build on this refrain, for Marx's political economy points to why, quite literally, the time is out of joint. But it only points. While Marx himself was obsessed with time (as the chapter headings of *Capital* make plain), the time factor in his value-theory has been obscured by his own emphasis on the subjective factor, on human labor-power as the key factor in profit. Used without this subjective emphasis, however, Marx's value-theory becomes a theory of time and speed, in which time is, quite literally, compressed in favor of distance. It is compressed by the binding of nature in the "fixed points" of commodities. These points are fixed relative to the reproduction-time of nature; they are fixed because they cannot reenter the natural reproduction process at the same rate as other natural substances. Their "time" is out of joint with the reproduction-time of nature. Once this is understood, it is plain that there can be no full environmental sustainability as long as large-scale or multinational capitalism persists.

But why adopt the labor theory of value to show this? It is the least used and possibly the most criticized aspect of Marx's oeuvre, yet it remains unique in its stress on the twofold nature of a commodity. A commodity, as Marx defined it, is always produced for exchange and always has exchange-value. But it also always has use-value, and there can be no use-value without nature, or natural substance. Because of Marx's emphasis on the twofold nature of a commodity, the labor theory of value can become a theory whose essential contradiction is between natural energy and the time or speed of exchange. Marx himself saw this basic contradiction in terms of labor-power and technology, where labor-power alone adds value, but where value will necessarily be diminished as more is spent on technology. Technology adds no value in itself, but more has to be spent on it in order for capital to produce in the fastest time possible and thus to compete.

Understanding of this contradiction has been limited because of Marx's subject-centered perspective, which singled out labor for special treatment. In all modes of production, across time and across cultures, labor for Marx is the subject, while nature is relegated to the realm of object. More exactly, nature and technology alike are the object. Together, they constitute the "means of production," which Marx defines as the "objective factors," with labor-power defined as the "subjective factor."[3] According to Marx, surplus-value, or profit, is due to the difference between what the subjective and objective factors add in production. The subjective factor (or "the subject"), labor-power, adds value, while the objective factors (or "the object"), nature and technology, do not. This is because the subject, labor power, is variable in its capacity to add value, while the object remains constant. Marx formalizes these different factors as "variable capital" and "constant capital," respectively. Variable capital is variable because it adds more than it costs in the production process. It does this because it adds more, within a given time in production, than the time needed to reproduce labor-power overall. Marx dwells at length on labor-power's ability to add more than it costs, but what it comes down to is this: Labor-power is living energy, and its livingness distinguishes it from constant capital (nature and technology), which is ostensibly dead. Its value is thus precisely constant. Being ostensibly "dead," nature and technology can give no more than they cost.

Despite all this, the profit maker will spend more on constant than on variable capital in order to compete, to get more and more products onto the market in the shortest possible time. More will have to be spent on constant capital as improved technologies make for faster production. If profit makers are to stay in the race for profit, they have to produce and distribute commodities as quickly as possible, which means spending more on those technologies and the natural resources that feed them. At the same time, they spend less on variable capital because the more sophisticated the technology (as a rule, and there are of course exceptions) the less labor-intensive the industry. In other words, while technological expenditure enables profit makers to compete more effectively in the short term, it leads, according to Marx, to a "tendency of the rate of profit to fall" in the long term. Profit depends on the difference that a living subject makes to a dead object.

Both theoretically and politically, the subject/object distinction is no longer a tenable place to begin. At the same time that Derrida was deconstructing binary oppositions and present time, the environment we inhabit was marshalling another critique of the subject-centered position. The practical critique begins with the ecological movements and environmental writings that are conscious of the diminution of certain natural substances and the degradation of the biosphere, a process wherein human beings have arrogated to themselves the right to control and direct their environment for their own benefit. The details of this practical critique are, of course, well-known. The odd thing is that, with the exceptions of Deleuze and Guattari, and Gayatri Spivak, attention to the subject/object distinction (and to binary oppositions in general) has stopped short of criticizing these oppositions and their effects on Marx. Spivak analyzes the use of oppositions and the subject-position in Marx's value-theory, but insists on a "materialist predication,"[4] in express distinction from Deleuze and Guattari.

It is time to take this materialist predication further. In fact, and obvious enough now, it is not only labor, or human beings, that live and add energy; it is also nature, although it was easy to forget this, to objectify nature, when it was abundantly there to be taken for granted. If nature (or certain natural forces) is shown to have an energetic property in common with labor-power, then Marx's "essential contradiction," between time and technology, has more explanatory power. Nature is the source of all value and, ultimately, of all energy, but the inherent dynamic of capital is to diminish this value and this energy in favor of time and technology.

Energy and Time. Labor-power, as Marx said quite precisely, is energy transferred to "a human organism by means of nourishing matter";[5] nourishing matter, in turn, is produced by other natural sources and the socially directed energy of human beings (usually women). Just as nourishing matter feeds labor-power, so is nourishing matter fed by other natural substances. Just as the reproduction of labor-power cannot take place without, or outside of, the cycles of natural reproduction, neither can the reproduction of other natural sources and forces. So, on the one hand, all these forces and sources are connected; on the other, they are not equal from the temporal perspective of capital. But, for the time being, I will refer to natural sources and forces without qualification whilst bearing in mind the obvious point that not all of them add energy (or useful energy) to the same extent. Some of them add more energy than others, including labor-power; some add less.

For Marx, energy could only be added by living labor; all other constituents of production were supposedly lifeless, although that distinction was irrelevant as far as the behavior of capital was concerned. But this does not mean that it is irrelevant to the inner workings of production—or to a value-theory that is not subject-centered. It is important to remember that Marx, in discovering what he thought was the source of capitalist profit, also showed how capital loses consciousness of that source, with more constant capital expended and less of the variable capital that adds value. This source was so obscured that it remained partly hidden even from Marx himself.

Since labor-power is precisely energy, even "tension,"[6] it has everything in common with other natural forces and is as capable of releasing energy. For that matter, it has a potential affinity with both animate and inanimate natural substances, insofar as these can be made into sources of energy. Of course, they still have to be *made* into these sources, and, on the face of it, only labor would seem to have this power of making. But our immediate concern is with their energetic dimension. Like labor-power, natural sources and forces are commodities capable of releasing and adding energy. Like labor-power, they have a certain time of natural reproduction, which means that, potentially, the value they add in production can be greater than their reproduction-time. Like labor-power, they can add more or less energy in the production process. Of course, we have to distinguish between these natural sources and forces in terms of (1) how much energy they generate and of what kind, and (2) how much it costs to acquire them, relative to one another and to labor-power.

The point here is that because Marx began from a subject/object world in which all things, artifacts and natural substances alike, are already commodities—objects for consumption by a subject—he made two mistakes: (1) He overlooked the affinity between labor-power and nature at the level of energy. Labor-power and other natural substances are alike in that they are living, as opposed to technology, which really is dead. Technology can only borrow energy from natural sources. (2) Because Marx ignored the vital energetic affinity between labor and nature, he then supposed that the only new substantial value added in the (industrial) production process is the energy newly materialized by *labor* in the product.

But once labor-power is treated as a source of energy—as one form of all natural sources of energy—once the opposition between subjective and objective factors is replaced by one between living nature and the commodified dead, then value-theory's logic can be extended. We can keep the logic that led Marx to break capital down into two components: constant and variable. We can even say that variable capital is the source of surplus-value, while constant capital is not. We can deduce, too, that the greater the outlay on constant capital in production the less the surplus-value extracted. We can deduce, furthermore, that the imperative to produce more in the shortest possible time will lead to a greater outlay on constant capital.

But the change we will make is to assume that *all natural sources of energy entering production should be treated as variable capital and sources of surplus-value*, and that some can be replaced by others. The logic of this replacement will encompass labor-power: if another natural substance can supply what labor supplies, it too will count as variable capital. Moreover, this series of assumptions entails that *there is no real check on the speed with which variable capital can be used up, apart from whether a particular form of variable capital can be replaced*, meaning that its reproduction has to be guaranteed. The absence of any natural check on speed is the short answer to why the time is out of joint. But we will approach this conclusion more slowly.

If all energetic sources entering production add value, the famous "tendency of the rate of profit to fall" will be offset.[7] It will fall only where constant capital is really "fixed" in relation to labor-power, fixed in that no other natural force—disguised as constant capital—figures in production.[8]

Energy, Reproduction-Time, and the Law of Substitution. Does this mean that any natural force or source of energy will do the same profit-making job that labor-power does? Only under certain circumstances, and with many qualifications. The extent to which one energy source can be replaced by another depends on what I term the *law of substitution*. The speeding up of production time, and its disjointedness with natural time, can only be understood in the context of this law: *all other things being equal, capital will take the cheapest form of energy adequate to sustaining production of a particular commodity at the prevailing level of competition*. Many such energy forms will be refined, that is, one to many times removed from their natural state. But this does not mean that they cease to be valuable. They cease to be valuable only when their capacity to add energy is exhausted. Up to that point, their value may even be increased as other forms of energy (including labor-power) are mixed into them, although this mixing can also diminish energy sources overall, especially when their reproduction-time is discounted. As we will see, the reproduction-time of other natural substances, aside from labor-power, will be discounted whenever possible; labor-power is the only source of energy whose reproduction-time capital *must* pay for—as a rule.

But our immediate concern is with qualifying "natural sources and forces." Some substances are readier forms of energy and add more energy than others. In everyday terms, the extent of the energy they have or add is precisely what makes them valuable. And this cuts both ways. If labor-power can stand in for another energy source more cheaply and more effectively, it will be the source chosen. The point is that at the level of substance, the material energetic level, the common denominator is energy, not labor-power—and all energy sources, including labor-power, vary in what they cost compared to what they add. At the same time, Marx's crucial distinction between labor and labor-power is massively amplified in the case of other natural sources and forces. His critical point was that *labor* added more in production than the reproduction cost of the commodity *labor-power*, although capital did not cheat: it paid for labor-power at its value. Other natural forces and sources also add more than their reproduction costs, but capital (and for that matter, state socialism) *does* cheat in terms of other natural forces by not paying for them at their value.

Do we have any reason (apart from my argument) to assume that capital operates by a law of substitution? In fact, a similar assumption about substitution was made by Marx in discussing the various permutations of labor-power as a commodity. Capital, he claimed, would not hesitate to force down the wage as much as possible (keeping "socially necessary labor-time" to the minimum) or to import (i.e., replace) labor-power from another source. This is why Marx assumed that the need to extract surplus-value could lead to the immiseration of the working class. He assumed that as the organic composition of capital changed—and a greater expenditure of constant capital meant less outlay on variable capital—the only way to make a profit or increase surplus-value would be to keep wages down, to the extent that the level of subsistence became the level of bare survival. Thus the advantage to capital of a reserve army of labor (the unemployed and the famous *Lumpenproletariat*) whose existence would in itself keep the cost of labor-power down: it weakens the bargaining power of the working class.

By the same logic, if certain natural forces capable of adding value within the sphere of industrial production are interchangeable, then capital's range of cheap options is greatly extended. It has in its back pocket not only Marx's "reserve army" but Heidegger's "standing reserve" of nature. In line with the logic of substitution that governs capital's selection of labor-power, where capital will always, all other things being equal, take the cheapest option, it should follow that capital operates by a general law of substitution where living forces overall are concerned. If one energy source can stand in for labor, and more cheaply, then it will be the chosen source. Thus, to take up at the tail end of the twentieth century Marx's famous nineteenth-century cloth example: natural fabrics will cost more than synthetic ones, whose raw materials can be "reproduced" at a faster rate, unless the natural raw materials as well as the fabrics themselves are reproduced and produced in "cost-effective," labor-intensive centers where the cost of labor-power is so low that the fabrics can compete internationally (*100% Cotton: Made in India*).[9]

The law of substitution can offset trends toward the immiseration of the working class to the extent that other energy sources can stand in effectively for labor. I say "to the extent" because, while the immiseration of the working class did not occur in the capitalist heartlands as Marx predicted, it has occurred in the global context.

The effects of the law of substitution here are similar to those wrought by imperialism and those leading to the creation of a labor aristocracy. When Lenin, following Marx and Engels, argued that a labor aristocracy, a richer segment of the working class, could be created through the exploitation of other sections of that class, nationally and internationally, he was pointing to how the rate of surplus-value extraction of a portion of the labor market could be lower in one place if it were higher elsewhere.[10] We can now see how a similar "benefit" to portions of the labor market can be effected through increasing the rate of surplus-value extraction of other natural entities and things. If coal or wood or oil provides energy that labor-power would otherwise provide, if they add value in the same way, and if they can be exploited more ruthlessly, then labor-power can benefit. Labor-power can be better off when coal, wood, or oil receives less than it needs to reproduce. As a rule, the reproduction-time of natural substances is not factored into capital's costs; as I said, frequently this reproduction-time is not paid for at all, let alone at its value.

In certain circumstances, and from its utterly ruthless perspective, capital might be concerned for the reproduction of natural forces and the substances on which they depend, but it will only be concerned insofar as these sources provide a continually cheaper option or if they are both irreplaceable and necessary. While capital has to be concerned about labor-power's capacity for resistance, it need only be concerned about resistance relative to natural forces when they are spoken for. Needless to say, natural forces, substances, and (nonhuman) beings are nonunionized and unrepresented, therefore frequently not spoken for.

Energy and the Speed of Acquisition. The question of the reproduction of natural sources returns us to time. Capital avoids paying for the reproduction-time of natural substances in order to make a profit. It is in this regard that a value-theory without the subject/object distinction reveals capital's basic contradiction to be between the time of natural reproduction and technology. By this theory, a particular capital stays in the race only by speeding up the materialization of energy—the value added by natural substances in production—and thereby speeding up the rate of surplus-value extraction. While this speeding up diminishes overall use-value in the long term, it works in the short term, yielding speedier profit via speedier production. But this speedier production is out of joint with the time needed for natural production. (This will become clearer when we consider two ways in which the extraction of surplus-value from natural substances is intensified.)

But first consider that, if we treat all natural forces capable of materializing energy or commodities produced naturally (agriculture) as variable capital, the problem with the idea of expanding nature's use-value, and therefore expanding the potential basis of exchange-value, would appear to be not that natural substances lack the "specific" quality of labor (for materializing energy, thereby increasing value), but that they cannot be measured in terms of "socially necessary labor-time"—the time required for a tomato plant to produce a tomato, say. This is a problem for agricultural capital in particular, in that agricultural commodities are more obliged to keep their natural forms and thus (it is implied) their natural time-cycles of reproduction. Yet it is not an insurmountable problem. Marx's concept of socially necessary labor-time is based on the average amount of time required to produce a given object at a given level of technology. Now, the average amount of time that a tomato plant takes to produce a tomato can in fact be calculated with some precision. The real point is that the plant's technology appears (or once did appear) to be fixed. One of the main historical limitations affecting the author of *Capital* was the assumption that the reproductive time of natural substances could not be speeded up, that the tomato plant's inner workings could not be regulated or controlled. It is now plain that this is not so and that capital has indeed found (socially necessary) ways of speeding up various modes of natural reproduction.[11]

Natural products that need to keep their forms in order to serve as agricultural commodities can be produced more speedily by regulating their conditions of production. These commodities are in general animals and animal products as well as trees, plants, and their produce. We now successfully breed pigs without trotters; unable to walk, they lie on shelves to speed up the fattening that takes them to pork. Cows are next in line for the same treatment, and wingless chickens are on the way. "Modern turkeys have been bred with breasts so large that it is impossible for them to mate." There is no doubt about the motive, not even a coating of palaver about science for science's sake. It is simply that "a wise farmer is not going to buy a patented animal, or any other item, unless it will increase profits. That is just what transgenic breeds are being engineered to do."[12] Chickens already lay eggs at several times their natural rate under battery lamps; the lactation of cows is artificially increased by BST; and tomatoes, like a great deal else, are planted in soil which has been artificially fertilized so that its fallow time is bypassed, with the plants themselves genetically recombined in order to increase their reproductive rate.

By such processes as these, which speed up the commodification of animals and plants (amongst other things), surplus-value is increased, but the long-term effect may well be an impoverishment of surplus-value based on use-value, to the extent that surplus-value must embody use-value. I say "may well be" because it is always possible to take account of the conditions of use-value in production (e.g., refertilizing soil naturally or artificially). However, with respect to the overall quantity of use-value, such measures must either diminish it or, if done by natural means, run counter to it. Natural means will be at odds with the speed imperative, while artificial means—and thus a profitable speed—depend on overdrawing somewhere else.

The price paid for speeding things up is a price paid in terms of overall productivity, and hence overall, long-term profit. There will be a decline in long-term profit to the extent that commodities embody less real substance, and this they must do as they become degraded of substance. Take the giant, airy American strawberry. Genetically recombined for enhanced size and grown in degraded soil, it looks great and tastes . . . like nothing. In the medium term, even its comparative price has fallen. A symptomatically postmodern commodity, it seems wonderful yet has literally less substance, hence less value. Its price nevertheless increased in the short term with the speed of its deceptively luscious production.

Short-term gain and a decline in long-term productivity and profit are also evident in the second way of speeding things up characteristic of industrial production: changing the form of natural forces and sources beyond recovery—and at an even more accelerated pace. Changing the form of a natural force or source can involve violent conversions, such as the one whereby coal is converted into electrical power or recombined in chemical conversions to make anything from plastic to CFCs.

It is arguably the case that reproduction-time, or real value, continues to be discounted as industrial production becomes more centralized. In fact, discounting the cost of reproduction is the other side of the coin of centralization. It is not only quantitatively, in terms of use-value, that centralization draws more from nature than it can return to support a political, juridical, and distributive apparatus beyond the one essential for local production, but also that the pathways of centralization proceed simultaneously with the pathways of extended acquisition. In one respect, this was anticipated by Marx: "The *smaller* the direct fruits borne by *fixed capital*, the less it intervenes in the *direct production process*, the greater must be this relative *surplus population and surplus production*; thus, more to build railways, canals, aqueducts, telegraphs, etc., than to build the machinery directly active in the immediate production process."[13]

Of course, energy cut off from its natural source of origin cannot continue to regenerate the natural energy that enabled it to come into being. However, as more and more natural substances assume this form, and as more and more natural substances are bound in fixed capital, they require greater and greater infusions of external energy to enable them to keep producing, due to two obvious facts: (1) the binding and fixing of natural substances in the form of commodities diminishes the quantitative supply of nature overall; and (2) these bound forms have no regenerative energy of their own. Yet as capital cuts back the supply of natural substances, it diminishes not only nourishing matter—one source of energy—but also the regenerative conditions of other natural sources of energy as well. Natural reproduction-time is seriously out of joint. Capital, to cope, has to speed up agricultural production, which of course makes things worse. Speeding up agriculture in turn fuels the speed of acquisition through consumption, which depends on wide networks of distribution, as does industrial production. In fact, this is where the two ways of speeding things up converge: acquiring more at a faster speed for production entails distributing more and consuming more, which puts pressure on agriculture to produce at a rate commensurate with other aspects of production and distribution. As available sources of energy—agricultural or industrial—are diminished, capital has to create new routes for the old sources of energy to come from farther away or find new sources of energy altogether, ranging from electricity and chemicals to "nuclear power."

The reproduction of natural substances and sources of energy goes according to a natural cycle that takes a certain amount of time. The hyperactive rhythm of capitalism, on the other hand, means that the conversion of substances into energy leads to its further conversion into other energy forms, which are increasingly coming to be the basis of energy overall, with lunatic environmental consequences. The reality, as by now should be abundantly plain, is this: short-term profitability depends on an increasing debt to nature, a debt that must be endlessly deferred, even at the price of survival.

Short-term profitability, with its inflated price, must lead to a reduction in long-term profit and productivity. Insofar as the substantial material embodiment in productivity and profit has to be reduced or rendered unreproducible by the logic of production geared to speed, capital is its own worst enemy. How this plays out in total terms should be reflected in the crisis of capital, in its "long waves" and "laws of motion." In sum, what Marx saw clearly and before all was the inherent contradiction in capital as a mode of production. He saw it in terms of labor and technology, or constant and variable capital, where the former, to keep pace, had to expand at the expense of the energy input of labor. That contradiction is recapitulated here, although its terms of reference have changed. Or, rather, its terms of reference have been stripped of their phenomenal forms so that the contradiction emerges as what it is, essentially: one between substantial energy and artificial speed.

How Space Replaces Time. The contradiction between energy and speed is not simple. Two kinds of time are at issue: the generational time of natural reproduction, and speed—the artificial time of short-term profit. Speed, as I have already indicated, is as much about space as about time as such. It is about space because it is about centralization and distance. Speed, measured by distance as well as by time, involves a linear axis, time, and the lateral axis of space. In the consumptive mode of production, the artificial spacetime of speed (space for short) takes the place of generational time. For, to the extent that capital's continued profit must be based more and more on the speed of acquisition, it must centralize more, command more distance, so, in this respect, space *must* take the place of generational time.[14]

It is clear that generational time suffers because capital tends inevitably to speed up the production of all commodities, including naturally formed or agricultural ones. While there are countervailing tendencies in agriculture (and in the very existence of labor-power and of scarce or apparently irreplaceable sources), the speed imperative will override them wherever possible. As capital speeds up, then, it will diminish or degrade the conditions for the natural reproduction of natural things. But this is not the only way in which generational time is short-circuited by short-term profit. As I have indicated in relation to fixed or constant capital, capital will also bind more and more living energy in forms which cannot reproduce themselves. These fixed or bound commodities are either not recyclable at all or are only recycled out of time, in that their recycling occurs at a pace far slower than other biospheric ingredients. The production of these kinds of commodities is the heart of industrial production, and this industrial heart has a temporal beat: the beat of instant gratification, a beat that gets more rapid by the minute. The substances in bound commodities are cut out permanently from the generational process of natural exchange at the same time that they are inserted, in their newly acquired objectified or bound forms, into the process of commodity exchange. Of course, it matters more to some substances than to others; trees lose more than rocks or minerals.

But what these erstwhile natural things lose in their ability to go on living, to reproduce down the generations, they gain in mobility. Not much of a gain, to be sure, for the things themselves, but a big gain for capital, which certainly requires the portability of most commodities. Moreover, since one cannot consume more products in production without having a market for those commodities outside production, both processes of consumption have to be speeded up. The more directly consumable a product is, the greater its use-value. Again, the most readily consumable product is the one that is most portable and involves the least expenditure of energy in consumption (a dishwasher is more valuable than a bucket, a shower has the edge over a pump). More time and energy is required to produce these products and make them portable, while less energy is expended in their consumption, especially if *they* come to *you*—and as fast as possible.

The point here is that time's disjointedness is a function of increasingly rapid movement through space. A commodity has to be shiftable, for it has to go to market. Aside from pigs and their ilk, commodities can only go to market in a movable form, which means being *removed* from the conditions in which they reproduce themselves. Only labor-power and animals continue to reproduce after being uprooted. In fact, one of the distinctive features of the commodity labor-power is that it is portable of its own accord. But no natural substance aside from the human and the animal can reproduce itself if it is uprooted, or literally removed from the earth. Centralization requires portability, however, and therefore uprooting; and portability is all the more required the faster production becomes, and the more extensively centralized. This should mean that, barring its replacement by something more cost-effective, portable labor-power's importance increases, both because it is a commodity that covers its own transportation costs and because it plays such a big part in shifting things around. And the scope of centralization must be extended, as the extent of acquisition depends on it.

Extending acquisition requires, first, some means of transportation, either to bring the desired good to you or to take you to it. Extending acquisition so as to consume more goods in the process of production automatically entails two things. The first is an increase in the scale of production. (With production no longer entirely on a local scale, the consuming producers are more likely to lose track of the source of value, in terms of the time of natural reproduction.[15]) The second is an increase in the speed at which the goods have to be brought to the point of production. That is how capital operates according to its own fantasmatic law of speed. Or rather, that is how the process we are renaming *centralized consumption* operates, a process of which capital is the greediest and most efficient exemplar. The more things are brought together from out of their habitat and locale, the more networks are needed to bring them to the place of consumption. The more they are brought together, following the paths of centralized consumption, the more they are cut out of their habitat and locale—and the more cut out they are, the less they can reproduce. The less they reproduce, the less they become. The less they become, the more substitutes for them must be found. The more substitutes needed, the greater the centralization needed to find and transport them. Centralization, speed, and spatial scope all increase because the goods have to be produced and distributed on a timescale at least comparable to that of local production in order to compete with it—a timescale that will, of course, be aimed at overtaking local production and same-scale competitors.

In other words, economic centralization creates energy demands and an energy field which can only be sustained by extracting surplus-value from nature. It is otherwise impossible, for even without the imperative to constantly speed up so as to stay in the race, the additional demands that centralization makes on the reproduction of nature (through transportation and such energy services as electricity, water, etc.) lead to more being extracted from nature than can be returned in terms of the time needed for natural reproduction. This process of extracting surplus-value from nature is inexorable, for it is necessary to maintaining the *centralized* apparatus of the state *and* advanced technological production, regardless of whether the mise-en-scène is capital's or that of an erstwhile state socialism.

Thus in production and distribution based on increasing economic centralization, distance overrides time. Moreover, distance overtakes time in inverse proportion to it so that, in general, lateral space increasingly substitutes for the (linear) time of local-generational production and consumption. Space thus takes the place of time via the denominator common to both, namely, speed: the speed at which the entities and substances traverse, or are transported, to the place of production increases, as does the speed at which they are consumed in production and the speed at which they are distributed—in accordance with the scale on which they are consumed in production—for further consumption. The idea that space takes the place of time in modernity has been put forward by others (Fredric Jameson especially), but the fact that this overtaking of time by space is integral to the process of surplus-value extraction has not been clear before now.

The speedy continuum of consumption for production and further consumption is the essence of why space has to override time in the CMP. In fact, the idea that centralization in itself demands more from nature than can be returned requires a formula: the condensed distance and imposed direction of spatial centralization is paid for by the time needed for natural reproduction. By this analysis, we are left with a world in which the price of centralized space is effectively the sacrifice of reproductive time. This world is made over on a lateral axis, which uproots to a vast extent the generational or "linear" one. In this making over, capital carries on like a parody of natural production. It has to have a means of "reproducing" its products, of enabling substance to turn into something else. In natural reproduction, this means is the energy generated by the natural cycles themselves. And we know that capital, like nature, uses energy to transform one substance into another. But capital garners its energy by violent conversions, and these conversions follow rhythms that bear only an attenuated relationship to the rhythms of natural production, whose temporal constraints they ignore.

In reproducing or producing its babies, capital follows its own "cycles" and "laws of motion." Its parody of nature is almost complete. In playing God and redirecting nature at its own speed and from its own subject-centered standpoint, capital is playing for high stakes because it is literally altering the *physis* of the world, adjusting nature's inbuilt logic and spatiotemporal continuum to suit itself. By its will, capital is imposing a direction on physical processes other than their own. In the meantime, the willful subject, the agency effecting all this, becomes more and more invisible among the diverse forms of power-without-accountability that mark the present era. The time is out of joint. We smell this around us and know it in our bodies. We console ourselves with myths of hybrids, while living the divide between a speedy fantasy that overlays us and a natural time that knows it is running out. The time is out of joint; we know this not only because of a sometimes romanticized sense of loss, but also because it is the necessary economic consequence of the present course of capital.

Notes

For Linda Burnett, because she supported this argument's initial drafting twenty years ago, and for Liana Giorgi, who persuaded me to revise it when I had all but abandoned it.

For an earlier version, see my *History After Lacan* (London and New York, 1993), 118–65. See also my "Arbeitskraft und Natur als Reproduktionskosten," *Das Argument*, No. 205 (Spring 1994): 341–57.

1 Jacques Derrida, *Specters of Marx: The State of the Debt, the Work of Mourning, and the New International*, trans. Peggy Kamuf (New York and London, 1994 [1993]), 37.

2 Ibid., 58–59.

3 Karl Marx, *Capital*, Vol. 1, trans. S. Moore and E. Aveling (Moscow, 1954 [1867]), 179.

4 See Gayatri Chakravorty Spivak, "Scattered Speculations on the Question of Value" (1985), in *In Other Worlds: Essays in Cultural Politics* (New York and London, 1987), 154–75, esp. 154–55.

5 Marx, *Capital*, 207 n. 1.

6 Ibid., 583.

7 In the literature on Marxism and the environment, it has been supposed that if capital has to make provision for environmental safeguards, the expenditure on constant capital will increase and therefore exacerbate the tendency of the rate of profit to fall. See the influential argument to this effect by André Gorz, *Ecology as Politics*, trans. P. Vigderman and J. Cloud (London, 1983 [1975]). There may be a minor increase, but the inflexibility of energy sources massively affects it and all other increases.

8 Other natural forces are readily disguised by Marx's original conceptual armory. Just as his definition of "objective factors" elided nature and technology, so too does the definition of another key term in Marx's vocabulary: "circulating capital." Referring to technological as well as natural forms of energy, circulating capital, as we will see, is the measure of just how fast money can move mountains (and rivers, dams, trees, and a few other things besides). The significance of circulating capital in this epoch has been recognized by Marxist political economy. For Ernest Mandel, it is probably the most important factor because of its increasing range and speed; see his classic and comprehensive *Late Capitalism*, trans. J. De Bres (London, 1975 [1972]). In my rereading of value-theory, this phenomenon is basic rather than incidental: the range and speed of circulation is one key to the extraction of surplus-value and the making of profit.

9 See M. R. Redclift, *Development and the Environmental Crisis: Red or Green Alternatives?* (London and New York, 1984); and *Sustainable Development: Exploring the Contradictions* (London and New York, 1987).

10 Although the concept of a labor aristocracy belongs more to the previous century than to this one, the logic remains the same; the labor aristocracy was more likely to perceive itself as middle class. See E. J. Hobsbawm, *Labouring Men: Studies in the History of Labour* (London, 1964).

11 While we are talking here of substances which need to keep their original form, and probably their ability to reproduce themselves, in order to serve as commodities, the same process applies to some natural substances capable of materializing energy as such (e.g., oil seed).

12 L. J. Raines, "The Mouse that Roared," in *Transgenic Animals*, ed. F. G. Grosveld and George V. Kollias (London and San Diego, 1992), 341, 342; cf. Patricia Spallone, *Generation Games: Genetic Engineering and the Future for Our Lives* (London, 1992).

13 Karl Marx, *Grundrisse* (1857–58), trans. M. Nicolaus (London, 1973 [1953]), 707–8; translation modified.

14 The same point has been made well by Elmar Altvater in the context of a discussion of thermodynamics, economics, and time; see his "Ecological and Economic Modalities of Time and Space," trans. M. Schatzscheider, *Capitalism, Nature, Socialism*, No. 3 (1989): 59–70. Altvater's article is in part a creative, critical discussion of Nicholas Georgescu-Roegen's thermodynamics-oriented "bio-economics" (in which Newton's second law is applied to space to support the argument that scarcity is inevitable). Georgescu-Roegen

differentiated between time "T" (a continuous sequence) and time "t" (the mechanical measurement of intervals). (Shades of Heidegger!) Mechanical time, which lacks the historical dimension that goes with a continuous sequence, is also opposed to historical time "T," which cannot be measured or predicted mechanically. For Georgescu-Roegen, according to Altvater, "a particular logic develops in the space and time co-ordinates (as in the social and economic co-ordinates): economic surplus production is guided by the quantitative imperative of growth by way of reducing the time spans of human activities (especially those of production and consumption). It does this by accelerating and transcending the quantitative and qualitative impediments in space in order to compress time, thus setting 'T' into 't.' There are thus two co-ordinating systems of space and time, which, in the form of two patterns of 'functional spaces,' are fixed upon a territorial-social reality" (63). Altvater goes on to conclude that "the expansionist pressure inherent in the economic logic of surplus production has a territorial dimension (as production is necessarily always spatial). Surplus production is thus identical to the economic conquest—exploration, development, penetration, and exploitation—of space, i.e., the 'production of space' " (69).

A different distinction between two kinds of time is made by Julia Kristeva, who distinguishes cyclical and monumental time from historical or linear time; see her "Women's time," trans. S. Hand, in *The Kristeva Reader*, ed. Toril Moi (Oxford, 1986). Cyclical time is the natural time of repetition, monumental time that of eternity. The problem with equating historical and linear time is that the sequential nature of generational as well as historical time is downplayed.

15 See Vandana Shiva, *Staying Alive: Women, Ecology, and Survival in India* (New Delhi, 1988).

Rosaria Champagne

Queering the Unconscious

Consider the following pair of intersecting anomalies: (1) the unconscious is always already queer, its queerness not lodged in sexual practices or affiliative identities; and (2) (anti-)queer Marxism and mainstream gay conservatism fail as *politically progressive heuristics* in their ontological retreat into historical determinism, on the one hand, and their pathological embrace of capitalist privilege, on the other.[1] Indeed, (anti-)queer Marxism and gay conservatism are unwitting partners in what may be the (*ur*-)queer marriage of our century. Their opposing positions on the relationship between capitalism and social progress, nullified by their projected disavowal of sexuality's inseparability from the unconscious, left open the possibility of such a nuptial. Marriages often flourish in hostile silence, and this one differs only in that its curious progeny is the divide between academic queer theory and community-based queer activism. Psychoanalysis can be brought to bear not for marriage counseling, but rather to diagnose the symbolic seductions that keep this queer couple together, in a perpetual dance of repetition, and that thereby stall any real progress toward queer liberation.[2]

The *South Atlantic Quarterly* 97:2, Spring 1998.

The fact is that you can't buy queer theory at Wal-Mart, and it's a good thing, too, for capitalism distorts the concept of material access by making commodification a precondition for exchange. "Queering the unconscious" can be understood as politically progressive when we differentiate queer liberation from problematic normative notions of sexual liberation; when we historicize our commitments to community-based queer movements on intellectual terms, not on the grounds of political allegiance; and when we resist turning queer theory into commodity queerness—all of which depends on the possibility of psycho-Marxism.

Gay Conservatism. Gay conservatism is a movement made up of mostly Republican-voting White gay men who see academic queer theory as monolithically "radical" and therefore nonpragmatic and out of touch with the *real* gay movement, the politically and sexually sanitized one that looks more like a golf league gone wine-tasting on a Saturday afternoon than a revolution.[3] Gay conservatives gained notoriety in 1996 when the Log Cabin Republicans (the national gay and lesbian Republican organization) sent a $1,000 check to Bob Dole's presidential campaign. (Bob returned the check.) Marriage rights and gays in the military are other notable movements initiated by gay conservatives, who maintain that both gender and capitalism are solid, self-evident, and, if not ahistorically true, then at least here to stay. Gay conservatism doesn't recognize bisexuals or transgendered people. These subjectivities are understood as fetishized icons, "shock tactics" deployed in Gay Pride marches as "men in tutus" and "dykes on bikes."[4] A founding text for this movement, Kirk and Madsen's *After the Ball* provides a "social code" for decorous gay behavior, behavior that these authors predict will translate automatically into social approval (hence their subtitle). Let's take a look at their "Self-Policing Social Code":

> *Rules for Relations with Straights*
> 1. I won't have sex in public;
> 2. I won't make passes at straight acquaintances, at strangers who might not be gay;
> 3. Wherever possible and sensible, I will come out—gracefully;
> 4. I will make an effort, when among straights, not to live down to gay stereotypes;
> 5. I won't talk gay sex and gay raunch in public;

6. If I'm a pederast or sadomasochist, I'll keep it under wraps and out of Gay Pride marches;
7. If I'm a transvestite, however glamorous, I'll graciously decline invitations to model lingerie for "Oprah" or "Donahue."

Rules for Relations with Other Gays
1. I won't lie;
2. I won't cheat on my lover—or with someone else's;
3. I'll encourage other gays to come out, but never expose them against their will;
4. Tested or otherwise, I'll practice safe sex;
5. I'll contribute money in meaningful amounts to the Gay Cause;
6. I will not speak scornfully or cruelly [about someone's] age, looks, clothing, or social class, in bars or elsewhere, lest I reveal my own insecurities;
7. When forced to reject a suitor, I will do so firmly but kindly;
8. I'll drop my search for Mr. Right and settle for what's realistic;
9. I won't re-enact straight oppression by name-calling and shouting down gays whose opinions don't square with mine.

Rules for Relations with Yourself
1. I'll stop trying to be eighteen forever and act my age; I won't punish myself for being what I am;
2. I won't have more than two alcoholic drinks a day; I won't use street drugs at all;
3. I'll get a stable, productive job and become a member of the wider community beyond the gay ghetto;
4. I'll live for something meaningful beyond myself;
5. When confronted by real problems, I'll listen to common sense, not emotion;
6. I will not condone sexual practices I think harmful to individuals or to the community just because they're homosexual;
7. I'll start making some value judgments.[5]

This social code is emblematic of the rhetorical and political priorities of gay conservatism, which values an uncritical participation in capitalism and a deep allegiance to the mass-media production of representations that will right the wrongs of bad press for queers. Gay conservatism holds the ahistorical belief that the origins of queer oppression can in fact be traced to "bad press," much of it self-generated. And gay conservatism is sometimes the only gay discourse available. As Michael Warner wrote recently, regarding the persuasiveness of gay conservatism, "If you don't know much about the past of the gay movement or AIDS activism, and if you get your information only from the press—if, in other words, you are in the position of nearly everybody on the planet—you might easily conclude that American gay politics is a minor offshoot of neoconservatism."[6]

We should not dismiss Kirk and Madsen's social code as merely tight-assed, for we need to understand the impossibility of queer political progress under conservatism. The sloppy psychologism inherent in their thinking reflects, among other things, the degree to which they naturalize capitalist patriarchy as inevitable, if not good for us all. One example of such psychologism is the authors' explanation for why failing to adhere to this social code creates a climate in which personality disorders can be "passed" among members of the gay community: "Although homosexuality isn't a personality disorder, the way gays are forced to live—by straights and by one another—lowers their resistance to personality disorders."[7] Kirk and Madsen are not alone in advancing wrongminded theories of the psyche and of the social order; such confusions pervade gay conservative writing.

Bruce Bawer, another defender of gay conservatism, throws down another gauntlet: "[Academic] queer ideology itself is ultimately selfish and immature [because] queer politics . . . serves the interests of those who would prefer not to see gay people become full . . . participants in mainstream society."[8] Gay conservatives point to Marxism as the *real* problem plaguing the academic and community "queer establishment." As Kirk and Madsen put it, "The radical gay cadre persists in seeing all issues in terms of an outmoded and inapplicable Marxist framework, which is not only annoying to reasonable people but the infallible sign of a rigid and simplistic mind."[9] Indeed, the gay conservative rallying cry to the "queer establishment" is, "Grow up."[10] Radical queers are ostensibly standing in the way of gay mainstreaming, the highest goal of gay conservatism.

(Anti-)Queer Marxism. (Anti-)queer Marxism takes the historical-materialist position that sexuality, like any other aspect of subjectivity, is historical,

not essential, and emerges in the particular history of class struggle, which is understood as a "causal determinant." Teresa Ebert explains the implications of this position for queer theory: "The very emergence of the 'queer' itself is the effect of the development of forces of production." And "the emergence of the 'homosexual' is . . . characteristic of a historical moment in which the forces of production have reached such a level of sophistication in their productivity that heterosexuality . . . is no longer necessary."[11] To Ebert, a historical-materialist understanding of queerness that posits "sexuality [as] an articulation of profit . . . determined by the mode of production" leads to the flat-out rejection of psychoanalytic theories of sexuality, which she dismisses as hopelessly "'ludic' (playful) and thus wholly inadequate in effecting political change or social betterment."[12]

Donald Morton, in the *Material Queer* and the "Class Politics of Queer Theory," brings Marxist historical materialism to bear on the entire field of academic queer theory and—amazingly enough—finds it readily reducible to the binarism of "desire theory" (the "ludic" domain of psychoanalysis, psychology, poststructural feminism, and liberal humanism) versus "need theory" (the "real" domain of Marxist theory and materialist history). Morton writes that, while desire theory "produces a politics of isolated localities in undecidable relation to each other," a chaotic condition that renders social progress impossible because of the multiplicity of issues and possibilities at stake, need theory returns us to a stable and controllable world: "Need theory . . . explains social change in relation to an objectively existing binary (base/superstructure) operating in the mode of determinate causality, such that changes in the (economic) base eventuate . . . in changes in the superstructure (politics, religion, culture, morals/ethics, sexual practices)."[13] Just as gay conservatives dismiss any challenge to mainstream orthodoxy as self-evidently childish and ineffective, Morton misreads "desire" so as to erase its meaning in queer theory, that is, its psychoanalytic rendering as a function of the unconscious that has no closure or end. He then relocates desire in its most commonsensical conceptualization, as sexual behavior. (If, as I suspect, he knows better, then Morton's move here is a self-serving and strategic gesture—and certainly not an intellectually grounded one.) Elsewhere, he asserts that "the different forms need and desire take have to do ultimately with . . . mode of production," since "materialism . . . envision[s] need and desire in relation to what is *socially productive*. Thus needs and desires have to be theorized in terms of their global social value, which would be determined—at a minimum—by the equitable distribution of resources of all kinds on a global scale."[14] In contrast to the "libidinal economy" of queer theory, which "formulates [a] future in terms of an ever-expanding region of sensuous pleasure," declares Morton, "gay theory was [genuinely] forward-looking: it had a historical vision of a differently ordered and more just future." Indeed, "today's queer theory is finally only part of that idealist bourgeois history currently being written through VR [virtual reality] goggles." His conclusion? "The most productive and responsible contribution will be made by a materialist . . . [response] that theorizes sexuality in relation to . . . social need."[15] Examples of this "virtual reality" perspective that Morton finds so offensive are AIDS-related survivor grief and attempts by some queer scholars to write about AIDS in a style that is at once personal and critical.

Both (anti-)queer Marxism and gay conservatism eschew subjectivity and its productions and effects for a rigid historicism whereby "truths" about our future appear as, say, a code for proper gay conduct or a Marxist critique of class struggle. I believe that politically progressive scholars need to draw on both materialist accounts of history and psychoanalytic interpretations of subjectivity in order to develop theoretically sophisticated refutations of "outward appearances" as the galvanizing force of social betterment, political change, and economic democracy. It is crucial for any politicized psychoanalysis to engage and make connections among, dialogically and dialectically, discrete traumas, motives, fears, fantasies, and desires, in whatever social guise, as historical and political forces. Lacanian psychoanalysis already sets some of the terms for such an engagement between the personal and the cultural. But to move wholly outside the subject is to proffer the hope that social forces not only exist apart from subjective interpretation, but are apprehensible outside of signification, a position that is both rigidly dogmatic and fundamentally reactionary. Their rejection of the nuances of interpretive matrices shows that (anti-)queer Marxism and gay conservatism are not-so-distant cousins of Bill Bennett, Lynne Cheney, and Dinesh D'Souza. As Eve Sedgwick observes, "Anti-intellectuals today, at any rate, are happy to dispense with the interpretive process and depend instead on appeals to the supposedly self-evident."[16] (One might also add to the list (anti-)queer Marxists and gay conservatives whose totalizing impulses elevate rigid "application models" of critical theory to revolutionary plateaus and, in the process, arrive at the same place as anti-PC pundits.)

The (Anti-Queer) Religious Right. Let's up the ante here and look outside of middle-class gay culture, specifically at an anti-queer text produced by the theocratic Right. A coalition of evangelical organizations that want to reframe Christian political practice, the theocratic Right also aims to revise the U.S. Constitution. If political savvy is no longer understood as worldly and therefore ungodly, it can be embraced as God's calling to his Christian soldiers—and the First Amendment separation of church and state can be redefined as an "attack" on Christians. While it is beyond the scope of this essay to explore the full complexity of the coalition of institutions we call the religious Right, it is important to know about some of its institutional components and their connections to the corporate Right (universities not excepted), such as the American Family Association, Campus Crusade for Christ, the Christian Coalition, Citizens for Excellence in Education, Concerned Women for America, Eagle Forum, Family Research Council, Focus on the Family, the Heritage Foundation, Operation Rescue, Promise Keepers, the Rutherford Institute, and the Traditional Values Coalition.

A good example of the imbrication of the religious and the secular—the signature representation of contemporary Christian nationalism—can be found on the cover of a recent issue of *Christianity Today*. It features a picture of Bill and Vonette Bright, founders of Campus Crusade for Christ. The Brights, with their tense, too-wide smiles, look like overstuffed angels. The angle of the shot suggests a heavenly perspective on the couple, while the accompanying text declares them "the Radical Brights. They call themselves 'slaves of Jesus Christ.' They founded a 300 million-dollar ministry. Their combined annual salary is $48,000. They are calling the American church to repent, pray, and fast. Their goal is 'to take the gospel to everybody on planet Earth.'"[17] The article describes how the Brights built their multimillion-dollar Campus Crusade for Christ industry, making it clear that "total quality management" is practiced by the religious Right.

In a number of well-funded media blitzes, other entities that shelter under the umbrella of the religious Right have sought to mobilize (if not to inform) a Christian citizenry by means of "infomercials" that provide the right Christian answers to questions, though not the processes of interpretation that make those "answers" tenable. Take, for example, a 1996 issue of *USA Today* that included a large advertisement in the Life section paid for by Americans for Truth About Homosexuality, which read in part:

> Bill Clinton's pro-homosexual position has not been an issue in this election because the American people haven't been told all the facts. The media . . . are strangely silent on an issue with such social and economic implications for our culture. Americans for Truth About Homosexuality is changing that by speaking the truth in the public square. We are a new organization launched by a former reporter for the *Washington Times* and publisher of the *Lambda Report on Homosexuality*, a critical monitor on "gay" activism. We believe, like most Americans, that homosexuality is WRONG and should NOT be encouraged . . . by governments, schools, popular culture, . . . or by the President of the United States. You can help spread the truth across America! Call 800-774-7989 today! Americans for Truth is dedicated to exposing and countering the powerful homosexual movement in America. But newspaper space is expensive. Please help us place ads like this in other newspapers by making your most generous donation. Call today for a free copy of this ad to run in your local paper. You will receive our special report, "President Clinton's Pro-Homosexual Record," and a free copy of the *Lambda Report* with any gift of $10.00 or more. Donations are not tax deductible. Please remit checks to Americans for Truth. Send all correspondence to: Americans for Truth, PO Box 45252, Washington, DC 20026-5252.[18]

What is significant about this advertisement is its unabashed display of self-righteousness, its implicit reliance on the Bible as a repository of self-evident truths (which is made explicit in the *Lambda Report* referred to here), and its confident deployment of a commonsensical normativity that resonates with nationalism and capitalism.

Other factions of the religious Right have produced home videos, distributed for free at participating-church services, on the evils of homosexuality (e.g., *The Gay Agenda*) and have published books and pamphlets, also distributed free of charge. One of these right-wing texts demonstrates a conservatism grounded on a theory that is common to (anti-)queer Marxism and gay conservatism as well. *Setting the Record Straight* was published by Focus on the Family, which has over a thousand full-time employees and an annual budget of $70 million (including its $4 million grant from the El Pomar Foundation for the purchase of fifty acres in Colorado Springs). It is run by Dr. James Dobson, a radio psychologist who believes, among other things, that homosexuality can be cured and that corporal punishment is a useful tactic in discouraging young, inchoate queers. In 1988, Focus on the Family merged with a Washington, DC, anti-queer think tank, the Family Research Council, and produced and distributed (free of charge) what they called "the homosexual packet." In 1992, it separated from the think tank after an IRS investigation concluded that such a merger made it ineligible for tax-exempt status.[19] *Setting the Record Straight* proposes that homosexuality be addressed from a public policy standpoint, not merely from a moral, Christian one. It gestures toward democracy and fairness in declaring that Christian moral outrage, though justified, should *not* result in the abuse of gay people ("love the sinner, hate the sin"). Instead, it suggests that reasonable and pragmatic questions about homosexuality be posed in a global context. These questions are derived, however, from highly contested notions about the transmission of AIDS and the role of women in the American family. In any case, the primary question posed by *Setting the Record Straight*, repeatedly throughout the various sections, is the following: "Are the qualities or consequences of homosexuality beneficial or detrimental to individuals and to society?"[20]

Need? Desire? Can the well-dressed gay conservative charm his way out of this one? The problem is not that the religious Right, (anti-)queer Marxists, and gay conservatives all want a global accounting of the social effects (including the consequences) of queerness; on the contrary, reading the personal through its meanings in the political was an early and important feminist strategy. The problem lies in the myopia of their "fixed" givens, whether expressed as "capitalism is here to stay," "materialist critique of class struggle = Truth," or "a kinder, gentler Christian dogmatism." All three movements position themselves ultimately in terms of the Hegelian master/slave dialectic—as masters, needless to say—and, accordingly stuck in the "impasse" of failed recognition, confuse power with success. By failing to recognize the slave as a subject, the master loses the opportunity to be recognized, to be accounted a subject himself, and reflected as such. The slave submits because she must, not because she recognizes the master as a subject, whose existence depends on the projection of the object. In Lacan's terms, the subject cannot recognize herself except in reflection, from or by some "other." On the basis of Hegel's failed master/slave relationship, Lacan concluded, as did Marx, that the slave triumphs by virtue of her knowledge of the other.

Gay conservatism, (anti-)queer Marxism, and the religious Right, in refusing a dialogical relationship with the "other" (radicals, "desire" theorists, and all-things-queer, respectively), therefore, become masters whose power is not earned in intellectual exchange but seized in strength. At the same time, gay conservatives see themselves as oppressed (by radical queers), while (anti-)queer Marxism traces its own oppression to the academic establishment of feminist and psychoanalytic theory. In the meantime, however, the religious Right marches into the next millennium with stunning political success. Indeed, of the three, only the religious Right commands a mass audience and wields a multimillion-dollar budget, which makes it the only "active" master. The "critiques" of (anti-)queer Marxism and gay conservatism, sticking to the U.S. cultural map at the turn of the century with all the might of gnats on a windshield, may blur your vision or annoy you, but they won't change your course.

The Queer Unconscious. Eve Sedgwick says that "something about queer is inextinguishable."[21] Lacan adds, "Since Freud the unconscious has been a chain of signifiers that somewhere (on another stage, in another scene, he wrote) is repeated, and insists on interfering in the breaks offered it by the effective discourse and the cogitation that it informs."[22] Sedgwick continues: "Queer is a continuous moment, movement, motive"; it is "recurring"; it means "across"; "the immemorial current that *queer* represents is as anti-separatist as it is anti-assimilationist. Keenly, it is relational and strange."[23]

Of course, the copula "is" misguides as it links, misappropriates as stable and fixed what it represents as it represents. The copula levels complexity and contradiction; it fails to perform.[24] Lacan defines the unconscious as "impediment, failure, split. In a spoken or written sentence something stumbles. . . . Discontinuity, then, is the essential form in which the unconscious first appears to us as a phenomenon—discontinuity, in which something is manifested as a vacillation." In an eerily Frankensteinian vein, Lacan writes that "at first, the unconscious is manifested to us as something that holds itself in suspense in the area, I would say, of the *unborn.* That repression should discharge something into this area is not surprising. It is the abortionist's relation to limbo."[25] Just as "queer" does not refer to a stable, conscious sexuality, gender, or history, the unconscious does not and cannot inscribe gender or sexuality. That we come to identify ourselves as gendered and sexual speaks not to anything inherent in the unconscious, but rather to the collective social invention by which a fundamental failure or lack in the unconscious would be resolved.

Regardless of (anti-)queer Marxism's intentional misreading of the term "desire," of gay conservatism's intolerance toward ideas and concepts that challenge their commonsensical pragmatism, or of the religious Right's protests against anything it cannot control, the want, need, or demand they express has nothing to do with desire in the psychoanalytic sense. While *need* seeks satisfaction, and *demand* a comprehending subject, *desire* relies on alienation from both its object and its recognition. A function of the unconscious, not a conscious wish for satiation, fulfillment, completion, or closure, desire literally sated yields only horror, as the gothic novel demonstrates. Desire spawns social identifications, but it does not mean "acting on one's sexual impulses," the libidinal economy that knots the underwear of (anti-)queer Marxists, gay conservatives, and the Christian nationalists of the religious Right. Just as "queer" cannot be contained by social codes of conduct, gay conservative enforcement efforts notwithstanding, the unconscious will not be had: "At the unconscious level, you cannot say: 'I am'; in fact, you are dispossessed of being. Thus, the unconscious is a level where there is no 'self-consciousness,' where the subject doesn't find a way of naming herself, because she lacks the fundamental referent, the 'I am.'"[26] This explains why "coming out" functions both in principle and in practice as an act of signification and resistance that is continual and never completed. Queer communities do not share a consensus about whether coming out is politically progressive, regressive, or neither. Our meaningful contradictions also explain why visibility does not automatically translate into liberation and why social change does not happen at the level of representation.

Understanding the unconscious as always already queer points to the limitations of totalizing theories for social progress, whether they emerge from (anti-)queer Marxism or the Lacanian Right. Here's a juicy example of the latter: observe how Jacques-Alain Miller, beginning in a progressive vein, then shifts from a politicized to a normativized psychoanalysis:

> The worst pervert is he who speaks in the name of morality. The true perverts, . . . the judge, the priest, and the professor—all those in a

> position of authority who control the jouissance of others. The worst perversion is righteousness. That is what Freud teaches us. Moral conscience is fed by exactly the same energy that would have gone into drive satisfaction but has been renounced. The criminal pervert is not the opposite of the righteous judge: the righteous judge is the worst criminal.[27]

Miller's conservatism slips out just at the moment when the queer unconscious activates terror: he advocates removing lesbianism from the psychoanalytic category of "perversion" on the grounds of its being a sexuality that precludes the penis. Of course, under patriarchy, there is no greater insult. Lesbianism becomes invisible and, as such, is unrepresentable and nonsymbolic. Of course, under Lacanianism, there is no greater insult. If female homosexuality is not a perversion, asks Miller, "what would you call it?" His answer? "It could rather be called . . . 'heterosexuality,' which Lacan defines as 'love for women.'" That Miller's slide into conservatism is a slide away from the radical potential of Lacanian psychoanalysis is even more evident when he explains that, "according to Freud, male homosexuality is a fundamental social bond: it is a principle of the social bond. Female homosexuality doesn't have that function; it may be of great *cultural* importance, but is not of fundamental *social* importance."[28]

Excuses, excuses. While my mother would be soothed by Miller's assurance that lesbians can be considered heterosexual, we need to remember that radical queer theory in recent years has been largely devoted to undermining the presumption of normative gender, a theoretic imperative we borrowed first from Lacan.

Marxism and Psychoanalysis: Mutual Recognition and Meaningful Contradiction. As I have already suggested, "queer" refers not to the *fact* of gay or lesbian, transgendered or bisexual identity, but to the *political and epistemic* meaning of homosexuality at this, the end of the century, when the religious Right is establishing a foundation for neofascism. The queer turn away from identity politics can be traced to Lacan, who saw identifications as one of the three sources of human aggression (along with cultural prohibitions and forced sacrifices).[29] Interdisciplinary queer theory is committed to two incommensurate and unsuturable systems: psychoanalysis, in which the sexual, more intimately linked to fantasy than to practice, is inseparable from the unconscious; and Marxism, in which the political, in a dialectical relation with the social, mirrors and demarcates the possible.

Queer theory espouses and enacts Hegel's concept of "mutual recognition" and its association with "freedom." When the self recognizes that its existence depends on an other which it cannot see, that recognition produces the freedom of "self consciousness." While I reject the notion of a "freedom" born of self-consciousness, I embrace the idea that social healing is made possible by mutual recognition, which enables strangers to become something other than enemies. If mutual recognition is the theoretical crux of queer theory's imbrication with psycho-Marxism (as I believe it is), then it challenges some basic tenets of both traditional psychoanalysis and Marxism. Mutual recognition renders politically impossible (and ethically suspect) the classical Marxist position on the dialectic as pointing toward class warfare, not difference. Indeed, such a turn misunderstands the radical potential inherent in totalizing social reality, which is not a leveling of differences but a materializing, in our social vocabulary, of the concepts by which we integrate the experiential with the epistemological so as to make meaningful political sense of our oppression.

In historical-materialist terms, the meaning of sexuality and sexual practices emerges from its historical "moment," a conceptualization distorted by (anti-)queer Marxists, who advance a misguided totalizing historical determinism whereby class struggle creates not only sexuality, but also the terms of its meaning. This conflation of historical origin with cultural effect points to an aspect of psycho-Marxism that is deeply relevant to queer theory: such a totalized and determined reading of history misconstrues the "real" as part of the symbolic order at the same time that it falls into the trap laid by the mirror stage. If the Real, as Ellie Ragland says Lacan defines it, is "the traumatic material of unassimilated memories and meanings that blocks the *dialectical* movement of symbolization,"[30] then the "trap" laid by the mirror stage is the ruse of historical linearity. As Richard Feldstein explains, in describing how "the temporal logic" of the mirror stage operates:

> A child peers into the looking-glass and experiences an anticipatory jubilance when piecing together a body image related to the ego's conception of itself. As the amorphous ego projects itself into a rigid

> body-image, it constructs the conceptual contours of subjectivity and experiences a jubilant anticipation of a future mastery that is connected to the acquisition of motor skills associated with this totalizing image of itself. This image of self-unification is constituted in part to repress anxiety-producing images of the body divided into bits and pieces. As a stage of chronological development, the dissociated body of bits and pieces would seem to precede the mirror stage, yet one can only measure part object and whole object representation in relation to each other. In actuality, the body in bits and pieces is constructed post facto from an anticipated future retroactively recognized.[31]

Historical determinism could thus be said to yield a sadistic form of cultural analysis, for by obfuscating the queer unconscious, (anti-)queer Marxists and gay conservatives reify the psychical as always already persecutory—and, in the process, they override meaningful relational conceptions of history.

Conceptualizing queer theory instead within the meaningful contradiction of Marxism and psychoanalysis, however, links personal experience with social history and creates a new avenue for public access and debate. Such access is a matter of political necessity, though not because "the public" or its standards should set the course of our work. Nor do I believe that prejudices can be overcome without the devising of a new language for social progress or that queer theory's public accessibility must proceed by way of a single, unidirectional route from the academy on down, gravitating with the force of privilege into the community. As I said before, you cannot buy queer theory at Wal-Mart, and it's a good thing, too. For if queer theory becomes commodified as identity politics, it will lose the power to change and grow, becoming distorted by the same process of commodification that warps all liberatory paradigms. That's what's wrong with gay conservatism, the political wing with the most power in mainstream gay organizations. But academic queer theory, with its critical trajectory stalled at social totalities and class warfare, is equally dysfunctional, at least if we define queer theory's function as enabling social and political emancipation. Indeed, there will be no queer liberation through only the leveling of class differences, in the terms of vulgar Marxism.

So here is my hope for the next generation of academic queer theorists: those who regard queer theory as hopelessly ludic will leave room for those of us who believe that there is no time like the present for a public teach-in; who believe that the religious Right is a genuine threat to the lives of all queer people and our allies in the United States today; and who believe that psycho-Marxism will help to shift our discussion from binary oppositions to mutual recognition—and to meaningful contradiction and difference.

Notes

1 (Anti-)queer Marxism conflates historical materialism with historical determinism and then positions "queer" as a signifier of the superstructure. It is, in theory and in practice, a conservative enterprise that levels the political potential of Marxist analysis. Gay conservatism, as typified by Andrew Sullivan, Bruce Bawer, Marshall Kirk, Hunter Madsen, and the Log Cabin Republicans, views social change as occurring at the level of representation, and capitalism as therefore capable of being marshaled to serve gay liberation.

2 I realize, of course, that the concept of liberation raises the eyebrows of both historical materialists (because it moves us outside of materially apprehensible constructs) and psychoanalytic critics (because it suggests that subjects can take control of social progress and that truths are not always bound up in lies). That's fine. I'm not advocating a normativized appropriation of psychoanalysis that would pit it against Marxism. Nor am I advocating that a psychoanalytic theory of the subject be inserted into a Marxist theory of history. Instead, I argue for a theoretic dialecticism in which differences can be recognized as rich sites of interpretive possibility rather than impasses to interpretive and political action.

3 On the subject of gay conservatism, see *The Advocate*, 29 October 1996, the cover of which announces "The Gay Republicans: If Dole is elected, these men may be your only hope."

4 Marshall Kirk and Hunter Madsen, *After the Ball: How America Will Conquer Its Fear and Hatred of Gays in the 90s* (New York, 1989), 114.

5 Ibid., 360.

6 Michael Warner, "Media Gays: A New Stone Wall," *The Nation*, 14 July 1997, 14.

7 Kirk and Madsen, *After the Ball*, 279.

8 Bruce Bawer, *Beyond Queer: Challenging the Gay Left Orthodoxy* (New York, 1996), x–xii.

9 Kirk and Madsen, *After the Ball*, 350. Of course, Marxism is not the only theory to be trashed for its lack of pragmatic utility. As Gore Vidal writes in the introduction to Jonathan Katz, *The Invention of Heterosexuality* (New York, 1995): "Freud was a romantic, school-of-Nietzsche, would-be novelist of the modernist-symbolist school . . . who put together a crackpot religion that would never have got off the ground had it not been for his personal brilliance and imperturbable megalomania" (viii).

10 Bawer, *Beyond Queer*, xiv.

11 Teresa L. Ebert, *Ludic Feminism and After* (Ann Arbor, 1996), 50, 65–66.

12 Ibid., 96, 217.

13 Donald Morton, "The Class Politics of Queer Theory," *College English* 58 (1996): 471–82; quotations from 474.

14 Donald Morton, "Changing the Terms: (Virtual) Desire and (Actual) Reality," in *The Material Queer: A LesBiGay Cultural Studies Reader*, ed. Donald Morton (Boulder, 1996), 1–33; quotation from 9.

15 Ibid., 14, 30.

16 Eve Kosofsky Sedgwick, *Tendencies* (Durham, 1993), 17.

17 *Christianity Today*, 14 July 1997.

18 *USA Today*, 31 October 1996.

19 See Jean Hardisty, "Constructing Homophobia: Colorado's Right Wing Attack on Homosexuals," in *Eyes Right! Challenging the Right Wing Backlash*, ed. Chip Berlet (Boston, 1995), 86–104, esp. 95.

20 Larry Burtoft, *Setting the Record Straight: What Research Really Says about the Social Consequences of Homosexuality*, Focus on the Family "Matter of Facts" report (Colorado Springs, 1994), 29.

21 Sedgwick, *Tendencies*, xii.

22 Jacques Lacan, "The Subversion of the Subject and the Dialectic of Desire in the Freudian Unconscious" (1960), in *Ecrits: A Selection*, trans. Alan Sheridan (New York, 1977 [1966]), 292–325; quotation from 297.

23 Sedgwick, *Tendencies*, xii. "The word 'queer' itself means *across*—it comes from the Indo-European root-*twerkw*, which also yields the German *quer* (traverse), Latin *torque* (to twist), English *athwart*."

24 My deep appreciation to Barbara Claire Freeman, who helped me to see this important point.

25 Jacques Lacan, "The Freudian Unconscious and Ours" (1964), in *The Four Fundamental Concepts of Psycho-Analysis*, ed. Jacques-Alain Miller, trans. Alan Sheridan (New York, 1981 [1973]), 17–28; quotations from 25 and 23.

26 Vicente Palomera, "The Ethics of Hysteria and of Psychoanalysis," in *Reading Seminars I and II: Lacan's Return to Freud*, ed. Richard Feldstein, Bruce Fink, and Maire Jaanus (Albany, 1996), 387–96; quotation from 388.

27 Jacques-Alain Miller, "On Perversion," in Feldstein et al., eds., *Reading Seminars I and II*, 306–20; quotation from 318–19.

28 Ibid., 320, 319–20.

29 Identities and identifications are produced, according to Mark Bracher, when subjects "turn against their own actual being and try to replace it (which means destroying it) with an idealized image of quality"; "Lacan's 'Civilization and Its Discontents,'" *Journal of the Psychoanalysis of Culture and Society* 2 (1996): 1–12; quotation from 4.

30 Ellie Ragland, "An Overview of the Real, with Examples from Seminar I," in Feldstein et al., eds., *Reading Seminars I and II*, 192–211; quotation from 197.

31 Richard Feldstein, "The Mirror of Manufactured Cultural Relations," in ibid., 130–69; quotation from 134.

Laurence A. Rickels

Giving Up the Ghost of a Fetish: Between the Couples Theory of Marxo-Freudianism and Nazi Psychoanalysis

Since the fall of the Wall (and the San Francisco earthquake on the other side of one bicontinental divide, drift, and slide), there's been time to underscore what I take to be the most grievous side effect of the disappearance of Marxism: the growing "disownership" of psychoanalysis, even or especially in all the discourses or projects that owe what foundation they have to Freud's science. This double disappearance act seems to me reflective and refractive of a split that emerged most fully perhaps by the 1930s, but which had been in preparation since World War I. I'm referring to the split-leveling between partners in a discursive coupling, the shotgun merger between the Marxist and psychoanalytic discourses that keeps on going without saying but never really goes through. It had already become a recycling has-been and, indeed, our biggest symptom (in theory as in therapy) by the time Marxism was at a loss to prepare or account for the group psychology that Nazi German psychological warfare so forcefully reformulated as the prescription of ingredients to be mixed and control-released along the thin line between inoculation and uncontrollability.

The *South Atlantic Quarterly* 97:2, Spring 1998.

The "hauntology" within which Derrida gave shelter to Marxism's effects, so readily scattered among all the warning signs and opportunisms claiming to bury, not to raise, Marx, pulled up short before the couple and addressed instead, directly, the corpus of Marxism that had thus been left home alone with its life and death. The frame of such a "decouplified" reading would be existentialist or post-existentialist if it were not implicitly advertised instead as the Heidegger aversion, I mean, version, that comes, free gift and all, with a certain deconstructive reception (which is syntonic with a Freudian reading of textual symptoms). But, as though enlarging a bit on the symptom, the up-front framing of psychoanalysis as out of this picture makes Freud's science out to be just one discourse among several with equal but separate rights to a certain precedence that philosophy, however, will always supersede—even in matters of media-technologization, haunting, and mourning.

Over the issue of Marxism's missingness, deconstruction goes down a second time for the body count of mourning. We remember the first time, the one that was so lasting. Paul de Man's corpus was identified with and assimilated, put to rest by being put to the test of already being deconstruction. Like the ghost or vampire animated by a survivor's split-off mixed feelings, the beloved man returned as Nazi teenager. What was thus brought back, as a necessity for all sentient beings, was a Freudian, nonphobic recognition of the corpus in all its parts, objectionable or not. The work of mourning, the Freudian reformulation which remains the frame for all analytic work, requires that all this resistance, defense, and transference be open to interpretation.

But this time, efficient mourning has a better chance. There are no mixed feelings, not about Marxism. Derrida just doesn't like the *ism*. The resistance here lies, definitely, in an unwillingness to be up front about it and give us our Bad Marx outright. The defense of dissemination is securely and preemptively in place; the projected enemy is now not the identifiable dead but any identifiable death or ontological mourning, any bereavement bent on absolute ghostbusting, on total success.[1] No more efficient mourning (except maybe, after all, by no default of his own, for Marx). The admission of a tension between efficient mourning and the interminability of a mourning that already outlasts the outcome of melancholic shutdown resurrects while eliding a tension that is always there, in the work of mourning as in (it's the same line of work) the work of transference. What I'm trying to suggest is that even in *Specters of Marx* Freud's always the spook, or he's spooked out of haunted site, out of haunted mind; in other words or worlds, he's the unidentified object, that ultimate object of identification. How soon we forget that in psychoanalysis there's always a tension, let's call it allegorical, which, from the bottom line on up, informs every conceptualization: the tension between the shorthand or shortcut of theory and the slow time, the in-session materiality of the transference.

In closing out the ledger of inheritance, Derrida reads Marx's concept of "commodity fetishism" as symptomatic of a certain split reception of and resistance to the ghosts that nevertheless crowd Marx's discourse with the bad-styling abandon of too many mixed metaphors.[2] Marxism's top notion within a psychosocial study of culture, a quick study which in turn pulls out all its unexamined supports from the commodity management of fetishism's concept, becomes in the retallying of Derrida's new closure nothing but pure or ghostly symptom, a false or foreign embodiment, and the kind of hunger that must transform itself into power. But Derrida's hauntological reckoning with Marxism's last and lasting effects leaves out the couple dynamics, the transfer and transference between partner discourses, within the big success story of commodity fetishism. How is it that the commodity version succeeded in obscuring the full range of Freud's intervention in matters of fetishism? Well, there are always greater contexts and questions that psychoanalysis just can't address, owing to its audience-captivity to a family setting, even or especially to the techno, TV setting of all that's in the family. Both the social-studies types (Marxists and "Deleuzers") and the Heidegger kids head psychoanalysis off at the impasse of a too-perfect fit with its objects of study. The familial fit keeps Freud tied to merely projective relations with the outside world; the techno-compatibility of his science zoning restricts psychoanalysis to being part of the problem and not being party to interrogating the essence of technology. Heidegger, who already came after Marx, was the first discourse-meister to be haunted not by the corpus that was history, but instead, though at the displaced remove of disownership, by psychoanalysis, even in its social or institutional forms. It might prove too circular to flash back to Heidegger's brother—hospitalized at a psychiatric institute known for its eclectic compatibilities with Freud's science—or forward to the *Zollikoner Seminare*, which offer substantial documentation of the philosopher's regular superintendence of his sphere of influence within eclectic psychotherapy. More to the point or period is to read Heidegger's emplacement as one of theoretic and therapeutic modality, with rights of passage across all corridors, departments, disciplines, in the era of what we can now call Greater Psychoanalysis.

The rise that National Socialism was getting out of its mobilization and metabolization of all the modernist disciplines which worked, including the "reversal of psychoanalysis" that Frankfurt-school theorists were quick to diagnose as the basis of Nazi thought and praxis,[3] provided the most pressing cause for attempting yet another forced marriage or couples-therapy session. Marxism required its vitalizing supplement in time, Big Time, for a first emergency of totalitarianism right in the midst of modernism. But Marxism got the free ride in what was supposed to be a dialectical booster or collaboration. Over the issue of fetishism, in particular, their union just got in the way. What the partners, for all their differences, might hold in common after all was the compatibility of Freud's group psychology with ideology, even if only as just another ideology subsumable under critique. (This was always the Marxist version of the "resistance" defense.) But the narcissism of the small difference between group psychology and ideology is, once again, captured in the complete nonrapport between Freud's and Marx's separate takes on fetishism. Thus I come to praise the conclusions of *Specters of Marx* but on Freud's terms and on his missing behalf: there is in fetishism, according to Freud, both acknowledgment of the ruinous materiality of loss and submission to a greater mourning, let's call it techno-mourning, that mourns over even those merely integrative moments in works of mourning and substitution. As techno-mourning, fetishism isn't about the identifiable or identified-with body. For once, it's not about couples. And it's not about losing, just because you lost. It is about winning, like a winner and not like a victim; it's about some power of emergency propulsion that gets us past the totalization and paralysis of loss to the wide open outer-spacing of what in a more couplified era or moment of mourning could only be seen as the closed and enclosing delusional states that were the determining limit and dead end of failed mourning. A change came over Freud's science by the end of the First World War, one that tends to get shortchanged by its confusion with and commodification as post-Freudian rereading or critique of Freud.

We already know going into this that Nazi research-happiness is legend. It's Nazi Germany's equal time-share in modernism. The Nazis were engaged in the all-out pursuit of whatever research project was out there, as long as it could be billed as war-effort promotional. But this proviso represents, within any history of modernism, no exceptional constraint. Wernher von Braun, for example, is not a stray projected, single-case overlap covering Weimar, Nazi, and U.S. aerospace projects. In other words, a circuitous, discontinuous "dialectic of Enlightenment" (or "case of California") is not the only way to test the endurance of National Socialism. There's also a direct hit or fit of continuity: within the limits and links of the one consideration given the total war service, Nazi research also mobilized psychoanalysis, and that means one of the most protected and progressive sources of "our" modernism. But on the wider range of a more eclectic *or* more reunified rapport with psychotherapy at large, it was in Weimar and then, nonstop, indeed with mounting urgency, in *Nazi* Germany that Freud's intrapsychic model (which, precisely, doesn't take it all so interpersonally) came to be pressed by wartime researchers into areas of scientific inquiry where no psychological model had gone before. In other words, the context otherwise obscured by make-believe oppositions between orthodox psychoanalysis and, say, the object-relations school (or between psychoanalysis proper, however its precise location is to be identified, and a mixed-up medley of psychotherapies) completes itself in the widest possible circulation of Freud's model throughout all departments of psychological interventionism. (This widest ranging of the Freudian model is what I mean by Greater Psychoanalysis.) It is the missingness of the era of Nazi psychotherapeutic eclecticism or correctness from our histories of modernism, National Socialism, and psychoanalysis which requires that we not see, or "Nazi," our complete investment in Freud.

Janine Chasseguet-Smirgel—the queen of perversion studies so conservative they're radical, even though all she basically says is good art object, bad part object—presided over the 1985 reconvening of International Psychoanalysis in Hamburg, back in Germany for the first time since the Nazi station break. But she, for one and for all, refused to dismiss Nazi psychoanalysis as the kind of contradiction in terms that belongs only to the category of aberration and discontinuity. Instead, she forecast the theoretical consequences that must follow for the reception, in the first place, of the concept of transference.[4] But every other fundamental concept of psychoanalysis really must line up for rereading within the missing continuity and context as well. The pressure already on, as a result of this repress release, to rewire the transference connections can only rise with the psychoanalytic conception of fetishism. What pushes fetishism to the front of the line is, first, that it is *the* overdetermined received notion or readymade, washing up out of a still-current contest between the intrapsychic axis of interpretation and the social study of whatever external force is out there with interpersonal relations. And what seconds the nomination of fetishism for the first forced entry into uncanny cohabitation with National Socialism is that it's the password for a genealogy of media in which modern group psychology can be followed up and out through the internalization and technologization of trauma.

It is true that fetishism, the concept noted most likely to secede from decidability, has at the same time, as theory and as the theory's practice or performance, been fine-tuning the reception of mass media within cultural studies for decades now. Along with the side effects of its conceptual performance, fetishism's outer-concept experiences, which even the cultural study of mass media cannot but promote, line up for a psychology not of the one-on-one or the one-by-one but of techno-reception and invention in group-effort format. In cultural studies today, fetishism still packs a sex or sexism charge, but, since one of the partners in the couplification is always a technical medium, the sex content shifts and the prospects for our technologization open up down lines of identification plugging along into another psychologization: the kind found in groups.

Sometimes a received notion drops by the wayside, way inside a missing context that doubles as rereading-invitational. The acupressure applied by the reintroduction of Nazi psychoanalysis tunes back both the jammed *and* the drifting receptions of the fetishism concept to the first takeoff of rocketry and cybernetics across intrapsychic airspace. That's right: the aerospace and psychotherapeutic connections were in it together, in the forgotten genre of invention called *psy-fi*. With this term I locate the three-way freeway jamming with science fiction, of course, and particularly with the forgotten or repressed history of German sci-fi production from 1897 to 1945, but also with the many *psywar* manuals for projected wars that were published in Germany from the First World War onward (soldiers!) and with the numerous case studies of psychotics that were fast becoming a German-language specialty as well.

In his World War I essay on war and death, Freud was already warning that every invention (including "attempts at mechanical flight") would stop dead in its tracks if mourning did not mediate the loss of irreplaceable relations.[5] After the war, fetishism became one of a series of new, shifting concepts that displaced the centrality of successful mourning. Although fetishism doesn't perform the work of mourning, it nevertheless describes a detour taken precisely around both mourning and the melancholic metabolism which threatens to die on the invention that must go ahead and cut its failures or losses. In the follow-up treatments administered in Nazi Germany, the fetishism concept opened onto a psychic (really, psychotic) war economy based on scarcity or lack *and* total mobilization that made it to an outside—an outside chance—where successful realization of the wished-for aim, in spite of its already accomplished total loss the first time around, could be scored.

But in the missing place of the continuity that was there, the outside, society-wide career of the fetishism concept has been the exclusive property of Marxism's take on the commodification of everyday life, which still gets awarded instant, unchecked credit for being the placeholder of Freud's missing public address system, while thus making us miss out on Freud's analysis of group psychology. The exchange-value which the Marxist half of the alliance assigned to psychoanalysis restricted Freud's fetishism license to the one one-sided side or wing that was leftover. In exchange, therefore, Freud's immediate focus on fetishism belonged in the home or, translating right away into the most repressed context, on the home front. But if we left it up to Freud's own theorization of fetishism, if we left it alone, this joint account or division of labor between the two master discursivities would give way, at the latest, along the dotted line of the air-splitting break Freud made between his inside view of conflict and the socioeconomic overenrollment of struggle in the classes. In his 1933 lecture tour of worldviews, Freud skywrites the line of irreconcilability between psychoanalysis and Marxism across the genealogy of media wars. That is, Freud goes ahead, skips a couple of classes, and reduces the First World War and its Second Coming, coming soon, to "the conquest of the air":

> That does not sound very illuminating, but the first links at least in the chain are clearly recognizable. English politics were based on the security which was guaranteed by the seas that washed her coasts. In the moment at which Bleriot flew across the Channel in his aeroplane this protective isolation was breached; and in the night during which (in peace-time and on an exercise) a German Zeppelin cruised over London the war against Germany was no doubt a foregone conclusion.[6]

These conveyors of velocity and death, which would strike psychologically across airspace before outflanking an enemy's sensorium and going in for the kill, belonged to a media pageant in which the side with the greatest surprise extension would always dominate. Freud says: Forget the other master discursivity's view that social change is an economic-conditions exclusive; the extension pageant is always the way historical change or chance is taken along the front lines of war.

A reading that gets stuck here on the positivism thinking of a machine history of discourses and institutions only libidinizes what we've all already given up on. But Freud's diagnosis of World War I readiness is less about machines in history than about the *internal* lead held by technology, a margin along which ego, with no place to go, pulls apart and turns into doubles. Our inevitable interest in technology, in other words, accrues from the narcissistic investments of the psyche. But that means narcissism was always less about one's own body and more about relations of remote control over missing bodies—and even more about the relation between the ego and its mastery. Once Freud admitted narcissism as a sexual force in its own right, one that did not first require exchange with the vows of object-related sexuality for its own potential (pathogenic or otherwise) to be realized, the conditions were met for his master mix of identification between technology and the unconscious. That's why, where the conveyors of war are (as in Freud's inside view of World War I), that's where the gadget lovers will be too.

During the Cold War, U.S. psywar specialist Harold D. Lasswell folded a warning label inside the narcissistic investment that comes between soldiers and their instruments. Even when subordination of one's own weapon to some larger unit is the official alternative that comes with training, overvaluation of the weapon or vehicle just won't go away. "Regardless of the physical weapon, or of the personnel devoted to the weapon, there is a vast concentration of understanding and loyalty, the result of which is to magnify the visible role of the weapon in the conduct of war. 'Gadget love' is a snare for the unwary in the same way that love of the horse, or the camel, or the elephant appealed to the cavalryman of the past."[7] Gadget love, fetishism by any other name, has since the world wars, in theory and in practice, given libidinal access to the mass psychology that stuck in the groove of a record—the war record, it turns out, of psychoanalysis. It's true that a symptomatic or synonymic reading of the libido that fuels planes, bombs, and rockets can be quickly mounted and satisfied. But before Gadget goes to war there are steps to be taken that fall in with Freud's internal reading of fetishism, which rebounds to the two bookends of his 1887–1902 thought experiment, the "Project for a Scientific Psychology," and his 1938 sudden take on splitting as the bottom line or borderline of all defense, "Splitting of the Ego in the Process of Defense." Between the two (and through the rereading of anxiety-as-signal in the interim), Freud caught up with his defense "Project," which did then compute. In the 1950s, editor James Strachey reset the trend of analogizing or digitalizing the "Project" with cybernetics to go off inside Freud's approach:

> To take a few instances of this similarity of approach, we may note first Freud's insistence on the prime necessity for providing the machine with a "memory"; again, there is his system of "contact-barriers," which enables the machine to make a suitable "choice," based on the memory of previous events, between alternative lines of response to an external stimulus; and, once more, there is, in Freud's account of the mechanism of perception, the introduction of the fundamental notion of feed-back as a means of correcting errors in the machine's own dealings with the environment.[8]

In Freud's theorization, fetishism stays together as a loner concept only so long as we not see that it has already taken off from itself—through the overlapping displacements that go into its formulation—and has exchanged its home-alone activities for mascot status in group efforts. In the brief 1927 essay on fetishism, in other words, the bottom falls out of the discrete perversion and onto disavowal, which then gives way to the defense formulation of splitting. This sliding scale of fetishism's administration of defense also encompasses and gets around the content points of castration and melancholia. Thus the fixity of boundaries all down the psychopathology continuum goes along for the slide. First Freud memorializes the fetish as the repeat and reversal of castration, as a substitution, yes, but the kind that only the one who cannot substitute must make. But, on second take, we don't have far to go before two cases of virtual melancholia are opened—onto a newfound outer space between neurosis and psychosis.

The fetishist gets around the one loss along the original trajectory bound to mother down another pathway, which leads not to a psychotic breakdown nor to the assignment of work of mourning, but to a successful realization, after all, of what Freud calls triumphs and victories. It is true that the original trajectory is now covered by repression and thus horror. But trauma's auto-monumentalization is not, not this time, some horror movie featuring mourning or melancholia. This memorial service is, after all, a substitution (so what if it's simulated and in some other place or cyberspace?), one that opens up its own new native habitat, the borderline or no-man's-land between neurosis and psychosis. The fetish, the invention that succeeds in the wake of a lost connection, a failed realization, remains, says Freud, "a token of triumph over the threat of castration and a protection against it."[9] With the erection of the fetish, then, the loss that threatens to traumatize you the first time around can, after all, be written off—as total. The fetish delivers the movement of invention from the shutdown of one approach toward its realization. Which is to say, even though the invention of the fetish was not aimed for, its realizability doubles back as the focus of the original loss all along. But you can't decide to go for the fetish. It takes you by surprise when you're at a loss.

Freud opens up fetishism for the admission of two cases in which a father's death goes without the son's realization, a shutdown of reality or realization which has not, however, turned the sons into melancholy psychos. This is where Freud must take exception to the distinction he has drawn elsewhere, between neurosis and psychosis, and formulate instead the breakaway notions of fetishistic disavowal and splitting, which pick up where a grief-stuck metabolism might otherwise have signed off. Thus two channels of reception, as different as wish and reality, both tune in, side by side, in what Freud calls fetishism's "oscillation" between psychosis and neurosis. But, following its near miss with melancholia, fetishism catches its hardest and fastest analogy with traumatic neurosis: "It seems rather that when the fetish is instituted some process occurs which reminds one of stopping of memory in traumatic amnesia. As in this latter case, the subject's interest comes to a halt half-way, as it were; it is as though the last impression before the uncanny and traumatic one is the one retained as a fetish."[10]

We would have tracked back only halfway, reached only another part-objective, if we had made only the one stopover at the uncanny. Freud's first public/published encounter with the uncanny double took place over the symptomatizing body of the psychological casualty of the First World War. Same time, same station as the essay "On 'the Uncanny,'" Freud's "Introduction to *Psychoanalysis and the War Neuroses*" characterizes the central conflict of war neurosis in terms of the internal doubling that pits one ego against the other one along this final frontier of defense: "The conflict is between the soldier's old peaceful ego and his new warlike one, and it becomes acute as soon as the peace-ego realizes what danger it runs of losing its life owing to the rashness of its newly formed, parasitic double."[11] The fixity and interability attributed to whatever fetishism is already in all the different disciplines at the start of the dialectic of Enlightenment, according to William Pietz's now standard historical study,[12] gives us one prehistory that would make this moment of overlap between fetishism and traumatic or war neurosis close the circle rather than close ranks on one continuum of trauma internalization. But more important for the future or indeterminacy of the concept is that both states, in Freud's accounting, are invoked as much for their overlaps as for the resulting label of their difference. Traumatic or war neurosis and fetishism also just miss each other on the scale of doubling. It's the overlap between the two that peels away from and opens up a zone of treatability all the way down the borderline between the transference neuroses and the narcissistic neuroses. It's this border zone over which fetishism's oscillation between neurosis and psychosis hovers, out of range of the repeater trauma that brings down war neurotics. Gadget love or fetishism therefore functions as user-friendly war internalization.

During World War I the place of fixation, of arrested fronts, movement, action—the so-called no-man's-land—had to be made habitable, comprehensible, its fixity or deadness reorganized, remetabolized, according to a new notion of shifting zones. This is what makes the analogy fit (like a fetish), the analogy between the reconceptualization of order at the new frontier of no-man's-land and the internal shifting of boundaries that Freud set going, by the end of the war, within a psychic space of oscillation. This analogy even extends its coverage to the borderline diagnosis, one of the latest arrivals from the analytic encounter with war neurosis.

In *Beyond the Pleasure Principle*, Freud sets up a frame for introducing the death-drive thesis into his thought. (His follow-up notion of group psychology would soon accept this thesis as the life-insurance policy of groups.) First, Freud gives consideration to the special psychic access afforded by the evidence of traumatic or war neurosis; second, and on the other side, he contemplates the scientific evidence that already advertises a time, coming soon, when human being will no longer come in generations, but will live on forever within one egoic span of attention through cell-like dividing and doubling. The two sides—the neurosis of trauma or war and the replication fantasies compatible with psychosis, perversion, or group psychology—first came together for Freud during the first total war. The modern legacy of doubling or replication thus splits the scene of war between what Freud referred to publicly in 1919 as "peace-ego" and "war-ego," then, renaming the partners one year later, as "ego" and "superego."

Freud's close encounter with the mass epidemic of traumatic or war neurosis during World War I opened up a no-man's-land or borderline zone between neurosis and psychosis for theorization and treatment. Along this opened-up borderline, group-psy and perversion were made equally accessible to psy-fi colonization for the survival of the species. Mourning, as the main therapeutic frame for the work of psychoanalysis, would appear modeled or dependent on the couple's reproductive function, which keeps open access to a libido pool of candidates for substitution. But Freud's emphasis from the First World War onward was on promotion (in theory) of ways or means beyond both mourning and melancholia. That's how the interest and investment in the diversified structures of psychosis, group psychology, and perversion took over even in psychoanalysis, where, pre–World War I, they had been left out as limit concepts.

The impact of the war record of psychoanalysis, which forced entry of Freud's model into the military, psychology, and military-psychology establishments worldwide, can be tracked through the outer reaches of its reception, when, after a delay, it scored on the Allied side the kind of recognition associated with surprise attack. Take, for example, a U.S. report on the neuropsychiatric casualties of the WWII Tunisian campaign: Roy Grinker and John Spiegel's *War Neuroses in North Africa*, which shows both acceptance of Freud's WWI intervention and the specialization that had gone into the war-neurosis portfolio by 1943.[13] It's also symptomatic of a take-by-surprise that the direct connection to Freud everywhere in evidence in this first, classified documentation seems to end only a couple of years later in a hang-up, when Grinker and Spiegel's postwar book version of their report, *Men under Stress*,[14] turns the airman into the unknown soldier of total warfare, no longer sharply outlining his psychoanalytic profile. This blur in focus, however, could also be taken as proof that the connection was there, following the digestive course of all genuine influence.

By this time, too, the psycho-technological lead the Allies were holding over Nazi psywar or group-psy had regrouped around the discovery of a smaller techno-relation, group or space, ranging from the military's buddy system, through the new formatting of group therapy for war neurotics and the plane's limited seating arrangement, to the family seated around the radio or TV set. In 1944, a kind of rewiring of the family unit was widely conceded by various U.S. military psychologists as an inevitable outcome of the return home of all the psycho-technologized boys, even if resistance to the changes would require treatment of the family itself. Family-systems therapy, which to this day remains the dominant modality of eclectic psychotherapy in the United States, took its inspiration, right after World War II, from Gregory Bateson. Over the course of the war, Bateson's relations with analysis had changed. At first he had promoted the so-called characterological understanding and production of propaganda (which was what German psywar took from Freud). But by the end of the war, he was envisioning a computer-compatible family-systems approach to understanding all mental disturbance as the "languistic" effect of a family's systemic dysfunction. At this time the notion of negative feedback got Bateson started on formulating a high-tech theory for the therapy that military psychologists had already commissioned during the war.

The German Freud "was there" when the authors of the 1943 report found that the gadget love binding pilot to plane had, in the special case of airpower, relocated the site of war traumatization. The ego-libidinal rapport with the flying machine was where the trauma would be too:

> The central unifying force through the Air Corps is the intangible and yet powerful devotion to aircraft felt in different degrees by all its members. . . . Planes receive an almost libidinal investment of interest. . . . The mechanic, the engineer, the radioman, the prop man, the navigator, the bombardier, and the pilot all take an intense interest in their plane. It becomes an extension of their own egos, so that they are affected by things that happen to the plane as if they had happened to themselves. . . . This continual preoccupation with the sight, the sound, and the fate of aircraft and their aircrews is the psychological background upon which the symptoms of the neuroses of war develop within the members of the Air Forces.[15]

This was the narcissistic axis of techno-relations that we saw first with the Nazis. Two years earlier, U.S. authorities had recognized that Nazi psychological research was way ahead of what the Allies were packing into their military complexes right down to psychoanalysis, which was enlisted as part of the Allied war effort only after the Nazis set the trend. A 1941 "survey and bibliography" entitled *German Psychological Warfare*, which was put out by the U.S. Committee for National Morale as part of the all-out attempt to catch up with Nazi research, placed two glossed Freud entries at the top of the Nazi military psychology greatest-hits list. The emergency manual documented how, ever since the World War I defeat, which had right away convinced the German military complex that wars had to be fought and won on psychological grounds, every method or theory that could contribute to the exercise of psywar, including Freud's science, had been mobilized by the Germans to prepare for the total effort. What the survey also showed was the extra-special consideration given to the psychology of air war by the Nazis.[16]

The U.S. compilation or reconstruction of Nazi reading lists that began in 1941 folds out the map of mass psychology's rerouting across intrapsychic airspace. One of the fetishes featured in the Allied reconstruction of the Nazi psychological canon adorns the (by all German accounts) classic 1919 study of everyday-life aspects of pilot vulnerability and psychopathology that precondition the military's hardest-to-treat outbreaks of war neurosis.[17] Pilots, who are under perpetual psychic stress brought on by being completely on their own and under constant threat, with only the heady sense of omnipotence on their side (which sets them up for the downswing), turn to the superstitious relief that the decoration of their fighter planes gives them: "These personal symbols seem to possess the significance of a talisman or fetish not only for individual pilots but for entire squadrons too." The fetish logo on the plane's tail co-signs the merger with the prosthesis that gets the pilot over getting stuck on loss. Traumatically self-aware that his "extremely inferior nerve apparatus" is not, on its own, up for flying, the pilot must be trained relentlessly until the air-technical operations of flight proceed "automatically."[18] To keep out of range of war neuroticization, the pilot must grow together with his machine in flight.

It is in the uncanny manual *German Psychological Warfare*, which documents the enlistment of intrapsychic theory and therapy in the Second Coming of Germany's total war effort (and then advertises the same service as a model for Allied war bonding), that we begin to get a fix on the at-once expansionist and trauma-fixated course of Freud's science. The restoration of this double account must, however, follow out the same psywar logic that got psychoanalysis inside every discipline, department, and market. It is a group-psy truth or truism that psywar observes: you know only what the other thinks you know. In other words, the Allied following or understanding of what the Nazis were up to is the best footnote to put forward. A post–World War II U.S. survey of Nazi aerospace therapy is the first place to register the high points of the Nazi airman's merger with his machine: "The plane—like any other prosthesis—becomes part of the tactile sensory organs in such a manner that sensory perceptions seem to be referred from the body directly to the corresponding parts of the aircraft. This is quite clearly the case in take-off, landing and banking. The incorporation of the flying processes into the tactile sensory system and into the tactile motor apparatus has been called by Metz . . . 'feel for flying' (*Fliegerisches Gefühl*)."[19]

We cannot restrict our consideration of the continued presence of psychoanalysis in Nazi Germany to that small group of certified analysts who didn't join their Jewish colleagues in exile, but stayed behind, finding their place at the central psychotherapy institute inside "Working Group A." It's in the so-called psycho-technical work of a military-psychology colleague like Paul Metz that we can detect the lasting influence of Freud's inside views of the prosthetic mergers and losses that run on narcissistic libido—the grade of fuel recommended for all technologization. These views came out of Freud's shifting focus on mourning and unmourning, which fixed ultimately on the fetishistic, gadget-loving movement he tracked across a functionalized outer space of accessible, colonizable psychopathology. The Pilot-I view of Freud's thought gives us the more complete range, in theory and in therapy, of what I am calling Nazi psychoanalysis. If we take the opening that the U.S. manual has given us back to the primary context (the one the Allies started covering in 1941), we can observe Metz, in his article on "functional and characterological questions of flying aptitude," connecting the internality of flight to the race to compensate, with in-flight prosthetic extensions or mergers, for the traumatizing incommensurability between the pilot's sensorium and the plane's "autonomy":

> Flying means to move in the three dimensions of airspace by means of the plane in such a way that corresponds to the conditions given by the airplane. . . . The pilot forms with his machine a unity. . . . The dead apparatus must merge with the living organism into a functional unity whereby the plane's parts at the same time become the external organs of the pilot. . . . The pilot . . . has become the center of the machine. The situation of the machine is his situation; both are identical and form a common "feeling picture."[20]

But the range of our sense organs, from vision power to the balancing acts of the vestibular organ, falls short. What Metz thus calls a "lack" or "gap" in the pilot's sensorium, specifically the senses that constitute him as an "orientation organism," cannot be bridged or overcome through coordination with the other senses and their extensions. This is where Metz sees, in any study of aptitude for flying, the necessary shift to the characterological register (the register often used in Nazi scientific discourse to represent and rename psychoanalysis, a science which, all its influence notwithstanding, could not always speak its names). At this point in Metz's presentation, analytic and therapeutic considerations compete for ascendancy, the former represented by the strict accounting of inevitable limitations and interminable efforts to supplement them, the latter by the functionalization of the allegory of this impasse or tension.

The half-life of active flying is brief, and the day always coming soon when the pilot will have difficulty getting back into his machine precisely because "flying, as such, already has the effect of psychic trauma. . . . Flying itself is . . . a biological problem. And if the person senses that he is inadequately equipped sensewise in biological matters, then this in turn has a lasting effect on the total personality. The person in the airplane exists always in psychic tension."[21] That's why the pilot must get "empathically" into the autonomy of the machine's manner of movement.

In his "preliminary reflections on a psychology of truck driving and flying," R. H. Walther drives forward the narcissistic empowerment which flight conditions promote. Training must keep this hypersensitive congruence with the machine's movements airborne all the way. To this end, "the [pilot's] use of the machine must have, in the truest sense of the word, crossed over into flesh and blood if he wants to free up all available energy for the flight." That is what enables Walther to read the psyche of man *and* machine in the open book of symptomatic movements of the apparatus: "Work on technical apparatuses has pointed up the advantage of offering the analytic psychological view a firm basis in the focus on the movements required for use of the apparatus. . . . We become conscious that movement possesses beyond its purposiveness a symptomatic value or expressive content which betrays something of the inner makeup of the personality."[22]

Where the psychology of and aptitude for flying comes up in Nazi research, radio aptitude isn't far behind. (Von Schroetter's 1919 study likewise recommended that radio abilities be kept in automatic readiness.) According to a 1936 study, at the microlevel the transmission of military broadcasts, right down to their reception and transcription at the other end, must, to save time, be conceived "intrapersonally."[23] The premier function of radio aptitude, therefore, is "empathic submission." The rhythmic shape entering the ear is admitted through free submission, and "the rhythmic oscillation discharges itself into the oscillating movement of the psychic field of oscillation, which fills the carrier in his totality. For this reason it imparts itself unconsciously and directly, almost automatically, even to the peripheral structures; it connects itself in the hand with the symbol which, in the course of training, is linked to this oscillation, and the hand writes down the letter."[24] Already in 1919 (in synch with the first intrapsychic takes on the pilot's apparatus in flight), Otto Lipmann was addressing the psychic disposition required for radiotelegraphic performance. Right from the start, his article makes clear that, whether you consider the giving or the taking of transmissions, it's a big mistake to assume that "interindividual" relations among the different aspects of radio operation can be extrapolated from what are in fact, one by one, independent or "intraindividual" functions in their own right.[25]

Just as Walther had analyzed, in his comparative psychology of truck driving and flying, the breakdown of communication with the apparatus for the symptomatic values of everyday functioning, so Karl Mierke sized up radio aptitude by reading broadcaster slips.[26] Through this study of radio control (in the wake of breaks with direct connection), Mierke discovered that, with radio, it's not so much aptitude or talent that counts anyway, but a certain attitude of the will which promotes constant practice. Those who qualify characterologically for radio service right away are "radio pious [*funkfromm*]." There are also those who must be disqualified from radio service, but, for the rest, training is the way to go. During the selection process acceptable candidates for training are identifiable as those who appear able to overcome the inevitable identificatory, intellectual, or emotional "inhibitions." The micro-barrier is where natural inhibition is the other side of trained skill: this is the premier "identificatory" relationship. At this semantic limit, "fusion between the radio sign and meaning must be so unambiguous and secure that the sign counts not just as the symbol of a letter or signal, but rather, beyond that, as in fact identified with it." While the complete absence of this ability can only be pathological, the capacity for making the connection can be heightened, all the way to automatization, through training. "But if the development of stronger identifications between sign and meaning can be 'practiced,' then it readily becomes clear that this process is concluded that much faster and surer the more the trained skill takes on the character of an automatic process. That is, this identification must proceed purely automatically and thereby seemingly unconsciously without the addition of the impulse of will or thought."[27] The double goal of training programs, then, should be "simultaneous identification" and "automatization."

The pilot, both video and audio portions, had already been sent to the other front: the assembly lines of cyborg production. His body and sensorium were the first in the military-psychological complex to be technologized and nonmachinically merged with the internalized apparatus. In his 1933 *Wehrpsychologie* (Defense Psychology), Nazi military psychologist Max Simoneit put the pilot highest on the charts of the internal doubling and defense that Freud saw go down in cases of war neurosis.[28] According to Simoneit, self-observation or doubling is the crucial condition of all military preparedness and achievement; it is a capacity for switching on and switching over that is comparable to long-distance measuring through technological media. The required self-observation or objectivity has to be enforced particularly when it comes to the selection of pilots. Firing while flying especially requires constant self-observation, which must tune out subjective and motile tendencies. Otherwise, in flight, you're constantly watching out for the subjective perceptual appearances and illusions that you must instantly delete on your inside-out monitors. That's why a disintegrative type is the one to look for, the type, you know the type, who can *sharply* distinguish the parts of his personality.[29] To this day, haunting manuals attribute some of the highest numbers of sightings of ghostly visitations to the air force, which sends the doubles of self-observation on time-travel missions of loss reversal.[30]

Flying touches down in all the haunts of modern group psychology. It rewires Preflight Man, who is over and out, to tune in or turn into the new airman, the Nazi Overman. This change of subject comes complete with a change in perspective. According to Major Alexander de Seversky, who addressed his 1942 work of caution to the Americans, the German investment in air force had succeeded in reorganizing the dimensionality of war. "In the past, too, there had been talk of 'total war.' But now it is being demonstrated for the first time. America is not being attacked piecemeal but *as a totality*. There is just one target: the whole country. A few farsighted aviation strategists had foreseen this type of third-dimensional warfare."[31] But by 1942 it was also already clear to Seversky that the Germans were on a losing streak with their one-sided and one-way staging of airpower. The RAF was able to push back the Battle of Britain because its planes were designed to attack and defend against enemy planes in flight. Whereas each German plane packed one machine gun in the back as an afterthought or ornament, its RAF counterpart blazed one-on-one in airborne conflict from many sides with as many guns.

The lack of defense capability in an instrument of total offense brings down planes and pilots, but it's not the same downer for rockets. Out of the loss of planes that utterly lacked defense—a loss that the sacrifice or self-sacrifice of pilots could not reverse—immediately came the invention of the rocket, which the Germans had all along been going for without knowing it. Out of losses within the register of automobilic technologies arose a high-tech analogue operation: automatic pilot, computer engineering, one-way rocketry. That's why, according to the haunting manuals, the phantom aircraft from World War I, which were seen (in the early portion of World War II) to take part in air battles, diverted enemy fire toward their one-way mission—and that's also why the ghost appearances of WWII planes that have been sighted since the closeout of that war have regularly been seen to be without any pilot.[32] The ghost of a loss models the success of the follow-up fetish invention.

It's not so much that the fetishist does not see a lack, loss, or difference as that he writes it off as total loss against the substitute realization, which, as substitute for substitution, is what he was aiming for right from the start when he was losing the first time around. The fetishist triumphs, gets what he wants and gets off, via the first misfire, which packs in its blast the surprise of success just the same, on the same plane of realization. Fetishism's near misses skip the down- or deadbeat of invention to get to the only realizable aim. It's gadget love, and it's always getting into automatic functioning: the automatic implementation of mathematics in computers and of flight in rockets through the primal service of feedback.

Feedback was the lip service on which the German war effort preyed. Follow-up to the production of ersatz or simulated alternatives to those supply items missing in Germany during World War I, feedback is associated not only with putting the flying machine on automatic pilot and keeping it internally (eternally) on track, but also with running it on virtual empty. Rockets shoot up a need to get around the running out of reserves. In other words, what goes down with what Metz calls the "incorporation of the flying processes" is another void inside fetishism-in-flight, the one that registers either full or empty. It comes up with all the one-way clarity of paranoid attack in Herhudt von Rohden's 1937–38 series of articles on airpower, in which he urges a total air offensive against enemy fuel resources; terrorization of the inner/outer *Bestände*, or reserve supplies, is what the air force is good for.[33] It's the only way out of the WWI fixation of war fronts which made that war one of supplies only. According to von Rohden, the premier targets of the offensive are to be the earthbound forces, their means of staying connected, in contact, and the system of their reserves. "The destruction of the 'heart' of the enemy corresponds to the essence of war and is therefore the set goal of the air force too." This brings up two aspects of air war that are connected in von Rohden's reflections, but only at their paranoid origin in the enemy's thoughts; von Rohden thus adopts a protective or projective position when it comes to thinking (1) air defense in flight and (2) reserve forces and supplies. When he declares tactical reserves a necessity, he points out that foreign nations have packed plenty of reserve planes into the organization of their war capacity to keep up the dueling strength of flying units. But even these reserves are already engaged, von Rohden counters, owing to the range of modern bombers. That's why reserves are finally less important than the maintenance of an economy of forces in the course of combat action. The strategy of cooperative offense (a view that's said to have originated with foreigners) requires "alternation between strikes against the power sources of the enemy and against his air force, against his army and his navy."[34] Due to their negative reaction to static-positional warfare (in other words, World War I), these foreigners have already been moved to prepare for this shift into the new three-dimensionality of warfare.[35] If air force was expended on one-on-one combat or dueling back in World War I, it was because the means were lacking then for a unified coordination of mixed weapons. Airborne showdowns are no longer part of the picture; now it's chain against chain: "There will be great losses. They will not only impact materially and physically, but will also have a significant influence on the troops' moral resistance and willingness to fight."[36]

The disavowals punctuating this forecast of future wars make it too long-range by half. Nevertheless, it is a disavowal or split that gets a lot of press. Already by 1935, in Wulf Siewert's reflections on airpower, which accepted flight's paradoxical dependency on the earth and thus opened onto the psychologization of the grounded group that must mobilize for air defense, there was also a surprising lack of dependency—on fuel reserves. For example, Siewert argued (without a glance at the gas gauge) that the oceans are no longer defensive spaces, having fallen away beneath the shadow of the airplane.[37] Airpower, argued von Rohden two years later, accelerates the metabolism of warfare and puts not only the usual energy sources but also the populace-at-large, and even time, on reserve. Owing to new developments in group-psy or psywar, the air-war effort in 1937 has a good enough view of the enemy psyche to give it close, careful consideration when selecting targets. These powers of psychological preselection are so crucial because speed, and that means supplies, must limit airpower. In other words, a war's duration can represent danger for air force. To keep air war from going in one year and out the other, the emergency brake of the leader function must be pulled. After all, the "character of the operative air war" is "collective war." And that means: "The basic conditions of technology, which make possible the conquest of space, must have entered every leader in flesh and blood."[38] Where the techno-leaders are, that's where the air-defense community will be too. The techno-interiority of war must already be there when you and the Führer look deep down inside yourselves: "The thoughts that give direction to the construction of an air force which are most important are whether and how the people and their Führer are able to think and act in a three-dimensional space."[39]

In Leni Riefenstahl's *Triumph of the Will* we get the primal view of this 3-D techno-fetishism and its incorporation or feedback. We watch Hitler summon the new Germany inside and around us from the techno-airspace his plane crossed all the way to the audio columns rising up out of the chorus funereally reciting the place-names of battles from the lost war. But the slogans for the future of the new or true Germany are still being pitched to the war dead. And so, as we get ready to take off for a Germany that's part crypt, part airspace, we hear the vanishing point: the war dead are *not* dead.

The projective rapport with the prospect of runaway reserve supplies, which turns on a three-dimensional axis, fits onto Heidegger's runway, the one where he parked one of his more famous examples of the essence of technology—the airplane that, even when stationary, is still in position and ready for takeoff. The plane on the runway thus models the standing reserve (*Bestand*), which is one essence of technology Heidegger comes up with, as though in denial of the fuel-bound half-life of the German mobilizations of world-war technology. What goes without saying is that the essence (or *essence*) of technology is the fuel that keeps the plane from falling back onto the strip of decontextualized loss and stranded objecthood.[40] What Heidegger was not alone in considering to be our technologization (i.e., our overcoming of object ties through the recycling and ready-positioning of standing reserve) thus runs on unacknowledged empty.

On the periphery of the same complex, Nazi military psychiatrist Klaus Conrad's treatment model, an existential brand of psychoanalysis based on the eclectic mix-up of Ludwig Binswanger (and thus also of Heidegger with Freud), enabled the reduction of the war psychosis he was treating in 1942 to depletion of a kind of psychic reserve fuel or energy, which is all your symptomatizing soldier really lacks. Take Case No. 10, whose spy-movie paranoia began with a dispute at the military gas station where the patient was responsible for rationing. When a couple of soldiers came to tank up, but without the required forms to fill out, the patient refused outright to dispense the necessary gas. But even after the soldiers had brought the paperwork, the patient had misgivings, which finally landed him in psychiatric treatment. He had already gone the night before, however, to another soldier's quarters to go over the gas station ledgers. Finding the door locked, he became convinced that everything was a setup designed to test whether he would notice. He knocked at another door, entered, and came across a soldier lying on a cot. The patient immediately concluded that this had all been planned to make allusions that would go without saying to his being homosexual. Like the gas-rationing misunderstanding on the morning after, the transgressive understanding in the barracks was just a test, a testing of the limits or reserve supplies that were giving way.[41]

Psychoanalytic case studies of psychotics have often served as vehicles for the homosexual component of a personality in whatever guise or degree of repression, projection, denial, acting out. It's the standard edition or identification of the narcissistic libido that's imploding and exploding whole worlds during the breaking out of psychosis. Freud regularly filled out the connections between technology and delusion "with repressed homosexuality." It's a near-miss connection. In his 1932 retelling of the Prometheus myth, Freud identifies homosexual flooding as the immediate response to the possession of fire and the suppression of this desire to shower the new energy source, to rub phallic stream against phallic flame, with the control of fire and thus with the onset of technologization, the ongoing control-release from this point onward of the original impulse to fight fire with fire.[42] The group-psy that's always along for the psy-fi drive reintroduces the problem of homosexuality, which Nazi therapeutic culture, in literal or efficient application of certain Freudian insights, was determined to face head-on within defense contexts of inoculation. By openly promoting homoeroticism on the very face of its popular culture, Nazi Germany sought to grant the race immunity from the real appeal of homosexuality in all techno-cultures where doubling or cloning cannot but represent the absolute desires. But homosexuality, according to "Freudian" energy-saving advice, would represent only a premature articulation of techno-desire, a quick fix that could only waste replicational activities and energies. How else to make sense of Freud's surprise observation that fetishism saves the man in crisis from becoming homosexual?[43] Techno-homoeroticism, fetishism, or gadget love (what Walter Benjamin referred to as aestheticization[44]) lubes the merger with the machine.

At the same time, fetishism represents a makeshift overcoming of the crisis in relations with heterosexual reproduction, a compromise formation between the fantastic prospects of doubling, replication, or merger with the machine and the human-all-too-human requirement of reproduction to restock the libido pool for the living on and evolution of the species (including our machines). The narcissistic portfolio of investments, which Freud opened up through his analysis of war neurosis, breaks down into shares of the ultimate sci-fi fantasy, that of replacing reproduction (which is death in life) with a new and improved immortality plan, that of amoeba-like and technology-compatible replication. Nazi Germany, which was, among other things, one big science fiction, resided within the tension that Freud's theory of fetishism described: the ongoing compromise between total techno-desire (represented most drastically in the how-to instructions the Nazi airman was given for overcoming the gravity or grave of the body and the earth through merger with the machine in flight) and the vestigial fact of life that still, however, had to be faced, namely, that, if only for the time being, reproduction was the only way for the race to be won and, at the same time, to go on.

Under the uniform lab conditions of his uniformed subjects, Conrad was able to study the stages of the coming out of psychosis in his soldier-charges, in whose inside-out condition or context the depletion of standing reserve conjoined with the breakdown of barriers that were, at the same time, the "resources or reserves of our current field." In the senseless and undisciplined behavior of the soldiers sent to him for treatment "two disparate situational fields communicate; again barriers were torn down and showed themselves to be ready to give way."[45] Case No. 28, for example, rode out his psychotic break all the way to the clinic, urging on the velocity of his transportation with cries of "Faster! Faster!" As it turned out, he was by then convinced that he was at all times participating in the entirety of the war effort. Somehow or other he was there, everywhere. When he urinated at night he just knew he was at the same time determining that bombs would fall on England. Back in bed, lying on his stomach, he was at the same time flying in a plane across English airspace. As the guardian or god of the bomber planes flying over England, he also exhibited a characteristic reciprocity of effects in the experience of breakaway psychosis. "Effects that the world and its supplies have on the ego—which the delusional perception thoroughly analyzes—are recircuited through a reverse direction of effects from the ego back to the world. There is reason to believe that where there is full-blown delusional experience both directions are always experienced at the same time."[46]

During the period of recovery from a psychotic break, Conrad observes a reverse movement that dismantles the delusion and (with the assistance of transferential psychotherapy) restores reality testing. But the patient does not then return to the starting point of some pre-illness integrated personality. In each case, the psychosis irreversibly reduces and depletes the patient's "energetic potential." Which is to say, the structural transformation that goes down with psychosis always sets itself up as enduring.[47] Following stabilization, the patient typically complains of a loss of energy, power, or excitement. There is never any talk of lack of energy during the psychosis. In their excited state, patients often exhibit enormous amounts of willpower. But already, during the onset of psychosis, a patient will experience a reduction of energy and thus attempt, as a kind of last stand, "to mobilize all reserves of the will" before inevitably leaving "the fight a changed person, one impoverished, depleted of energy." The "energy potential" here, Conrad admits, is "comparable to a country's 'war potential,' which, in peacetime as during a war, in other words at a time of heavy use of war materials, remains a constant quantity."[48] Conrad breaks down these cases of psychosis according to the degree of energy potential lost or depleted by the time of recovery. Only in certain nonschizophrenic psychoses could this loss be kept to a minimum, leading him to conclude that the loss is what defines schizophrenia. "If one could only discover some energetic substitute which could be given the patient from without—analogous to a missing hormone—then one would have, in the true sense of the word, 'healed' his schizophrenia, for the patient lacks nothing else at this stationary stage of his process. As severely disturbed as the catatonic asylum patient appears, he lacks nothing but the fuel which could put the psyche back into gear."[49]

While intrapsychic conflict is bigger than life, the reserve, or *Bestand*, structure (which, according to Heidegger's forecast, would pick up where humanity left off) puts everyone, one by one, on standby. The fuel tank inside the soldiers Conrad analyzed is what they represent in the bigger picture of total mobilization. Here we touch down again on Heidegger's runway, his runaway recourse to denial and projection. But, then, the fuelless and pilotless plane triumphs as fetish over those same old dependencies and setbacks. With the takeoff of the total war's final phase on an automatic plane of realization, feedback propelled a new rocket age away from the earthbound dependency of automobilic technologies on the reserve fuel tank. It was a sci-fi front of survival set up on the borderline inside psychosis. The zone of nontransferential disconnection otherwise set aside as melancholia or schizophrenia was a new frontier for future colonization through the evolving super- or survivor-body growing out of equal machine and human parts up and down the axis of intrapsychic space. The V-1 and V-2 "miracle weapons [*Wunderwaffen*]" follow Daniel Paul Schreber, Freud's favorite psycho, across the delusional or cyberspatial trajectory that begins with a wound (*Wunde*) of loss and separation (or takeoff) and ends up with the wonder or miracle (*Wunder*) of the new sci-fi world waiting to be colonized in place of the one that has been lost.[50]

By the time psywar took over from where the war neurotic had been let off, the inside trajectories of narcissism, having come into focus through Freud's close encounter with war neurosis, were being made user-friendly or war-ready. The internal doubling of war neurosis had to be remetabolized, technologized, group-psychologized in order to contribute to future war efforts all the benefits of, say, psychotic transference or loyalty-versus-betrayal, but without the bad side effects. Ernst Simmel's 1918 view that the neuroses were safety catches or fuses that helped to prevent psychotic blowout (which is just one self-help step away from his follow-up reflection that membership in mass psychosis or psychological warfare issues group protection against breaking down one by one) could be seen as opening up access for control of the internal doubling of the ego in wartime.[51] Soldiers were to be sent to the borderline between neurosis and psychosis, a newfound no-man's-land that from the First World War onward was the front for psy-fi expansionism into the outer reaches of psychosis. German military psychologists were the first to see brand-new training grounds for the defense and offense industries opening up. This spread of Freud's science washed up on the Allied side, too, during World War II. In *The Shaping of Psychiatry by War*, J. R. Rees notes the lead that U.S. military psychology had held for World War I. But, in the meantime, "Germany borrowed much of [this U.S.] . . . war work and built on it the psychological department with its elaborate selection techniques, out of which grew the still wider department of psychological warfare."[52] As Rees tells the story, a British officer who was instrumental in setting up the special selection boards for the war effort "had, before the war, the distinction of being the only serving British officer who had seen the German army officer selection work in progress. On his return to this country he had pressed the authorities to start some similar work in the British army, but the suggestion was turned down and he was told, '. . . You're the bloody Freud of the British Army.'"[53] But, as Rees settles the account, by the time Britain too had come up for total air war, even the British military, like the Freudian German one, was shooting up with so-called battle inoculations—the inoculations, in sum, of Greater Psychoanalysis.

Notes

1 See Jacques Derrida, *Specters of Marx: The State of the Debt, the Work of Mourning, and the New International*, trans. Peggy Kamuf (New York and London, 1994 [1993]), 9.

2 Ibid., 149–56.

3 See the introduction to *The Essential Frankfurt School Reader*, ed. Andrew Arato and Eike Gebhardt (New York, 1985), 18.

4 Janine Chasseguet-Smirgel, "'Time's White Hair We Ruffle': Reflections on the Hamburg Congress," *International Review of Psychoanalysis* 14 (1987): 433–44.

5 Sigmund Freud, "Thoughts for the Times on War and Death," in *The Standard Edition of the Complete Psychological Works of Sigmund Freud*, 24 vols., ed. and trans. James Strachey (London, 1953–74), 14: 289–300.

6 Sigmund Freud, "The Question of a *Weltanschauung*," *New Introductory Lectures on Psycho-Analysis* (25), in ibid., 22: 158–82; quotation from 177–78.

7 Harold D. Lasswell, "Political and Psychological Warfare," in *A Psychological Warfare Casebook*, ed. William E. Daugherty and Morris Janowitz (Baltimore, 1958), 23.

8 James Strachey, Editor's Introduction to "Project for a Scientific Psychology," in Strachey, ed. and trans., *Standard Edition*, 1: 283–93; quotation from 292–93.

9 Sigmund Freud, "Fetishism," in ibid., 21: 147–58; quotation from 154.

10 Ibid., 155.

11 Sigmund Freud, "Introduction to *Psychoanalysis and the War Neuroses*," in ibid., 17: 207–10; quotation from 209.

12 William Pietz, "The Problem of the Fetish, 2," *Res* 13 (1987): 23–45.

13 Roy R. Grinker and John P. Spiegel, *War Neuroses in North Africa: The Tunisian Cam-*

paign (January–May 1943), a special report prepared and distributed for the Air Surgeon Army Air Forces by the Josiah Macy, Jr., Foundation, New York.

14 Roy R. Grinker and John P. Spiegel, *Men under Stress* (London, 1945).

15 Grinker and Spiegel, *War Neuroses in North Africa*, 99–102.

16 *German Psychological Warfare: Survey and Bibliography*, ed. Ladislas Farago (New York, 1941), 21.

17 Hermann von Schroetter, "Zur Psychologie und Pathologie des Feldfliegers," *Wiener Medizinische Wochenschrift*, Nos. 12–18 (1919). The study appeared in 7 parts or installments.

18 Ibid., 1: 4, 2: 1, 3: 3; my translations here and elsewhere unless otherwise indicated.

19 *German Aviation Medicine: World War II*, a special report prepared under the auspices of the Surgeon General, U.S. Air Force, n.d. (New York, 1971), 1: 1036. The report's quotation is from Paul Metz, "Die Eignung zum Flugzeugführer als Anlagenproblem," *Zeitschrift für Psychologie* 143 (1938): 12–14.

20 Paul Metz, "Funktionale und charakterologische Fragen der Fliegereignung," *Zeitschrift für angewandte Psychologie*, Supp. 72 (1936): 153–72; quotations from 154–55.

21 Ibid., 171.

22 Rudolf Hermann Walther, "Ansätze zu einer Psychologie des Kraftfahrens und Fliegens," *Soldatentum* (1934): 14–22; quotations from 21 and 14–15.

23 W. Dietsch, "Über Funkveranlagung," *Zeitschrift für angewandte Psychologie*, Supp. 72 (1936): 140–48.

24 Ibid., 142.

25 Otto Lipmann, "Die psychische Eignung der Funkentelegraphisten," *Zeitschrift für angewandte Psychologie* 15 (1919): 301–40.

26 Karl Mierke, "Versageranalyse bei Funkern," *Archiv für die gesamte Psychologie* 55 (1938): 297–370.

27 Ibid., 299, 307.

28 Max Simoneit, *Wehrpsychologie: Ein Abriss ihrer Probleme und praktischen Folgerungen* (Berlin, 1933).

29 Ibid., 38, 40–42.

30 See Nigel Blundell and Roger Boar, *The World's Greatest Ghosts* (New York, 1988), 134–38, 143–46.

31 Alexander P. de Seversky, *Victory through Air Power* (New York, 1942), 11.

32 See Martin Caidin, *Ghosts of the Air: True Stories of Aerial Hauntings* (New York, 1991), 108–12.

33 Herhudt von Rohden, "Betrachtungen über den Luftkrieg," *Militärwissenschaftliche Rundschau*, Nos. 2–5 (1937–38): 2: 198–214; 3: 347–61; 4: 504–17; 5: 623–31.

34 Ibid., 3: 511, 516.

35 Ibid., 1: 199.

36 Ibid., 4: 631.

37 Wulf Siewert, "Flugzeug und Erdraum," *Zeitschrift für Geopolitik* 8 (1935): 508–16.

38 Von Rohden, "Betrachtungen über den Luftkrieg," 2: 349, 348, 352.

39 Ibid., 3: 504.

40 See Martin Heidegger, "Die Frage nach der Technik," in *Vorträge und Aufsätze* (Stuttgart, 1954), 20–21; *The Question Concerning Technology and Other Essays*, trans. William Lovitt (New York, 1977), 17. "Yet an airliner that stands on the runway is surely an object. Certainly. We can represent the machine so. But then it conceals itself as to what and how it is. Revealed, it stands on the taxi strip only as standing-reserve, inasmuch as it is ordered to ensure the possibility of transportation. For this it must be in its whole structure and in every one of its constituent parts, on call for duty, i.e., ready for take off." Heidegger then continues, "Whatever is ordered about in this way has its own standing. We call it the standing-reserve [*Bestand*]"; and concludes, "Whatever stands by in the sense of standing-reserve no longer stands over against us as object." With the establishment of this melancholia, proof or proofing, the airplane example can be parked on the runway in the next line.

41 Klaus Conrad, *Die beginnende Schizophrenie: Versuch einer Gestaltanalyse des Wahns* (Stuttgart, 1958), 52, 51.

42 Sigmund Freud, "The Acquisition and Control of Fire," in Strachey, ed. and trans., *Standard Edition*, 22: 187–93.

43 Freud, "Fetishism," 154.

44 See Walter Benjamin, "Das Kunstwerk im Zeitalter seiner technischen Reproduzierbarkeit," in *Gesammelte Schriften*, 4 vols. in 12 parts, ed. Rolf Tiedemann and Hermann Schweppenhäuser (Frankfurt a.M., 1980), 1: 2; 435–508, esp. 506–8.

45 Conrad, *Die beginnende Schizophrenie*, 35.

46 Ibid., 74, 76.

47 Ibid., 128.

48 Ibid., 125, 126.

49 Ibid., 143, 139.

50 Regarding Schreber's rapport with the wonder-enriched dead, see Samuel Weber's Introduction to the 1988 Edition of Daniel Paul Schreber, *Memoirs of My Nervous Illness*, ed. and trans. Ida Macalpine and Richard A. Hunter (Cambridge, MA, and London, 1988), vii–liv, esp. xiv–lx.

51 See Ernst Simmel, "Zweites Korreferat," in *Zur Psychoanalyse der Kriegsneurosen*, Internationale Psychoanalytische Bibliothek 1 (Leipzig and Vienna, 1919), 42–60, esp. 45.

52 John Rawlings Rees, *The Shaping of Psychiatry by War* (New York, 1945), 11, 34.

53 Ibid., 67.

Abdul-Karim Mustapha

Meta-Prolegomena for a Study of Psychoanalysis and Imperialism

> Philosophy is rather the reverse, a knowledge that leaps ahead, opening up new domains of questioning and aspects of questioning about the essence of things, an essence that constantly conceals itself anew. That is precisely the reason this knowledge can never be useful.
>
> —Martin Heidegger, *Basic Questions of Philosophy*

What can we gain, if anything, by juxtaposing *psychoanalysis* and *imperialism*? With this arrangement, do we intend to illuminate the historical role which psychoanalysis has had in the discourse of imperialism, itself a mode of knowledge and a form of territorialization? Do we intend to discover once and for all that enigmatic kernel of truth lurking within the body of psychoanalysis, a truth regarding the psyche of imperialism? Is it, furthermore, our intention to uncover through this arrangement (a fictive network, a genealogical pairing) the *plane of immanence* in the relationship between these two terms? If these lines of escape were sure to pull us toward real names and objects, would we therefore be within an order of questioning that claimed to speak politically, beyond the immedi-

The *South Atlantic Quarterly* 97:2, Spring 1998.

ate knowledge of psychoanalysis and its profound populism, of the unconscious and of Freud's research? What founding gesture indeed links these two seemingly urgent, diversified, and historiographically unconnected themes together in a space which calls on the reconfiguration of their objects as well as their places within that incalculable constellation we so comfortably label, without immunity from the pressures of the signifier, *poststructuralist thinking*?

It would come as no surprise if we were to suggest that this combination, unappealing as it is to the eyes and ears of the professional psychoanalyst and the practitioner of psychoanalytic discourse alike, cannot take on the same form as another series of equivalences that would breathe new life into the Euro-American practice of literary psychoanalytic theory by extending the tentacles of this discourse into such spaces as *race*, *nationalism*, *multiculturalism*, and the like. Here, perhaps, it is not simply a matter of revealing the knowledge that psychoanalysis represses about the phenomenon of imperialism or of investigating the role of psychoanalytic institutions and practices in the ever-increasing criminalization of the social, as Derrida would suggest, along with a postcolonial reiteration of Fanon's unmatched critique of psychoanalytic practice.[1] Beyond the privileged knowledge that such projects might yield, the possibilities for thinking psychoanalysis and imperialism together in one sentence beckon to a different order of things not yet even within the grasp of the formula itself. As such, there is a risk involved that goes beyond the limits of academic commitment, a risk primed by the political experience of the will to will.

Today, however, against the reigning tendencies of the Anglophilic gesture toward psychoanalysis (a gesture which maintains a rather cynical attitude toward the history of that discourse), the proposed realignment of psychoanalysis with imperialism should be recognized as a means by which the ideological structurations and ethical constraints stemming from its social function and philosophical/nonphilosophical demands can be suspended, disrupted, in order to *read* what Althusser put forth as a direction toward recovering "the non-thoughtness of these problems which derive from an epistemological history of psychoanalysis and a social (and ideological) history of the world of analysis."[2] Althusser's reading—his prescription for dismantling the history of psychoanalysis as simply an adventure in reading, a fruitful if appropriative reading of Freud—compels us to retreat from the initial question, although this *diversion* is as important as that question of a bridge between psychoanalysis and imperialism. Indeed, Althusser's question regarding the distance between history and the reader, his intervention into the fields of psychoanalysis and the philosophy of history, is as much a part of this questioning as of the answer we seek. Why? Because in Althusser we learn for the first time that the map of history does not necessarily succeed the land called Man; we learn that too often they have changed costumes under our noses.

The Althusserian question is not merely a matter of asking about the history or character of something. Althusser (i.e., the name and the signature works) can be accorded a foundational authority for the precociousness of his perspective—a forceful impression upon selected texts, a rigorous process of *meaning bending,* a betrayal of the chronology of concepts—in effecting what he calls a *reading.* Reading is no less important than questioning; they must stand together on the same horizon because they are equally indeterminate. Althusser's *techne* of reading seeks determinacy, however; it appeals to a systematic unfolding of connectives, transitions, transpositions, and ultimately flight—a leap, as it were, from the text. It was Althusser who initiated that radical flight from the text, a flight characterized by its conservation of the political pressures which incite a particular reading by a particular author—Marx reading classical political economists, say, or Lacan reading Freud alongside Russian linguistics—reading as a return, an overturning, a sublation, and, in the last instance, a shrewd questioning of the question. In this regard reading, *pace* Althusser, takes as its starting point the historico-material situation of the Occident and disunites the discourse of that situation from its calculable and incalculable objects as it moves toward its national and global destinies in the form of knowledge. Isn't Althusser, then, perhaps the most astute disciple of Heidegger, whose teaching, despite its own lapses, excited by delusions of grandeur and the parabolic calling of Spirit, asks that we forgo hermeneutic assurances by simply accepting the inconclusivity of philosophical thinking, a "knowledge" that, according to Heidegger, "can never be useful"?[3]

The singularity of any interpretation (reading in the immediate sense) compels us to possess and to be dispossessed by the artifacts of political education, a requisite condition prior to our will to understand, to come forward and claim responsibility for a text and the words of which it is constituted, fashioned as a mere act of irresponsibility necessary for accomplishing any reading.[4] With the idea of a reading as a ritual political offering in a time of fanaticism and voluntaristic appeals to sacred texts and godly authors, the author of *Reading "Capital"* advises his readers that a compelling reading is one which disengages itself only to return later with a mouthful of words. If reading is in fact always already subverted by the historical conjuncture which allows the act to be performed as it "takes into account and includes within itself in full the moment constituted by the theoretical validity of a thought *qua* judgement," it is curious to read Jacques Derrida's announcement, at the outset of one of his many deconstructions of psychoanalysis, that he is "psychoanalytically irresponsible, and it is perhaps so that certain things might be said through the mouth."[5] What might appear to be a frank, intellectualist mode of disavowal must be viewed in the opposite light, against Althusser's reading. Derrida's initial move, as narrated here, enacts an acceptance of the opacities of the psychoanalytic enterprise, then proceeds to make statements about its disciplinary and political status while claiming to know little or nothing; Althusser, who understood things differently, detected and distrusted the levels of transparency in psychoanalytic practice and theory prior to his revaluation of the discourse and its objects. Perhaps the reflexive aspects of these approaches are unique to psychoanalysis—Derrida relies on the cunning laughter of the deconstructionist modus operandi, while Althusser preferred the calculated refrain of the dialectician. In their radical refusal to come close to the object, however, both Derrida and Althusser adumbrate a style of philosophical questioning/reading which relies on an *absence* of literary authority. This absence is, of course, characteristic of a general intersubjective destitution occasioned by a broader social trend toward a phenomenology of reading in reverse—of *rearchivization*—and toward upending disciplinary formations in the wake of the crisis of the university, movements in which Althusser, like other New Philosophers (as they were termed by their contemporaries), participated. Along these lines, Rodolphe Gasché is quite correct to dislocate Derrida's work from the rather misleading context and contents of Americanist deconstruction by restaging it as a dialogue within the long history of philosophy of reflection, for this is the wider context of the absence as such.[6]

The Absence. What is the power of the absence? *Absence* ultimately marks a strategy of *enclosure*, whereby the reader annihilates his being in the immediacy of canon formation, of ordering a series of texts so as to pronounce it a system, only to then recover his scattered flesh, stitched together by the threads of necessity on the shadowy terrain of the goddess Aletheia and expressed in the proverbial, orthodox spirit of Truth as the Heideggerian discourse of philosophical disclosure. Absence as a strategy of disclosure (*die Eröffnung*) is not a common practice, a gift of the philosophical experience. It is, by its own order of necessity and conformity to the will to truth, provoked in advance of a given theoretic insight, a derivative conscience instituted and extracted from the "dialectical gap" in the mise-en-scène of knowledge formation.[7]

It is this *perspectivism* of the absence, then, that effectively prepares the reader to be a witness: a witness to the silent drama of the antagonistic and sometimes repetitious theater of transformations of philosophical perspective. Contrary to Derrida's pronouncement of "irresponsibility" as an ethics of reading in the context of reading the constitution of the International Psychoanalytic Association, the Althusserian absence embodies and "takes the responsibility for its crime as a 'justified crime' and defends it by proving its necessity" against the positivism of self-reflection and self-enclosure.[8] It would appear that this Althusserian *absence of Lack*, the same thing that animated the critical conscience of Althusser's Marx when he read Quesnay and Smith "out loud," was Lacan's starting point for speaking out loud when he returned to Freud in an effort to fill a void with a body that would placate their distinctive analytics of reading, speaking, and writing through and outside the philosophical. And here is Althusser, the genealogist of reading, thinking out loud: "The first man ever to have posed the problem of *reading*, and in consequence, of *writing*, was Spinoza, and he was also the first man in the world to have proposed both a theory of history and a philosophy of the opacity of the immediate. With him, for the first time ever, a man linked together in this way the essence of reading and the essence of history in a theory of the difference between the imaginary and the true."[9] One must always invoke Spinoza in order to reveal the skeletons in Althusser's thinking. Here, he offers us not Hegelian history or a critique of materialist historiography, but rather the productive tensions in the foundation of the "positive form of negative thought," which "is not freely constituted by the masses," as Antonio Negri notes.[10] Is it possible, bearing in mind this tradition of reading and the exigency it has imposed on political theory and social thought from Spinoza to Althusser himself, for us to think out loud about the consequences of Althusser's reading of Lacan? By reading Freud and Lacan against the backdrop of the French intellectual scene, Althusser could transform the ends and the beginnings of history, as told, through and through. The weakness he discovered in Lacanian psychoanalysis as a knowledge formation, as a substitutive engagement with philosophy, was its failure to confront history as the representation of subjects re-presenting themselves in the immediacy of a crisis, albeit a failure that was not novel but in fact common to all traditions of questioning limits in philosophy. This implied a necessary and contingent paradox which, for Althusser, was less an embarrassment than a simple matter of fact: performing an epistemological history always entails describing (and occupying) a less evident epistemological position. As discomfiting as this situation may be, it merely demonstrates that Althusser's readings were undertaken neither to supersede nor to transcend the texts of Marx and Lacan, but to deploy them wisely in the process of discovering the dividing line between discourses and their objects, "the *real determinations* of the historical process," according to Etienne Balibar.[11] Isn't Althusser, then, the subject of a lack? Under the restraints of this paradox, we must avoid any immediate identification of Lacan with Althusser, heeding the rather stern warning by Slavoj Žižek that "the great debate occupying the foreground of today's intellectual scene, the Habermas–Foucault debate, is masking another opposition, another debate which is theoretically more far-reaching: the Althusser–Lacan debate."[12] Surely, with Žižek's exposure of what he calls the "traumatic kernel" in contemporary poststructuralism, this is not the moment to announce an ideological, if not personal, closeness between Lacan and Althusser. Instead of cosigning such a reductionism then, let us proceed with reading through Althusser's Marx and Althusser's Lacan, conjoined by the causes of truth and knowledge, standing on this bridge over the abyss of the absence.

The Question of Form. In his reading of Marx reading the classical political economists, Althusser announced a precious finding, his own version of the discovery of the unconscious, a discovery he described as "an internal dislocation (*décalage*) in the real, inscribed in its *structure*,"[13] hence a *fetishism* of reading—and of the real. Althusser's version had deeper resonances, following as it did Foucault's plea for such a history of psychoanalysis in

Madness and Civilization. For both Althusser and Foucault, the ideological investigation of psychoanalysis was part of a larger project to do with the history of science/science of history as a form of value. Foucault's inquiry enabled us to pursue the dividing line, or caesura, between psychoanalysis and imperialism in order to "recreate the negative part of the concept, that which has disappeared under the retroactive influence of present day ideas and the passage of time."[14] Moreover, Foucault's attempt to "recreate the negative part of the concept" would be achieved by Althusser in "Freud and Lacan." That essay had a paradoxical reception within the besieged life-world of 1960s psychoanalytic France. Lacan and his school were then under attack from both anti-Freudians (remnants of the International Psychoanalytical Association, which had excommunicated the Master) and some former Lacan students. When "Freud and Lacan" appeared (on the eve of May '68), it was received by Lacan and his cohort as a congratulatory appraisal by an "outsider," a sympathetic listener and an academic defender of the French Freudian tradition extending from surrealism to Lacan. "Freud and Lacan," however (Lacan's wishes, ego, and self-perception notwithstanding), had been purposefully written by a renegade intellectual as an intervention into Lacan's teaching. Althusser assumed that Lacan's students (many of whom were also at the time his own students) would heed the warning by becoming more aware of, and interrogating more fully, the *relevance of their place in history* and, as a consequence, would become more aware of *their relationship to the Master*. Before Lacan himself became aware of the effects of Althusser's theoretic challenge to his teaching, it was already clear that the continual ruptures, breaks, divisions, and fissures within the psychoanalytic movement, as well as Lacan's refusal to have his "thoughts" formalized by his students (a refusal which took the form of a series of returns to Freud, each time with a new interlocutor), all stemmed from the perennial question of form, from the desire for form and the impossibility of form.

Thus, within this speculative economy that Althusser had established under the rubric of an "epistemological history of psychoanalysis," he risked the scientificity that was his own desire by embracing a historical project about knowledge formation, the praxis of which would be sought in the interstices or between the forms of desire, condensed in the difference between the question of being and the limits of philosophical knowledge (apropos of Deleuze and Guattari's desiring-machines, those instruments for coding and overcoding, for the territorialization of floating signifiers, in a sense fields of *constitutive condensation*). To be sure, the theoretic demand of Althusser's essay would meet with theoretic silence from Lacan and his students, for this intervention displaced psychoanalysis, arguing that the term itself was an effect of a decentered approach to Freud's work. Theoretically speaking, "Freud and Lacan" posited desire in every Lacanian reading of a Freud text, that is, an implicit desire on Lacan's part for a "theoretical space," a "theoretical embodiment" through which the assertions, claims, and objects of that new reading might actualize the text's essence and thereby reproduce a self-identity consonant with its transition from one form to another: hence Lacan's use of Saussure, and of Kojève's reading of Hegel, to read Freud, as well as his appropriation and use of mathematical inquiries into causality, and of the surrealist conception of madness and paranoia as modes of knowledge, in his readings of Freud. Herein lies the enigma behind Althusser's epistemological history of psychoanalysis.

In "The Direction of the Treatment and the Principles of Its Power," Lacan, already struggling to reveal this kernel himself, had formally declared the *question of form*, the *desire for form*, as particularly apparent in the analytic situation.[15] To be more precise, Lacan linked the desire for form to the impossibility of constructing a cogent analytic practice, of devising a set of transcendent laws which would guarantee a correct interpretation for the analyst and the analysand. (Perhaps there is a political lesson here for us all, namely, that a total and complete form of pedagogy is equally impossible.) Hence speaking itself, the conversation between analyst and analysand, emerged as a problem of form. Such "speaking" recalls Derrida's and Althusser's references to the mouth as an opening and a means of yielding useful words; a paradigmatic example of the Nietzschean dialectic of the anus and mouth as essential to the biographical poetics and politics of an author in the face of philosophical blindness, this charged but nevertheless differentiating tactic has been deployed in philosophy since Hegel, especially by Nietzsche in *Ecce Homo* and then by Derrida in *Otobiographies*. Returning to Lacan, we find that there is no absolute form of "the analytic situation":

> My doctrine of the signifier is first of all a discipline in which those I train have to familiarize themselves with the different ways in which the signifier effects the advent of the signified, which is the only conceivable way that interpretation can produce anything new.

> For interpretation is based on no assumption of divine archetypes, but on the fact that the unconscious is structured in the most radical way like a language, that a material operates in it according to certain laws, which are the same laws as those discovered in the study of actual languages, languages that are or were actually spoken.[16]

For Lacan, the question of form (which is also a silent reminder of the Althusserian epistemological history) can be accounted for as the necessary effect of the translation of and transition between the signifier and the signified. Interpretation as such is inessential without the recognition of its own determinacy by the translation of the movement of forms; rather, the essence of interpretation, the desire for form, lies in that continually shifting phenomenality of the movement between the signifier and the signified. This movement is essential to Lacan's questioning of limits in philosophy insofar as that tradition, since Hegel, has looked into the connection between the signifier and the signified, although Lacan would surprise himself and his enemies by an inversion—attempting to explicate the movement of the separation between the signifier and the signified over time. (It is important to note here that his understanding or conceptualization of interpretation is grounded in historical materialism and seeks to overcome the binding effect of the hermeneutic circle; we must bear in mind that these references are especially true for Ricoeur's important contribution in *Freud and Philosophy*, a text on which the Lacanian school still remarks for its so-called misunderstanding of Freud's relationship to philosophy and of his importance within that eruptive scene of philosophical fervor in 1960s Paris.) To grasp the significance of Lacan's inversion, it simply amounted to his realization that telling the truth has more to do with time than with (not excluding or concealing) words or facts.

Returning to Althusser's problematic—the discourse on the discourse of psychoanalysis—we can begin to approach the consequences, historical and political, of the question of form in determining the ideological structuration of psychoanalytic discourse. Through Althusser (and, perhaps, through the later, more reflexive and doubtful Lacan), we can apprehend the *new form* of psychoanalysis as an antipsychoanalytic psychoanalysis. What does this mean? It means that if we grant Althusser the epistemological privilege he demands of psychoanalysis in calling for a properly "epistemological history . . . and a social (and ideological) history of the world of analysis," it would appear that the categories essential to psychoanalysis must undergo a radical revision, not retroactively but within the Now, under the sign of a new process of synchronicity. It is indeed the case that this new process of synchronicity—or what Derrida has aptly labeled the "constitutive outside," the general economy of which is not far from Althusser's own insistence on the primordial necessity of the *décalage* (or "dislocation in the real")—must come into focus. Opening up this other space, in which a complex of heterogeneous modes of symbolization coincides with an abundance of signifiers, compels us to look into an alternative psychoanalytic constellation and territory where the Imaginary, the Symbolic, and the Real are not merely technical terms but active elements in the production of history. In other words, if this epistemological history of psychoanalysis renders it as an impossible complete form, perhaps that is why we must ask what we stand to gain from juxtaposing *psychoanalysis* and *imperialism*.

This is a difficult question, and I cannot claim to have even begun to imagine its structural force, much less to have developed any representation of the dispersion of its epistemic singularity within poststructuralist thought. However, our point of reference for this and other questions still lies in the contradictions set within that proposed epistemological history. The hesitations and contradictions lodged in Althusser's "Freud and Lacan" are largely expressed as proposals, like its closing sentence: "This has opened up one of the ways which may perhaps lead us some day to a better understanding of this *structure of misrecognition*, which is of particular concern for all investigations into ideology."[17] Ultimately, this thought, so rooted in its time and immersed in the act of radically settling accounts with itself through others, turns out to be a detour through, and in the last instance subsumed under, the global order of all investigations into ideology. For the same reason, psychoanalysis-and-imperialism is *not* a detour to a more direct confrontation with psychoanalysis or to a reconsideration of psychoanalysis-and-Marxism, hyphenated late in the twentieth century; it is rather the double, or a metafiction, of epistemological history itself, one that appreciates the specificity of the practice of knowledge which results from its questions, "but above all for the close association of the problem of the object and the objectivity of a science with that of the *domain* of validity of its concepts."[18] Epistemological history distrusts the formalism exemplified by critical enterprises such as Marxism that would claim to supplement or liberate some or all elements in psychoanalysis by unveiling its First Cause through the realism of materialism. And I doubt that Althusser himself would have subscribed to such a predication.

The articulation of psychoanalysis and imperialism, like that of psychoanalysis and Marxism, even in the late twentieth century, can serve only in an introductory capacity vis-à-vis the unexpected problematics arising from the consciousness that wills a reading. No doubt, this late in the century, the task of any possible discourse such as psychoanalysis-and-imperialism is less one of comparative description (i.e., of both systems and their elements) than of a motion to abjure the stylistic exceptionalism, as well as the epistemic singularity, often proclaimed by and attached to the self-representations of current critical practices. That is why, after praising and deriding Lacan, Althusser claimed not to have proven anything new about psychoanalysis as such, but to have revealed a new dimension for all investigations into ideology, the dimension of the *break*.[19] Perhaps ideology itself is the system, and psychoanalysis-and-imperialism or psychoanalysis-and-Marxism its elements, for, as Althusser noted,

> if this thesis is correct, analytic practice (the cure), which absorbs all the attention of those interpreters and philosophers eager for the intimacy of the confidential couple in which avowed sickness and professional medical secrecy exchange the sacred promises of intersubjectivity, does not contain the secrets of psycho-analysis; it only contains one part of the reality of psycho-analysis, the part which exists in practice. It does not contain its theoretical secrets. If this thesis is correct, neither do the technique and method contain the secrets of psycho-analysis, except as every method does, by delegation, not from the practice but from the theory. Only the theory contains them, as in every scientific discipline.[20]

"If this thesis is correct. . . ." The problem and semantic effect of imperialism remains a blind spot for psychoanalysis; it is neither incidental nor merely another factor to be plugged into the overextended permutations of late-twentieth-century psychoanalysis. The judgment of the everydayness of imperialist reality and the place of such judgment in the home of psychoanalysis will shed significant light on the imbalances of the archive and its modes of delegation through oppositional readings, which cannot

be reduced to individual or collective cultural artifacts—the ideological misgivings of the racialist, nationalist, feminist, and postcolonialist appropriations of psychoanalysis (and the criticism which seeks to deconstruct them) notwithstanding. By marshalling the lessons of reading and the questions gathered from reading, psychoanalysis-and-imperialism might give itself over to a supplementary staging of an epistemological history, that is, a modest effort by which new areas of silence and underdevelopment can be heard or made visible through a critical engagement with psychoanalysis. Such an effort would be bound to redraw the frontiers of both psychoanalysis and imperialism, of their political legitimacy and possibility, through the mediation of a philosophy which would remind us "that it is the peculiarity of scientific discourse to be *written*; and that it therefore poses us the question of the form of its *writing*."[21]

Notes

The larger project of which this essay is a part is modestly aimed at disentangling the figure of psychoanalysis from its contemporary literary-pragmatic uses by way of revisiting and gathering the thrust of Althusser's "Freud and Lacan" and putting to work the rigorous philosophical and political demands that his essay made of Lacan and his followers, raising questions about veridicality, the ethics of reading, and the paradoxes of disciplinary formation. Imperialism emerges here as the other, the exterior through and against which psychoanalysis can translate and redistribute its objects. I am not interested, however, in applying psychoanalytic concepts, as some scholars have, to race, nation, or gender. While such projects may have their uses in giving a new face to post–Cold War New Criticism, my own focus is on the constraining factors and conditions of possibility which Althusser recognized in 1968 as constitutive of the formation of psychoanalysis. My primary goal in this and other, forthcoming essays is to mark and question the philosophical imperatives of psychoanalysis as a knowledge project. For more on the philosophical approach to Lacan, see Jean-Luc Nancy and Philippe Lacoue-Labarthe, *The Title of the Letter: A Reading of Lacan*, trans. François Raffoul and David Pettigrew (Albany, 1992 [1973]).

1 Jacques Derrida, "Geopsychoanalysis: '. . . and the Rest of the World'" (1981), trans. D. Nicholson-Smith, *American Imago* 48 (1991): 199–231.

2 Louis Althusser, "Freud and Lacan," in *Essays on Ideology* (London and New York, 1984 [1976]), 147–71; quotation from 170.

3 Martin Heidegger, *Basic Questions of Philosophy: Selected "Problems" of "Logic,"* trans. Richard Rojcewics and Andrew Schuwer (Bloomington, 1994 [1974]), 4. See also Martin Heidegger, *What Is Philosophy?*, trans. William Kluback and Jean T. Wilde (New Haven, 1956). In both works, Heidegger places tremendous emphasis on the idea of questioning, pushing it to the level of a category. Moreover, the infrastructure of a question or a reading opens up the way for our understanding of how the production of a narra-

tive—the ultimate goal of a question or a reading—is constrained and conditioned by an opposing value formation pointing toward politics and history, congealed in the entity of the social as a cluster of references deriving from and included in the narration. In America, it is not good business to relate Althusser to Heidegger; any historian of French twentieth-century philosophy worthy of the name, however, would see obvious similarities in their methods.

4 See Rodolphe Gasché, *The Tain of the Mirror: Derrida and the Philosophy of Reflection* (Cambridge, MA, 1986), 35–54.

5 Derrida, "Geopsychoanalysis," 203–4.

6 In addition to Gasché's *Tain of the Mirror*, see two impressive texts by Vincent Descombes, *Modern French Philosophy* (Cambridge and New York, 1980 [1979]); and *The Barometer of Modern Reason: On the Philosophies of Current Events* (New York, 1993 [1989]).

7 See Mikhail Bakhtin's formulations of what I am describing as "the absence," in *Toward a Philosophy of the Act*, trans. Vadim Liapunov, ed. Vadim Liapunov and Michael Holquist (Austin, 1993), 9:

> Any kind of practical orientation of my life within the theoretical world is impossible: it is impossible to live in it, impossible to perform answerable deeds. In that world I am unnecessary; I am essentially and fundamentally non existent in it. The theoretical world is obtained through an essential and fundamental abstraction from the fact of my unique being and from the moral sense of that fact—"as if I do not exist." And this concept of Being is indifferent to the central fact—central for me—of my unique and actual communion with Being (I, too, exist), and it cannot in principle add anything to it or subtract anything from it, for it remains equal to itself and identical in its sense and significance, regardless of whether it exists or not; it cannot provide any criteria for the life of practice, the life of the deed, for it is *not* the Being *in which I live*, and, if it were the only Being, I would not exist.

See also Louis Althusser, "On the Young Marx," in *For Marx* (London, 1990 [1965]), 50–86: "The Young Marx emerged into the world of thought of his own time, to think in it in his turn, and to enter into the exchange and debate with the thoughts of his time which was to be his whole life as an ideologue. At this level of the exchanges and conflicts that are the very substance of the texts in which his living thoughts have come down to us, it is as if the authors of these thoughts were themselves absent. The concrete individual who expresses himself in his thoughts and his writings is absent" (64).

8 Louis Althusser, "From *Capital* to Marx's Philosophy" (1965), in Louis Althusser and Etienne Balibar, *Reading "Capital,"* trans. Ben Brewster (New York, 1970), 13–69; quotation from 15. See also the Maspero edition of *Lire "Le capital"* (Paris, 1968).

9 Ibid., 16–17.

10 Antonio Negri, *The Savage Anomaly: The Power of Spinoza's Metaphysics and Politics*, trans. Michael Hardt (Minneapolis, 1991 [1981]), xix.

11 Etienne Balibar, "Althusser's Object," *Social Text*, No. 39 (Summer 1994): 157–88; quotation from 162.

12 Slavoj Žižek, *The Sublime Object of Ideology* (London and New York, 1989), 1.

13 Althusser, "From *Capital* to Marx's Philosophy," 17.
14 Michel Foucault, *Madness and Civilization: A History of Insanity in the Age of Reason*, trans. Richard Howard (New York, 1965 [1961]), v.
15 Jacques Lacan, "The Direction of the Treatment and the Principles of Its Power" (1958), in *Ecrits: A Selection*, trans. Alan Sheridan (New York and London, 1977 [1966]), 226–80.
16 Ibid., 233–34.
17 Althusser, "Freud and Lacan," 171.
18 Balibar, "Althusser's Object," 159.
19 Ibid., 161–70.
20 Althusser, "Freud and Lacan," 151.
21 Althusser, "From *Capital* to Marx's Philosophy," 69.

Elizabeth Jane Bellamy

"Intimate Enemies": Psychoanalysis, Marxism, and Postcolonial Affect

Beginning with the efforts of the Frankfurt school, there have been a number of ambitious attempts at a synthesis between psychoanalysis and Marxism, a kind of meta-theory that could negotiate the "individual" focus of psychoanalysis with the more "collective" political concerns of Marxism.[1] Such a synthesis has long remained elusive and, in what many refer to as a post-Marxist era, now often seems irrelevant and obsolete. More specifically, in a postcolonial era (broadly defined as the aftermath of the ruinous effects of centuries of imperialism) psychoanalysis and Marxism, those two major "master narratives" emerging from European modernity, have been judged as directly complicit in colonialism; and doubts (not to mention resentments) persist that psychoanalysis and Marxism can ever be effectively imported into postcolonial contexts. Because of their status as dominant, first world, metropolitan theories, psychoanalysis and Marxism have frequently been rejected as useful tools for postcolonialist critique. In this context, we can consider the comments of Gayatri Spivak not just because she so often serves as a predictable spokesperson for the general topic of "postcolo-

The *South Atlantic Quarterly* 97:2, Spring 1998.

nialism and its discontents," but because her own work has been so heavily influenced by "European" theory, even as she expressed reservations about its overall usefulness for the postcolonialist project. Generally critical of any attempt at a totalizing theory, over the last decade Spivak has been particularly sensitive to "high" theoretical discourse's incommensurability with the political urgencies of postcolonialism. In "A Literary Representation of the Subaltern," for example, she expressed concern about "the overtly imperialist politics of psychoanalysis"; and in "The Political Economy of Women as Seen by a Literary Critic," she urged an investigation of "the insertion of psychoanalysis" into third world countries.[2]

Such justifiable postcolonialist concern about the complicities of psychoanalysis with imperialism notwithstanding, psychoanalytic theory has a long and somewhat troubled history of incorporation into colonial and postcolonial contexts—a history deserving of at least a brief overview here. In *Prospero and Caliban: The Psychology of Colonization*, for example, Octave Mannoni analyzed psychological disturbances in postwar Madagascar and depicted (highly problematically) the Madagascan native as suffering from an unconscious "dependency" syndrome, a "desire" to be colonized.[3] Another key, and much more politically efficacious, use of psychoanalysis for cultural critique within a (neo)colonial context was, of course, Frantz Fanon's analysis of the imbrications of the psychical (particularly in association with French colonial ethnopsychiatry) and the political. His reformulation of Lacan's mirror stage around colonial difference was particularly significant: "When one has grasped the mechanism described by Lacan, one can have no further doubt that the real Other for the white man is and will continue to be the black man. And conversely."[4] Fanon's psychoanalyzing of colonial racism in *Black Skin, White Masks* has been a major influence on the work of Homi Bhabha, who, among recent postcolonial theorists, demonstrates the most persistent and explicit engagement with psychoanalysis. In "The Other Question," for example, he made heavy use of Freud's concept of the fetish for an analysis of racial stereotypes within colonial discourse.[5] And in such essays as "Remembering Fanon" and "Sly Civility," Bhabha has followed Fanon's lead in using Lacan to theorize the identity of the colonizer as a "lack" that can only be filled by the colonized other.[6]

Like psychoanalysis, Marxism too has experienced an uneven and often contradictory fate within postcolonialist theory, despite its presumed status as the more politically engaged of these two European master discourses. In his vastly influential *Orientalism*, Edward Said (his expressed interest in Gramsci and downplaying of Marx's own criticisms of colonialism notwithstanding) denied Marxism any efficacy in postcolonial contexts: "In the end it is the Romantic Orientalism that wins out, as Marx's theoretical socio-economic views become submerged in [a] classically standard image" of the East.[7] But more recently, Aijaz Ahmad, who unabashedly supports orthodox Marxism as an explanatory model for postcolonial experience, has gone so far as to attack much postcolonialist theory as anti-Marxist. In his essay "Marx on India," Ahmad, attacking Said's critique of an "Orientalist" Marx, accused him of ignoring the complex issues raised by Marx's two 1853 *New York Tribune* articles on India.[8] However, Kalpana Seshadri-Crooks has criticized Ahmad in turn, arguing cogently that his denunciation of postcolonialism as anti-Marxist "seems highly dubious given that Marxism is not some sort of ready-made grid that can be imposed upon social realities; rather, Marxism is itself a highly conflictual discourse whose terms and concepts must be constantly negotiated if they are to be made useful."[9]

What has emerged so far from this overview is that the master narratives of psychoanalysis and Marxism, despite a sustained postcolonialist attack on their Eurocentric biases, have each found a "place," however precarious and contingent, within the discourse of postcolonialism. And thus it is possible to point to a critical, if often contradictory, history of psychoanalysis "and postcolonialism" or of Marxism "and postcolonialism." But, to return to the central problem, how can we talk—and how much can we say—about the complex intersection between psychoanalysis and Marxism, let alone how that intersection *itself* intersects with postcolonialism? Such a line of inquiry is treacherous ground indeed, for not only does it inherit the still vital and vexed question (legacy of the Frankfurt school) of how the Marxist and psychoanalytic discourses can themselves achieve a meaningful mediation, but it must now also confront the intense political critique of their Eurocentrism, which is potentially incommensurate with any postcolonial context.

My own line of inquiry will be pursued via the work of Bhabha and Spivak, specifically, the use of the psychoanalytic concept of *affect* in their efforts to articulate subaltern experience. Although much has been written on the postcolonialism of these two prominent theorists, to the best of my knowledge there has been no analysis of how they have brought affect to bear on postcolonialist critique. Throughout their careers, Bhabha and Spivak have each been instrumental in refusing to view Marxism and psychoanalysis as monolithic and prescriptive; rather, they have been receptive to both discourses as (echoing Seshadri-Crooks) "highly conflictual" ones "whose terms and concepts must be constantly negotiated if they are to be made useful." Bhabha's and Spivak's uses of affect represent two intriguing sites of just such a negotiation—and by way of a concept that ranks among the most difficult and inadequately theorized in the Freudian corpus, its difficulty hinging on the less than well-understood but highly significant relationship between the libidinal and the unconscious.[10] Moreover, although neither Bhabha nor Spivak seems inclined to explicitly position affect in relation to the rest of Freudian theory (and orthodox, doctrinaire Freudians might judge their respective deployments of the term so labile as to be theoretically meaningless), each theorist's invocation of affect within a postcolonial context constitutes a valuable attempt to revitalize this inadequately theorized concept for cultural critique; furthermore, no genealogy of subaltern agency should fail to take into account Bhabha's and Spivak's reconfigurations of affect as a politically resonant site for a postcolonialist mediation between Marxism and psychoanalysis. Although Bhabha's work tends to be more psychoanalytically inflected than Spivak's, which tends (on the subaltern at least) to be more Marxist-inflected, with each accordingly deploying affect for (sometimes significantly) different purposes, both regard the concept as crucial to their articulations of subaltern experience. In the final analysis, their deployments of postcolonialist affect, far from simply being a "catachresis" too grounded in Western psychoanalysis to have any relevance for postcolonialism, borrow from and radically alter the original valences of Freudian affect such that a postcolonial psycho-Marxist discourse which eludes complicity with Eurocentrism is forged.

Spivak and Bhabha have built this discourse on the figure of the subaltern as the point where the complex (and never fully "locatable") intersection between Marxism and psychoanalysis occurs within postcolonialism. As is well known, the Subaltern Studies Group was founded to provide a countermovement to mainstream South Asian history in terms of defining national identity in the context of decolonization. Ranajit Guha, arguing that certain forms of peasant insurgency could not be subsumed within colonialist or nationalist narrations of nation, posited subaltern studies as a revisionist historiography that would focus (contra mainstream bourgeois/nationalist historiography) on rural, non-elite sectors of decolonized countries. The significance here for any intersection between psycho-Marxism and postcolonialism is that the revisionist historiography of subaltern studies has inevitably led to efforts to define an essential "subaltern consciousness," with the reality of material exploitation informing considerations of the psychical experience of decolonization. As Guha has observed, bourgeois/nationalist historiography "den[ies] a will to the mass of the rebels themselves and represent[s] them merely as instruments of some other will. . . . If any consciousness is attributed at all to the rebels, it is only a few of their leaders—more often than not some individual members or small groups of the gentry—who are credited with it." And even in radical historiography, the specificity of rebel consciousness is too often portrayed as an "Ideal Consciousness . . . ill-equipped to cope with contradictions which are indeed the stuff history is made of."[11] For Guha, the contradictions and "self-alienations" of rebel consciousness elude the oversimplifying categories of a quasi-Hegelian "Ideal Consciousness" and require a more nuanced attention to the intersection between individual psyche and political collectivity. Thus, in its efforts to define "subaltern consciousness," subaltern studies poses such questions as the following: How is antagonism within the contingencies of decolonization represented? Where is the agency of change in the subaltern? How is rebel consciousness to be represented, given that it lies outside the regulative logic of political independence and the nation-building project and is accessible only in what Guha refers to as "the prose of counter-insurgency"? In one form or another, all these questions attempt an imbrication between the psychical and the political within the complex cultural context of colonialism and decolonization.

Given Bhabha's ongoing engagement with psychoanalysis, it is not surprising that any genealogy of postcolonial subaltern agency must begin for him with a particular attention to what he calls "social pathologies" or, more specifically, "the affective experience of social marginality," with affect defined vis-à-vis postcolonialism as "the uneven development and the differential, often disadvantaged, histories of nations, races, communities, peoples."[12] These "disadvantaged histories" are not simply narratives of class antagonism (as conceived by orthodox Marxism), but rather what can be more productively viewed within a psychoanalytic framework as fragmented "contingencies" or counter-hegemonic strategies of emancipation and social antagonism fractured in turn by "disjunctive temporalities." A genealogy of postcolonial agency proper, then, is an attempt to articulate those disjunctive moments in history that render the "present" an impossibility, an attempt mandating attention to the affective "social pathologies" that arise in the wake of such uneven, fragmented temporalities.

The psychoanalytic concept of affect (or what Bhabha also terms "intersubjective affect") thus takes on signal importance for subaltern studies. Picking up where Guha's description of subaltern consciousness as "self-alienated" leaves off, Bhabha's concept of postcolonial affect emerges from the "incommensurable demands and practices" entailed by social survival, with the cultural and psychical displacements that characterize the process of decolonization tracing, at best, "the liminal edge of identity."[13] In an explicitly psychoanalytic (indeed, explicitly Lacanian) moment, Bhabha depicts postcolonial agency not as something that exists in/of itself, but rather as an unlocatable aftereffect: "The agent emerges as a form of retroactivity, *Nachträglichkeit*. It is not agency as itself (transcendent, transparent) or in itself." Subaltern consciousness is most productively viewed as an aftereffect, therefore, because the rebel, as the agent of change, is traversed by an interruption in sign systems, specifically, an incommensurability between the religious and the militant that serves as the "origin" of affect within subaltern insurgency. In this context, Bhabha quotes Guha quoting from Sunil Sen's account of the Tebhaga movement in Dinajpur (*Agrarian Struggle in Bengal*): "Muslim peasants [came] to the Kisan Sabha 'sometimes inscribing a hammer and a sickle on the Muslim League flag' and young maulavis '[recited] melodious verses from the Koran' at village meetings 'as they condemned the jotedari system and the practice of charging high interest rates.'"[14] Here, it is simply inadequate to speak of a rebel "Ideal Consciousness." Rather, rebel insurgency is to be interpreted as disjointed, contradictory, self-alienated, for even as the Muslim peasants protest the jotedari system and its high interest rates (which might tempt the historian to read their revolt solely as an orthodox Marxist narrative of class struggle) they also deploy, as their nostalgic (or "affective") means of protest, the neither fully "religious" nor fully "socialist" Muslim League flag while chanting "melodious verses from the Koran." These disjunctive and only partial modes of opposition militate against a truly collective action. Thus the Muslim peasants are less the site of "individuation" (in the bourgeois, Western sense of the term) than the site of "ambivalence" as "an intersubjective affect" induced by the incommensurability between the religious and the militant.

Bhabha's concept of postcolonial affect can be viewed, then, as one of the more innovative renegotiations of psychoanalysis for postcolonialist critique. No longer simply Freud's physical discharge of instinctual energy, affect is endowed by Bhabha with an explicitly political resonance, perceived as a subjectivity (or "liminal edge of identity") that (dis)appears retroactively as the aftereffect of the peasant experience under colonialism. Or, put another way, the postcolonial "affective experience of social marginality," oscillating as it does between (conscious) nostalgia and (unconscious) self-alienation, (dis)appears in the interstices between psychoanalysis and Marxism.

Spivak's deployment of affect in her work on the subaltern is potentially more complex than Bhabha's, given her explicit engagement with the thorny thickets of orthodox Marxism. Like many of her terms, Spivak's reconfiguration of affect within postcolonialist critique is often enigmatic and provocatively unelaborated. For example, at the beginning of "Asked to Talk about Myself . . . ," she observes, enigmatically, that "the notion of origin is as broad and robust and full of affect as it is imprecise."[15] Affect is then not pursued, a decontextualized use of the term that exemplifies her tendency to weave it into her discourse. Spivak's deployment of the concept achieves more coherence, however, in her works on the subaltern, especially "Woman in Difference."[16] This essay is in my view perhaps the most sustained theorizing of affect within postcolonialist critique, as well as one of the most significant attempts to establish the relevance of psycho-Marxism to postcolonialism. As we shall discover, Spivak's interpretation of affect, though not entirely unrelated to Bhabha's reconfiguration of it as subaltern nostalgia, is less invested in affect's relationship to (un)consciousness than in its capacity, as a Marxist category of economic and social coding, to disguise the real of the body within material exploitation.

Several of Spivak's essays are especially important contributions to the effort to define subaltern consciousness and the role of colonialism and decolonization in shaping a subjectivity and an agency that are at once indebted to and departures from the traditional aims of psychoanalysis and Marxism.[17] For example, true to her abovementioned insistence that postcolonialism must seek a Marxism "rescue[d] from its European provenance," Spivak has located her work within "the nooks and crannies of Marx,"[18] yet she has also faithfully deployed such orthodox Marxist concepts as "labor" and "value." Indeed, examining her early "Marxist-deconstructive" phase can lead to a fuller understanding of her most recent work on subaltern consciousness within a reconfigured psycho-Marxism.

In terms of the relationship between labor and value, Spivak has observed that Marx "left the slippery concept of 'use-value' undertheorized." She teases out the "slippery" nature of use-value by establishing what she calls its "textuality": exchange-value allows use-value to occupy "the normative inside place of the host as well as banishing it as that which must be subtracted so that value can be defined."[19] Moreover, "use makes 'value' vanish, yet without the moment of consumption of the commodity as use-value the value would not be 'real'-ized."[20] Rey Chow summarizes Spivak's deconstructive focus on the "textuality" of value and its not readily apparent relationship to labor thus:

> "Value," in other words, functions in the same enigmatic manner as "writing." While it is supposed to be secondary (since it occurs as a result of labor, as writing is thought to occur after "natural" language—speech), it seems shamelessly usurping. . . . Like writing also, value poses the question about origins: does the value/worth of value come from what "precedes" it, namely, labor, or does it come from itself?[21]

Is "value" intrinsic to itself, or does labor *create* use-value? In the earlier, more Derridean phase of Spivak's career, she saw the asymmetry between labor and value as the site of *differance* itself. But more recently, as her ongoing interest in the reality of material exploitation has led to her work on the subaltern (particularly on unorganized peasant labor), this asymmetry has become the precursor of both Spivak's own postcolonialist psycho-Marxism and, as we shall see, her reconfiguration of affect.

Spivak's earlier "Marxist-deconstructive" interest in the indeterminacy of use-value thus sets the stage for her later focus on the question posed by the Subaltern Studies Group: Where do we "locate" the agency of the subaltern? In Spivak's summary, the subaltern experiences "no firmly established agency of traffic with the *culture* of imperialism."[22] Because the subaltern is positioned outside of organized labor, the challenge for postcolonialist discourse is to arrive at new ways of theorizing Marx's concepts of labor and value and their relationship to psychical experience. While Bhabha claims that subaltern identity cannot be located in "consciousness" (i.e., peasant solidarity as a sign of "consciousness"), but rather in a subaltern "subject effect," Spivak would make the additional point that such a subaltern "subject effect" originates in Marxist value-form and its yet-to-be theorized relationship to labor. Even more significantly for Spivak (and herein lies her own negotiation with not only Marxism but also psychoanalysis in a postcolonial context), subaltern agency is specifically "located" in the vulnerability of the body: "It is the body's susceptibility to the production of value which makes it vulnerable . . . to insertion into the economic."[23] Labor-power renders the subaltern body susceptible to the production of value: while the alienation of the subaltern body originates in the very nature of labor-power, the body's material reality is directly implicated in the "textuality" of use-value.

For Spivak, of course, a glaring absence in subaltern studies has been not just the body in general but the specific body of the gendered subaltern subject—hence her interest in Mahasweta Devi's fiction as texts about the "(im)possibility of 'making' the subaltern gender the subject of its own story."[24] As we shall see, that impossibility is what also precludes, for Spivak, any kind of glibly premature mediation between Marxism and psychoanalysis in a postcolonial context. Rather, the "space" of the subaltern woman is located in what she describes as a "paralogical" displacement that falls ambiguously between psychoanalysis and Marxism, as illustrated by such Mahasweta heroines as Draupadi, who stands naked before the Army Chief, "her breasts mangled and her vagina torn and bleeding"; Jashoda, who lies dead, "her breast putrefied with cancer"; and Douloti, whose decaying corpse was once ravaged by venereal disease.[25] Spivak, emphasizing that these unaccommodated female bodies have no relationship to the political activism of the male subaltern, also argues that they elude the traditional Marxist-feminist thematics in which Marx's value-theory has been downplayed with the claim that women's work does not typically produce value.

Taking the vivid case of Mahasweta's story "Stanadayini" (Breast-Giver), Spivak demonstrates the ways in which labor-power renders the female body directly susceptible to the production of value. The heroine, Jashoda, supports her crippled husband and family by serving as a wet nurse to the infants of a wealthy household, with her labor-power thus constituted by her "production mode" of gestation and lactation. But, as Spivak points out, Mahasweta's story depicts an oddly overdetermined aporia, one that is stalled between the categories of "sex" and "class," between the domestic and the "domestic" (or, more broadly, between the discourses of psychoanalysis and Marxism). "Stanadayini" is less about mothering than about *professional* "mothering," focusing as it does on the concomitant emergence of both exchange-value (i.e., the newly emergent value of Jashoda's milk, which is consumed by another mother's children, not her own) and "surplus labor" (as opposed to "necessary labor" in the strictly domestic sphere). In such a scheme (the crux of which, for Spivak, is affect and its relationship to labor and value), "professional mothering" is removed from the "affective" realm of private, domestic maternity, since value emerges from Jashoda's labor-power. Spivak reads Mahasweta's story, which concludes with Jashoda's death from breast cancer, as less about Jashoda's "consciousness" (within the affective realm of mothering) than about the material real of her body and the nonaffective realm of professional fostering, with the dying Jashoda's cancerous breast (normally the maternal signifier par excellence), in Spivak's provocative phrasing, "blast[ing] mothering right out of its affective coding."[26] Mahasweta, accordingly "sees mothering in its materiality beyond its socialization as affect, beyond psychologization as abjection."[27]

For Spivak, then, affect assumes a much more rigorously Marxist valence by contrast to Bhabha's deployment of it as subaltern "nostalgia." In her conception, affect is a process of socialization that obscures the subaltern female body's insertion into the economic sphere, which leads to its production of value (and, ultimately, to its premature death). Spivak thus treats Freudian affect not so much as a psychoanalytic term than as an economic process of recoding, whereby "private" emotions reemerge in the larger economic realm as the origin of exchange-value and surplus labor. In response to the question of where we are to "locate" the agency of the subaltern woman, a female subjectivity that is not, in some sense, always already implicated in such "affective" realms as mothering, she points to the material real of the female body, which "blasts" womanhood "right out of its affective coding."

"Woman in Difference," which includes her dense and complex commentary on another Mahasweta story, "Douloti the Bountiful," also represents Spivak's most comprehensive and coherent articulation of the importance of affect for postcolonialist critique. "Douloti the Bountiful" depicts an even more complex instance of how the female body "blasts" womanhood "right out of its affective coding," that of prostitution as an "affective" realm where female labor-power renders the body even more brutally and directly susceptible to the production of value. Spivak's commentary on this story illustrates most effectively her concern with uncovering those ineffable moments *prior* to affect, when the material real of the female body is presented in all its intractability—an intractability (neither fully psychoanalytic nor fully Marxist) that actually serves as the site of agency for the gendered subaltern.[28]

Before returning to "Woman in Difference," however, let us briefly glance at Spivak's "Marginality in the Teaching Machine." Her analysis there of affect within a strictly Marxist context begins with Deleuze and Guattari's *Anti-Oedipus*, which is particularly interesting to Spivak because it has been so instrumental in extending the range of Marxist value-form from economic to social, or "affective," coding.[29] "Their suggestion was that, since capital decoded and deterritorialized the socius by releasing the abstract as such, capitalism must manage this crisis via many reterritorializations, among which the generalized, *psychoanalytic* mode of production of affective value operates by way of a generalized systemic institution of equivalence spectacular in its complexity and discontinuity."[30] For Deleuze and Guattari, capital (and its inevitable traffic in economic-value coding) releases a libidinal energy of desire that capitalism must then *recode* back into the terms of the social realm. Specifically, desire must be recoded as affect so as to extract surplus-value, which Deleuze and Guattari interpret as capitalism's process of crisis management. As we have already seen in the context of Spivak's commentary on "Stanadayini," one major consequence for her of the "production" of affective value is its attendant gender coding. Gendering (or "the theoretical fiction of sexual identity") depends on an affective coding of exchange and surplus—or, in the final analysis, "negotiating 'sexuality' rather than sexual identity."[31]

In "Woman in Difference," Spivak aims to extend Deleuze and Guattari's economic analysis of the operations of affect, "spectacular in [all their] complexity and discontinuity," to the tribal subaltern on the "decolonized terrain" outside of national space, a position from which the subaltern cannot participate in the transition from colonialism to nationalism. " 'Empire' and 'Nation' are interchangeable" for the subaltern (especially the subaltern woman), with "nation" still a marked term within political discourse, a "regulative logic" derived from the old colony.[32] For Mahasweta, then, the district of Palamu in "Douloti the Bountiful" is just such a "decolonized terrain," where bond labor becomes the only means of repaying a loan at an extortionate interest rate and where the term "bond slave" displaces "citizen." On such "terrain," bond slavery constitutes a collectivity that bypasses the concept of nation. Within this system of hereditary bond slavery, affect is interpreted by Spivak (following Deleuze and Guattari) as part of the value-coding apparatus. She observes that "family life is still possible here, the affects taking the entire burden of survival." This "regulative logic of loans" effectively binds women and men to one another in a collective legitimizing of struggle, with bond labor socially vested in the collective "we." The men consider the options of armed struggle versus agitating for legislation, even as the old *kamiya* women sing songs by the fire, lamenting, "We will never be free."[33] But the central focus of both Mahasweta's story and Spivak's subaltern reconfiguration of affect in "Woman in Difference" is prostitution. Beneath the family life of bond slaves a system of bond prostitution operates, whereby women are abducted from bond labor (*kamiya*) households and reduced even further as bodies for economic exploitation: "Woman's body is thus the last instance in a system whose general regulator is still the loan. . . . But it is also the last instance on the chain of affective responsibility."[34] What, precisely, does Spivak mean by "the last instance on the chain of affective responsibility"? Here, where family ties are broken, she insists, "woman's body," is "elsewhere." Since, for Spivak, the "separate place of the woman's body" is a space *prior* to the traffic in affective-value coding, the body of the bond prostitute is both separate from and implicated in prostitution as a mode of production.

In the course of their copulation with clients many bond prostitutes become pregnant. Spivak quotes Mahasweta's simple but resonant observation that "even under such circumstances, children are born."[35] More to the point, even under such circumstances "the affective coding of mothering" still operates. Here Spivak draws on Simone de Beauvoir's *Second Sex* for insight into how motherhood renders the woman's body (affectively) abstract: "However much the woman might want *a* child, however much she may bestow intentionality upon it, she cannot desire *this* child." In other words, child rearing is a chosen (or an "affective") commitment. On the surface, it would seem that the system of subaltern bond labor must work against such maternal commitment because, in these houses of prostitution, the inscription of the female body in gestation would presumably be coded economically rather than affectively. After all, as Spivak notes, "children are not written into mother right" for bond prostitutes.[36] However, even here the affective coding of motherhood is possible, for when these children are born their prostitute mothers must give them up to missions and orphanages, then hope that they will escape the *kamiya* life; and it is in this very hope for or commitment to their children's future that mothering among the bond prostitutes is affectively coded.

The "separate place" or "elsewhere" of woman's body cannot, in Spivak's reading, be located in the prostitute-mother's body, given its preoccupation by/with affective commitment. Thus Spivak turns to Mahasweta's heroine Douloti as a figure for the virtually unlocatable "separate place" or "excess of the woman's body" that exists *before* its affective-value coding. How, precisely, does the "excess of the woman's body" evoke a space *prior* to affect? Douloti is only a child: she accepts bond slavery as a law of nature, and her relationship with her mother, who resides in the village, is, in Spivak's words, "filled with affect," hence falling decidedly within the affective-value coding of sentiment. It is Douloti's "excess," in fact, that Spivak regards as the narrative's most crucial indeterminacy. Neither the male *kamiya* militants nor the other bond prostitutes present such a crisis of representation: the militants, who plot insurgency, readily represent "the coding of intention into resistance," while the bond prostitutes readily represent "the resisting acceptance of victimization."[37] But Douloti, who has been abducted into bond labor prostitution, is portrayed by Mahasweta as *neither* an intending subject of resistance *nor* a resisting victim. Instead, Douloti experiences an "unresisting nostalgia" and sees *kamiya* resistance as futile. Thus Mahasweta presents Douloti's nostalgic affect (for mother, for village) as an impasse; Douloti is a sympathetic character, yet one whose affect (as a function of value coding) works against social change. In Spivak's view,

> Mahasweta presents Douloti's affect and, ultimately, Douloti herself, as the site of a real aporia. You cannot give assent to both on the same register. I am also arguing that, in terms of the general rhetorical conduct of the story, you also cannot give assent, in the same register, to the evocation of a space prior to value-coding, on the one hand, and the sympathetic representation of Douloti as a character, recognizable within an earlier discursive formation, on the other.[38]

Although Douloti's affective nostalgia for her village is politically regressive, it produces real consequences nonetheless for the formation of "nationhood"; in the end, it is her broken body, ravaged by venereal disease, that represents "the figuration of the woman's body before the affective coding of sexuality," whereby woman is both fully implicated in the mode-of-production narrative and distanced from it—and by which "the *Aufhebung* of colony into nation is undone."[39] Unlike the prostitute mothers, Douloti does not position herself as a (sexual) identity in the chain of affective-value coding. Thus, at the conclusion of the story, when she lies down to die on a large map of India in the clay courtyard of the village school (with the map serving as a kind of synecdoche for "nationhood" itself), Douloti, as "the space *displaced* from the Empire–Nation negotiation," in effect makes nationalism impossible.[40]

As in her analyses of other Mahasweta stories and their presentation of the crisis of a "speaking" subaltern, Spivak's analysis of "Douloti the Bountiful" places the "excess" of the marginalized woman's diseased, broken body at the very center of the narrative. In doing so, she seems intent on bringing traditional psychoanalytic, feminist, and Marxist critiques to crisis by means of a differently configured subaltern agency, one that stands apart from resistance and intentionality (i.e., Douloti as an "intending subject-agency"). Central to her reconfiguration of subaltern agency is Spivak's repositioning of the "excess" of woman's body vis-à-vis affect. That excess prior to affect is also the excess left in the wake of any attempted mediation between Marxism (here, the case of bond prostitution) and psychoanalysis (here, the affective commitment of mothering, or to one's village, etc.). For Spivak, Douloti's excess, or the "separate place of the woman's body," is, as it were, beyond the "affective" principle—an ineffable moment of agency *before* the socializations of affective commitment.

By way of conclusion, Spivak's Marxist-inflected use of affect can be productively juxtaposed with Freud's original concept (which, given her engagement with Freud throughout her career, is left curiously unacknowledged in more recent essays). However vast the theoretic, not to mention geographic, distance between Mahasweta's Palamu and Freud's Vienna, there are nevertheless some intriguing similarities between Spivak's concept of affect and Freud's that should not be overlooked. Freud's insistence that affect cannot become unconscious (in "The Unconscious") suggests a fundamental gap in psychoanalytic discourse between the body and its representation—as witness his own unsuccessful attempts to forge a specific relationship between affect and the hysterical body, a relationship that Freud viewed as representationally overdetermined. The difficulty for him in interpreting hysteria is that the utterance (of pain, of loss) is replaced (or, more accurately, *displaced*) by the affective symptom—a symptom that is not readily interpretable due to its implication in the enigmas of bodily experience. Thus we might ask, with respect to Douloti's broken body, is it *prior* to affect (in Spivak's sense of economic coding) or *constitutive* of affect (in its original psychoanalytic sense)? To what extent can we see the "excess" of Douloti's body as demonstrating not only affect as "unresisting nostalgia" (on the Marxist level of the traffic in affective-value coding), but also affect as a (Freudian) corporeal state that precludes its own representation? In other words, Douloti's broken body lying on the map of India arguably returns us to the original somatic valences of Freudian affect, for in that body can be read the fundamental gap in Freudian affect between the body and its representation (a gap that in a Marxist scheme would be prior to any value coding). If, moreover, affective symptoms are not readily interpretable due to their implication in the enigmas of bodily experience, then it could be argued (elaborating from Vienna to Palamu) that the (im)possibility of "nationhood" is likewise implicated in the enigmas (or Spivak's "excess") of Douloti's bodily experience. Although Spivak claims that one must get to a point prior to affect (as a Marxist process of economic coding) in order to find the bedrock of a truly postcolonialist critique, perhaps it is Freudian affect, rather, that best renders this "impossible" (unrepresentable, unnarratable) space of nationhood. Perhaps it is Freudian affect that best theorizes the "impossibility" of nationhood's representation and narration as woman/mother in particular, and thereby its affective coding, within the histories of decolonized and nationalist struggle.

Let us give not Freud but Bhabha and Spivak the last word here, however, for it is they who have succeeded in resuscitating his vexed and unresolved concept by endowing it with an important historical and cultural specificity. By means of their highly original respective renegotiations of affect with postcoloniality, Bhabha and Spivak have established the concept's value for a psycho-Marxism that is far from irrelevant or obsolete.

Notes

I wish to thank Sandhya Shetty for her valuable comments on this paper.

1 Although now over twenty years old, Fredric Jameson's analysis of the difficulties of such a project is still relevant. In pinpointing the intellectual challenge of forging a true synthesis between psychoanalysis and Marxism, he warned that such an articulation must avoid "ideological ion-exchanges, in which a molecular element of one system is temporarily lent to the other for purposes of stabilization"; "Imaginary and Symbolic in Lacan: Marxism, Psychoanalytic Criticism, and the Problem of the Subject," in *Literature and Psychoanalysis: The Question of Reading, Otherwise*, ed. Shoshana Felman (New Haven, 1977), 338–95; quotation from 386.

2 Gayatri Chakravorty Spivak, "A Literary Representation of the Subaltern: A Woman's Text from the Third World" (1987), in *In Other Worlds: Essays in Cultural Politics* (New York and London, 1987), 241–68; quotation from 261; and "The Political Economy of Women as Seen by a Literary Critic" (1989), in *Coming to Terms*, ed. Elizabeth Weed (New York, 1990), 218–29; quotation from 226. Spivak's relationship with psychoanalysis (like her relationships with deconstruction and, as we shall see, Marxism) is complicated, to say the least. Throughout her career, she has been consistently engaged with Freud and Lacan; and, in "Echo" (1993), a feminist psychoanalytic rereading of Ovid's myth of Narcissus, she confesses, "I have always felt uneasy about the use of psychoanalysis in cultural critique since it is so culture-specific in its provenance. . . . Yet Freud has remained one of my flawed heroes, an intimate enemy"; *The Spivak Reader: Selected Works of Gayatri Chakravorty Spivak*, ed. Donna Landry and Gerald MacLean (New York and London, 1996), 175–202; quotation from 177. Spivak is equally guarded about the relevance of Marxism for postcolonial studies. Although over the years she has frequently turned to Marx for much of her theoretic energy, Spivak wrote of seeking a Marxism "rescue[d] from its European provenance" in her 1985 essay "Scattered Speculations on the Question of Value" (*In Other Worlds*, 154–75; quotation from 157).

3 Octave Mannoni, *Prospero and Caliban: The Psychology of Colonization*, trans. Pamela Powesland; Foreword by Maurice Bloch (Ann Arbor, 1990 [1950]). For studies of the institutionalization of psychoanalysis in India, see Durganand Sinha, *Psychology in a Third World Country: The Indian Experience* (Delhi, 1986); and Ashis Nandy, *The Savage Freud and Other Essays on Possible and Retrievable Selves* (Princeton, 1995). See also Kalpana Seshadri-Crooks, "The Primitive as Analyst: Postcolonial Feminism's Access to Psycho-

analysis," *Cultural Critique*, No. 28 (Fall 1994): 175–218, for a valuable overview of "the untenability of [psychoanalytic] theory for Indian analysts" (177).

4 Frantz Fanon, *Black Skin, White Masks*, trans. Charles Lam Markmann, Foreword by Homi K. Bhabha (London, 1986 [1967]), 161.

5 Homi K. Bhabha, "The Other Question: Difference, Discrimination and the Discourse of Colonialism," in *Literature, Politics, and Theory: Papers from the Essex Conference, 1976–84*, ed. Francis Barker, Peter Hulme, Margaret Iversen, and Diana Loxley (London and New York, 1986), 148–72. Specifically, Bhabha argues that racism is predicated on fetishism as a need to assert mastery and pleasure: "In the act of disavowal and fixation the colonial subject is returned to the narcissism of the Imaginary and its identification of an ideal-ego that is white and whole. . . . The construction of colonial discourse is then a complex articulation of the tropes of fetishism—metaphor and metonymy—and the forms of narcissistic and aggressive identification available to the Imaginary" (163–64). For a feminist psychoanalytic rereading of Fanon's construction of gender, see Gwen Bergner, "Who Is that Masked Woman? Or, The Role of Gender in Fanon's *Black Skin, White Masks*," *PMLA* 110 (1995): 75–88.

6 Homi K. Bhabha, "Remembering Fanon: Self, Psyche and the Colonial Condition," in Fanon, *Black Skin, White Masks*; and "Sly Civility," in *The Location of Culture* (London and New York, 1994), 93–101. Although Bhabha, like Fanon, is both appropriative and oppositional in his stance toward Lacan, he has frequently been attacked for an unquestioning reliance on psychoanalytic paradigms. See, for example, the critique of Bhabha's alleged attempt to portray Fanon as "a premature poststructuralist" by Benita Parry, "Problems in Current Theories of Colonial Discourse," *Oxford Literary Review* 9 (1987): 27–58, esp. 31; Robert Young's criticism of Bhabha for deploying "the transcendental categories of psychoanalysis for the analysis of the historical phenomenon of colonialism" in *White Mythologies: Writing History and the West* (London, 1990), 144; and Abdul R. JanMohamed's attack on Bhabha for a depoliticizing use of Fanon that "represses the political history of colonialism" in "The Economy of Manichean Allegory: The Function of Racial Difference in Colonialist Literature," in *"Race," Writing, and Difference*, ed. Henry Louis Gates, Jr. (Chicago, 1986), 79. For a cogent overview of some of the attacks on Bhabha, see Henry Louis Gates, Jr., "Critical Fanonism," *Critical Inquiry* 17 (1991): 457–70.

7 Edward Said, *Orientalism* (Harmondsworth, 1978).

8 Aijaz Ahmad, "Marx on India: A Clarification," in *In Theory: Classes, Nations, Literatures* (London and New York, 1992), 221–42. Ahmad has also expressed his discomfort with Bhabha's emphasis on the contingent nature of class and his notion of "hybridity," in particular, which allegedly dispenses with "a sense of place, . . . of some stable commitment to one's class or gender or nation [that] may be useful for defining one's politics" (*In Theory*, 14). In light of my earlier citation of Jameson (n. 1), I might also mention Ahmad's attack on his "Third-World Literature in the Era of Multinational Capitalism," *Social Text*, No. 15 (Fall 1986): 65–88; see Aijaz Ahmad, "Jameson's Rhetoric of Otherness and the 'National Allegory,'" *Social Text*, No. 17 (Fall 1987): 3–25, where he takes Jameson to task for a "Eurocentric" Marxism that essentializes the category of "Third World."

See also David Scott's recent call for postcolonialism to "distance itself from the

Enlightenment project of Marxism," in "The Aftermaths of Sovereignty: Postcolonial Criticism and the Claims of Political Modernity," *Social Text*, No. 48 (Fall 1996): 1–26.

9 Kalpana Seshadri-Crooks, "At the Margins of Postcolonial Studies," *Ariel* 26 (1995): 47–71; quotation from 65.

10 In "The Unconscious," where Freud addressed affect perhaps most theoretically, he treats it as virtually axiomatic that affect, as a physical discharge of a quantity of instinctual energy, does not belong to the realm of the unconscious, but is a psychical phenomenon quite distinct from repression. Since repression aims to inhibit affect, Freud theorizes that "there are no unconscious affects as there are unconscious ideas"; "The Unconscious" (1915), in *The Standard Edition of the Complete Psychological Works of Sigmund Freud*, 24 vols., ed. and trans. James Strachey (London, 1951–74), 14: 166–204; quotation from 178. There is virtually no relationship, for Freud, between the unconscious and the corporeal (the affective). Affect is not a representational sign (since affects are never repressed), but rather a somatic *conversion* that continually shifts the ground of (psychical) interpretation. Perhaps because of the interpretive difficulties that accrued in attempting to distinguish affect from repression, Freud stopped short of a fully worked out theory of the concept.

11 Ranajit Guha, "The Prose of Counter-Insurgency," in *Writings on South Asian History and Society*, ed. Ranajit Guha, Subaltern Studies 2 (Delhi/Oxford/New York, 1983), 1–42; quotations from 38 and 39.

12 Homi K. Bhabha, "The Postcolonial and the Postmodern: The Question of Agency," in *Location of Culture*, 171–97; quotations from 172 and 171.

13 Ibid., 177, 179.

14 Ibid., 185, 187.

15 Gayatri Chakravorty Spivak, "Asked to Talk about Myself . . . ," *Third Text*, No. 19 (Summer 1992): 9–18; quotation from 9.

16 Gayatri Chakravorty Spivak, "Woman in Difference," in *Outside in the Teaching Machine* (New York and London, 1993), 77–95.

17 See Gayatri Chakravorty Spivak, "Limits and Openings of Marx in Derrida," in ibid., 97–119; "Speculations on Reading Marx: After Reading Derrida," in *Post-Structuralism and the Question of History*, ed. Derek Attridge, Geoff Bennington, and Robert Young (Cambridge, 1987), 30–62; "Can the Subaltern Speak?" (1988), in *Colonial Discourse and Post-Colonial Theory: A Reader*, ed. Patrick Williams and Laura Chrisman (New York, 1994 [1988]), 66–111; and "Scattered Speculations."

18 Quoted in Robert Young, "Neocolonialism and the Secret Agent of Knowledge: An Interview with Gayatri Chakravorty Spivak," *Oxford Literary Review* 12 (1991): 220–51; quotation from 244.

19 Spivak, "Limits and Openings of Marx," 97; "Scattered Speculations," 162.

20 Spivak, "Limits and Openings of Marx," 106.

21 Rey Chow, "Ethics after Idealism," *diacritics* 23 (1993): 3–22; quotation from 4.

22 Gayatri Chakravorty Spivak, "More on Power/Knowledge," in *Outside in the Teaching Machine*, 25–51; quotation from 49.

23 Spivak, "A Literary Representation of the Subaltern," 252.

24 Ibid., 246. See also Gayatri Chakravorty Spivak, "Subaltern Studies: Deconstructing Historiography" (1985), in *In Other Worlds*, 197–221, esp. 215–21.

25 Spivak, "More on Power/Knowledge," 49.

26 Ibid.

27 Gayatri Chakravorty Spivak, "Marginality in the Teaching Machine," in *Outside in the Teaching Machine*, 53–76; quotation from 64.

28 In this context, see also Spivak's account of Bhubaneswari Bhaduri's *sati* suicide and the crisis of representing gendered subalternity in "Can the Subaltern Speak?"

29 Gilles Deleuze and Félix Guattari, *Anti-Oedipus: Capitalism and Schizophrenia*, trans. Robert Hurley, Mark Seem, and Helen R. Lane (Minneapolis, 1983 [1972]).

30 Spivak, "Marginality in the Teaching Machine," 62.

31 Ibid., 63. The larger context of this assertion is Spivak's acknowledgment of the influence of Kalpana Bardhan's work on the gendered subaltern in "Women's Work, Welfare and Status: Forces of Tradition and Change in India," *South Asia Bulletin* 6 (1986): 3–16. Bardhan, says Spivak, "shows the presupposition that gender determinacy is the coding of the value-differential allowing for the possibility of the exchange of affective value, negotiating 'sexuality' rather than sexual identity."

32 Spivak, "Woman in Difference," 78.

33 Ibid., 82, 84.

34 Ibid., 82.

35 Ibid., 89.

36 Ibid.

37 Ibid., 92.

38 Ibid., 93.

39 Ibid.

40 Ibid., 94.

Eugene Victor Wolfenstein

Michel Foucault and Psychoanalytic-Marxism

In the *History of Sexuality*, Michel Foucault develops his own interpretation of capitalist civilization and its sexual discontents in opposition to the one put forward by Wilhelm Reich, Herbert Marcuse, and their French New Left heirs.[1] This dimension of his argument has been largely disregarded. Yet when we attend to it, we not only bring the distinctive features of his interpretive project into sharper focus, we also find ourselves forced to reconsider the premises of left Freudian theorizing. Reich, Marcuse, and their heirs argue that capitalist production depends upon sexual repression of the sex drive, while Socialist revolution requires sexual liberation. Foucault thoroughly undermines this position. If we are not to consign the left Freudian project to the historical dustbin, we must find a way to obviate Foucault's criticisms.

There is a second feature of the *History of Sexuality* that should be brought forward. The text was originally titled *La volonté de savoir*—the will to know. The will to know is the scientific, philosophical, or epistemological form of Nietzsche's will to power. Reduced to its simplest

The *South Atlantic Quarterly* 97:2, Spring 1998.

form, the will to power is the overcoming of resistance: "The will to power can manifest itself only against resistances; therefore it seeks that which resists it."[2] I see Foucault as interpreting sexuality from roughly this vantage point. Such a reading can be contested.[3] But it is the Nietzschean conception of power in the *History of Sexuality* that most distinguishes it from the left Freudian narratives Foucault criticizes.

My own perspective, I should note, is not left Freudian but rather psychoanalytic-marxist. The hyphen is intended to signify a dialectical tension—an identity through difference, if one wishes to be Hegelian about it. The terms themselves signify traditions of theorizing rather than the founders of these traditions. Hence we have "psychoanalytic" in preference to "Freudian" and the impersonalizing "marxist" in preference to "Marxist."

This yields the polemical, perhaps even dialectical, structure of inquiry: Foucault against the left Freudians, psychoanalytic-marxism against Foucault.

Foucault against the Left Freudians. Foucault begins by characterizing the model of historical development he is going to contest. The core of this model is the empirical claim that, from the seventeenth century on, sexual repression became increasingly characteristic of European society. Earlier, "a certain frankness was still common. . . . It was a time of direct gestures, shameless discourse, and open transgressions." But "twilight soon fell on this bright day, followed by the monotonous nights of the Victorian bourgeoisie."[4]

How is this shift to be explained? For the left Freudians, it is a function of capitalist development:

> By placing the advent of the age of repression in the seventeenth century, after hundreds of years of open spaces and free expression, one adjusts it to coincide with the development of capitalism: it becomes an integral part of the bourgeois order. The minor chronicles of sex and its trials is transposed into the ceremonious history of the modes of production; its trifling aspect fades from view. A principle of explanation emerges after the fact: if sex is so rigorously repressed, this is because it is incompatible with a general and intensive work impera-

> tive. At a time when labor capacity was being systematically exploited, how could this capacity be allowed to dissipate itself in pleasurable pursuits, except in those—reduced to a minimum—that enabled it to reproduce itself?[5]

But, so the argument continues, the darkest hour comes just before the dawn. Sex is a drive, an imperative force in human nature; repression eventuates in a return of the repressed. "And the sexual cause—the demand for sexual freedom, but also for the knowledge to be gained from sex and the right to speak about it—becomes legitimately associated with the honor of a political cause: sex too is placed on the agenda for the future."[6]

Thus Foucault establishes the polemical framework of his investigation. He does not discuss the proponents of the repressive hypothesis in any depth, but it is clear whom he has in mind. He cites Reich as an early advocate of this position; he alludes to the "great Refusal" and "hyper-repressive desublimation," hence to Marcuse's version of critical theory; and he invokes the New Left sexual rebellion of the 1960s, in which Reichian texts and Marcuse himself played a part.[7] At times he even engages in an imagined dialogue with an anonymous critic who speaks from the position of the French Freudian Left.[8] So, while one might complain about his scholarliness and the depth of his engagement with psychoanalytic-marxism, Foucault did take on the version of the theory that in practice was most closely tied to the emancipatory project of modernity—precisely Reich's interwar-era sex-pol movement and the New Left theories of sexual-cum-political revolt.

Foucault's relationship to this left Freudian history of sexuality is complex. On one level he does not challenge it. He, too, sees important changes beginning in the seventeenth century. At times he seems to grant that sexual repression is at least a significant feature of the last several centuries, if not the most basic one, and he also evinces a certain respect for the Freudian achievement. Although he raises doubts about the repressive hypothesis, he claims that the doubts are "aimed less at showing it to be mistaken than at putting it back within the general economy of discourses on sex in modern societies since the seventeenth century." And he holds, if not very strongly, to the project of going beyond the existing sexual regime. The questions he poses, however, show that Foucault is rather more than a doubting Thomas:

> Is sexual repression truly an historically established fact? . . . Do the workings of power, and in particular those mechanisms that are brought into play in societies such as ours, really belong primarily to the category of repression? . . . Did the critical discourse that addresses itself to repression [i.e., that of Freud and his leftist successors] come to act as a roadblock to a power mechanism that had operated unchallenged up to that point, or is it not in fact part of the same historical network as the thing it denounces (and doubtless misrepresents) by calling it "repression"? [9]

It is plain that, in raising these questions, Foucault is executing a glissade through which he has already answered them. He intends nothing less than a radical shift in the perspective from which sex and sexuality are to be analyzed, a shift that will bring to light a very different history of modern sexuality.

Let's cut directly to the central issues and see how the text and the argument are organized around them. In its earliest and simplest version, psychoanalysis characterizes sex as a drive with highly determining effects on apparently nonsexual mental processes and modes of social interaction, as well as upon sexual behavior itself. Repression, an intrapsychic technique for managing this disruptive force, prevents the sexual wishes of infancy and early childhood, especially, from emerging into consciousness. It is reinforced by repression in the more general social sense (e.g., religious prohibitions). Together, the two forms of repression can be said to mobilize social pressure against the force of the sexual drive through the institution of internalized moral authorities. The kingdom of the mind becomes hierarchically ordered, in a veritable image of the political kingdom. Morality is enthroned and the sexual drives are either domesticated or outlawed. Thus the classical psychoanalytic model combines the notion of sex as a drive with a conception of power relations as hierarchical and restrictive. In the left Freudian instance, capitalism is introduced as the power behind the throne, that is, as the situational explanation for sexual repression. Power mediates the relationship between capitalism as a mode of production and the sexual drives of individuals in such a way as to turn sexual energy, libido, into labor power: labor is alienated libido.

Foucault sets out to challenge the foundations of this argument. Instead of taking sex as a biologically given drive, he asks the historical question: How does sex come to be seen as a drive? Sex may be the god in the machine, but who built the machine, under what circumstances, and with what consequences? Instead of begging the question of how sexuality evolves historically by positing sex as an a priori principle, he wants to call the sex drive itself to historical account. To borrow from Marx, in this regard Foucault is undertaking a critique of the fetishism of the sex drive.

In sexual repression, one party (social or psychological, as the case may be) is exercising power over another. Power is prohibitive on the one side, rebellious on the other. Foucault does not deny that such relationships exist. He does deny that this is the general model of power relationships. He contends that power in general more nearly resembles a contingently interwoven network of strategic interactions which only occasionally takes on the form of stabilized and repressive hierarchies. When prohibition is put forward as the paradigmatic form of power, consequently, a part is allowed to (mis)represent, indeed to disguise and occlude, the whole. It is this larger domain of power relationships that the Foucaldian critique aims to bring to light. Foucault not only broadens the definition of power, however; he also relocates it. Both psychoanalysis and Marxism include analyses of power, but each casts power in its familiar role as mediator, as a means to an end that remains external to it. Broadly rather than technically speaking, power can be said to serve utilitarian ends in the case of Marxism, hedonic ends in the case of psychoanalysis. But for Foucault power itself is the interpretive perspective, hedonic and utilitarian concerns its fields of operation. Ends and means have been inverted in such a way as to remind us of the wisdom of Zarathustra: "And life itself confided this secret to me: 'Behold,' it said, 'I am *that which must always overcome itself.*' "[10]

No, that is going too far. There is no "life itself" for Foucault, nor any a priori principle of self-overcoming or overcoming resistance. He is, rather, bent on keeping ontological claims to an absolute minimum. As "Maurice Florence" puts it, Foucault's "first methodological rule" is "to circumvent anthropological universals to the greatest possible extent, so as to interrogate them in their historical constitution."[11] This is the skeptical approach he takes to the claim that the sexual drive is constitutive of human nature—the same approach he would have had to take to the anthropological universalization of a will to power. But short of this perhaps metaphysical extreme, Foucault does press the claims of power as a privileged interpretive perspective.

Foucault plays out these opening critical and constructive moves along three dimensions: (1) a challenge to the empirical-conceptual claims of the "repressive hypothesis," along with an initial reconstruction of the discursive history of sexuality; (2) an articulation of the perspective of power, especially in the form of the will to knowledge; and (3) a more general historical narrative within which to place power, knowledge, and sexuality. In sum: critique, alternative perspective, and alternative historical interpretation. Empirically, Foucault does not deny that "new rules of propriety" and "a policing of statements" developed during the modern period, but the appearance of censorship and silencing is misleading because, "around and apropos of sex, one sees a veritable discursive explosion." The Catholic confessional of the premodern period, in which sex was to be both directly named and spoken about in detail, changed in one respect but not in the other: while sex came to be spoken of less directly, the confessional mode was maintained and enlarged. The essential point is this "incitement to discourse": "Western man has been drawn for three centuries to the task of telling everything concerning his sex; . . . since the classical age there has been a constant optimization and an increasing valorization of the discourse on sex; and . . . this carefully analytical discourse was meant to yield multiple effects of displacement, intensification, reorientation and modification of desire itself." Or, more concisely: "What is peculiar to modern societies, in fact, is not that they consigned sex to a shadow existence, but that they dedicated themselves to speaking of it ad infinitum, while exploiting it as *the* secret."[12]

This incitement to sexual discourse involved several general modalities—new lines for the penetration of power into sexual life, the incorporation of perversions and the specification of individuals within a system of sexual knowledge, the pleasure to be gained in the course of developing this power/knowledge relationship, and the evolution of various devices for saturating society with sexual meaning.[13] More particularly, a science of sexuality emerged with (a) characteristic means of gaining knowledge and (b) characteristic objects of knowledge created by those very means. With regard to (a), what emerged was a confessional science, of which psychoanalysis is clearly the most elaborated form. Its attributes include a clinical codification of the inducement to speak; the postulating of sex as a general and diffuse causality for even manifestly nonsexual phenomena, hence a sexual latency or unconscious sexuality that could be forced to speak; a method of interpretation for unveiling this truth about sexuality; and the medicalization of that process, or the inscription of sexuality within the domain of medical therapy.[14] With regard to (b), four principal objects of knowledge emerged: "the hysterical woman, the masturbating child, the Malthusian couple, and the perverse adult."[15] Thus the analytical question concerns not only the how and why of a sexual science, but also the reasons for its construction of precisely those objects of knowledge. While Foucault, like the psychoanalytic-marxists in their own way, does ultimately tie these developments in the history of sexuality to the evolution of the capitalist system, unlike them he does not anchor the analysis of capitalism in the problematics of labor and libido. As I have already indicated, he operates both from the perspective of power and with a distinctive conception of power itself.

Foucault begins his discussion of power by imagining the reaction of a French psychoanalytic (Lacanian) critic to his critique of the repressive hypothesis. This critic accuses Foucault of conflating the early Freudian or Reichian model of sexual drive and moral prohibition with the sophisticated psychoanalytic view of the constitutive role of the law (i.e., the Law of the Father) vis-à-vis desire. The latter view, in which desire is never outside the power of the law, is itself a refutation of the earlier model. Their conflation, his critic claims, permits Foucault to play a double game: "You confuse your adversaries by appearing to take the weaker position, and, discussing repression alone, you would have us believe, wrongly, that you have rid yourself of the power of the law; and yet you keep the essential practical consequence of the principle of power-as-law, namely, the fact that there is no escaping from power, that it is always-already present, constituting the very thing which one attempts to counter it with." Not so, Foucault responds. He is perfectly willing to acknowledge the variations in psychoanalytic theory. But whatever differences there may be between the two versions of the theory, both models identify the exercise of power with prohibition:

> Underlying both the general theme that power represses sex and the idea that the law constitutes desire, one encounters the same putative mechanics of power. It is defined in a strangely restrictive way, in that, to begin with, this power is poor in resources, sparing of its methods, monotonous in the tactics it utilizes, incapable of invention,

> and seemingly doomed always to repeat itself. Further, it is a power that only has the force of the negative on its side, a power to say no; in no condition to produce, capable only of posting limits, it is basically anti-energy.[16]

This conception of power has a historical foundation. It grew up alongside European monarchies and the legal systems associated with them (even where that association took the form of opposition). But such a "juridico-discursive" conception of power—of "power that has its central point in the enunciation of the law"—is only part of the story.[17] The conception must be expanded if the manifold ways in which power interacts with sexuality are to be grasped.

It is just here that we come to the Nietzschean, or neo-Nietzschean, heart of Foucault's analysis ("neo-Nietzschean" because, as indicated above, he does not fully embrace a will to power). His expanded conception of power appears to be more descriptive than explanatory, more a way of mapping interactive processes than a way of theoretically explaining them. Of course, this appearance may be deceptive. A power drive may be implicit in or even required for Foucault's conception of power relations. Alternatively, it may be that he has rid Nietzsche's philosophy of a residual homunculus of subjective causality. Either way, however, his conception of power bears an unmistakable Nietzschean stamp:

> Power must be understood in the first instance as the multiplicity of force relations immanent in the sphere in which they operate and which constitute their own organization; as the process through which, through ceaseless struggle and confrontations, transforms, strengthens, or reverses them; as the support which these force relations find in one another, thus forming a chain or a system, or on the contrary, the disjunctions and contradictions which isolate them from one another; and, lastly, as the strategies in which they take effect, whose general design or institutional crystallization is embodied in the state apparatus, in the formulation of the law, in the various social hegemonies.[18]

When Foucault adds that "where there is power, there is resistance," and that "resistance is never in a position of exteriority in relation to power," he comes very close to Nietzsche's contention of a pervasive will to power that "can manifest itself only against resistances" and therefore "seeks that which resists it."

When sexuality is viewed from this broadly Nietzschean perspective, its Freudian features fade away. Sex is no longer seen as "a stubborn drive, by nature alien and of necessity disobedient to a power which exhausts itself trying to subdue it and often fails to control it entirely." It appears "rather as an especially dense transfer point for relations of power: between men and women, young people and old people, parents and offspring, teachers and students, priests and laity, an administration and a population. Sexuality is not the most intractable element in power relations, but rather one of those endowed with the greatest instrumentality: useful for a number of maneuvers and capable of serving as a point of support, as a linchpin, for the most varied strategies."[19] The task is then to see how power relations immanently constitute the field of sexual knowledge, as well as to explain the historical evolution of this power/knowledge relationship.

Foucault approaches this task from two, mutually reinforcing directions. First, he contends that within the ruling classes the system of kinship alliances tended to be replaced by the surveillance of sexuality. Second, and more broadly, he depicts a shift from juridico-discursive power to bio-power. Both transitions found expression in and were mediated through the creation of the sexual sciences.

The first point might be approached negatively. As Foucault accurately states, the left Freudians, Reich and Marcuse in particular, also depict a two-stage modern history:

> The first phase corresponded to the need to form a "labor force" (hence to avoid any useless "expenditure," any wasted energy, so that all forces were reduced to labor capacity alone) and to insure its reproduction (conjugality, the regulated fabrication of children). The second phase corresponded to that epoch of *Spätkapitalismus* in which the exploitation of wage labor does not demand the same violent and physical constraints as in the nineteenth century, and where the politics of the body does not require the elision of sex or its restrictions solely to the reproductive function; it relies instead on a multiple channeling into the controlled circuits of the economy—on what has been called a hyper-repressive desublimation.[20]

Foucault reads this depiction of sexual history as backwards and upside down. Sexual discipline and surveillance began with the bourgeoisie, who imposed it upon themselves, and spread only belatedly and incompletely to the lower classes.[21] Hence the historical question becomes: What functions did the sexual sciences perform for the bourgeoisie? To put the answer in Nietzschean terms, the deployment of the sex/power/knowledge relationship was the vehicle for the bourgeoisie's self-overcoming—the discipline through which it created itself as a class—while the effect of this new regime on the lower classes was a secondary matter:

> The primary concern was not the repression of the sex of the classes to be exploited, but rather the body, vigor, longevity, primogeniture, and descent of the classes that "ruled." This was the purpose for which the deployment of sexuality was first established, as a new distribution of pleasures, discourses, truths, and powers; it has to be seen as the self-affirmation of one class rather than the enslavement of another: a defense, a protection, a strengthening, and an exaltation that were eventually extended to others—at the cost of different transformations—as a means of social control and political subjugation.[22]

Or, to extend the Nietzschean interpretation of this passage, the deployment of sexuality derived from the will to power of the bourgeois classes, just as the deployment of alliances derived from the will to power of feudal and early modern aristocracies.

The history of the deployment of sexuality, Foucault now claims, "can serve as an archaeology of psychoanalysis."[23] On the one hand, psychoanalysis is the archetypal confessional science for the bourgeoisie, the characteristic vehicle for its sexual self-formation. On the other, it helps effect the transition from the system of alliance to that of sexuality by symbolically preserving the former in the latter:

> But despite everything, psychoanalysis, whose technical procedure seemed to place the confession of sexuality outside family jurisdiction, rediscovered the law of alliance, the involved workings of marriage and kinship, and incest at the heart of this sexuality, as the principle of its formation and the key to its intelligibility. The guarantee that one would find the parents–children relationship at the root of everyone's sexuality made it possible—even when everything seemed to point to the reverse process—to keep the deployment of sexuality coupled to the system of alliance.[24]

Hence the logic and limits of the Reichian intervention: Reich waged war against the system of alliance as it presented itself within the deployment of sexuality; he did not, however, call into question the deployment of sexuality itself. It is therefore "apparent why one could not expect this critique to be the grid for a history of this very deployment. Nor the basis for a movement to dismantle it."[25]

If the Reichian/Marcusean version of psychoanalytic-marxism could not provide a "grid" for the history of the deployment of sexuality, what could? Or, to rephrase the question: What is the relationship between the deployment of sexuality and the evolution of capitalism? Again, there is first the negative answer: the deployment of sexuality is not a function of the purely economic requirements of the capitalist mode of production. This point was made explicit in Foucault's Collège de France lecture of 7 January 1976. There, he took up the question of how to analyze power (which, as we already know, is the perspective from which we are to view the development of sexual knowledge), asking, "Is the analysis of power or of powers to be deduced in one way or another from the economy?" Is it that "the constitution of political power obeys the model of a legal transaction involving a contractual type of exchange" (as we find in liberal versions of economism)? Is it that "power is conceived primarily in terms of the role it plays in the maintenance simultaneously of the relations of production and of a class domination which the development and specific forms of the forces of production have rendered possible" (as we find in the instance of Marxist economism)? Or does the assumption of a primary economic causality have to be dropped for a "non-economic analysis of power" to become possible, even if "it effectively remains the case that the relations of power do indeed remain profoundly enmeshed in and with economic relations and participate with them in a common circuit"?[26] To put it no doubt too simply, Foucault advocates viewing capitalism as a system of power relations, a view that, if adequately conceptualized, would constitute the grid for the history of the deployment of sexuality.

Here we return, at a historically more concrete level, to the misleading tendency to subsume all power relations within the juridico-discursive model, which, Foucault contends, developed around early modern monarchical claims of sovereignty. The monarch's sovereignty was materialized in practices of "deduction" (*prélèvement*). The populace lived as it would live, outside the monarch's control, but he imposed himself at its boundaries through processes of economic extraction, on the one hand, and the right to kill offenders (those who threatened his power), on the other.[27] Power in this juridico-discursive sense was associated with the system of ruling-class alliances. And this conjuncture was both symbolized and mediated by blood: "*a reality with a symbolic function*."[28] Bloodlines were to be maintained in their purity, blood was to be appropriately shed, and so on.

These practices and their symbolization have not disappeared; nevertheless, since "the classical age the West has undergone a very profound transformation of these mechanisms of power." Power now flows through the (individual and social) life process itself. In one sense this could not be a novelty, given Foucault's general definition of power as a productive force which generates its own resistances. Hence the prior invocation of Nietzsche: where there is life there is power, if not exactly the will to power. Juridico-discursive power is a form of the more general phenomenon, as is *bio-power*, the term Foucault uses to designate the novel, modern form of power that "brought life and its mechanisms into the realm of explicit calculations and made power–knowledge an agent of transformation of human life." Bio-power operates through two modalities: the disciplines of the body, and the regulation of populations. Here we have the historical explanation for the emergence of the sexual sciences, in that sex was the "pivot" linking these two modalities. "On the one hand, it was tied to the disciplines of the body: the harnessing, intensification, and distribution of forces, the adjustment and economy of energies. On the other hand, it was applied to the regulation of populations, through all the far-reaching effects of its activities. It fitted in both categories at once."[29] Both modalities converged in constituting the objects of sexual knowledge. The sexualization of children, "hysterization" of women, reproductive narrowing of marital sexuality, and the psychiatrization of the perversions all functioned to bring the life processes into the domain of bio-power.

It might be protested (as, indeed, Foucault himself protests) that the analysis of bio-power presupposes sex, precisely. How else could sex function as the constitutive medium of bio-political relationships? Foucault's response is to distinguish between embodied sexualities and "sex *in itself*."[30] He does not intend any exclusion of biology and the physiological realities of sexuality from history. Quite the contrary: bio-power is a conceptualization of a specific mode of their historicization. But he insists on a distinction between these multiform sexualities and an a priori sexual principle, a sexual essence with a variety of existential manifestations. The latter is both constituted through and the symbolic center of the former. Just as commodities and money function as fetishes in political economy, so does sex function as the fetish in the sexual economy. In short, "sex is the most speculative, most ideal, and most internal element in a deployment of sexuality organized by power in its grip on bodies and their materiality, their forces, energies, sensations, and pleasures."[31]

From this perspective, the left Freudian project of human emancipation is doubly misguided, in that it is both anchored in an economistic conception of power and it fetishizes sexuality. It worships at the bio-political church. No wonder, then, that its attacks upon the capitalist system are unavailing. Left Freudianism could also be considered merely a resistance internal to the regime of bio-power, less a challenge to the system than a vehicle of bio-political self-overcoming. And thus emerges an ironic reversal of the emancipatory claims put forward within the psychoanalytic-marxist tradition: for Reich and his successors, left Freudianism appeared to be a genuine force of liberation (whatever its efficacy in our ever-more capitalist age), while here it would seem to be constituted by and reconstitutive of the very power it opposes.

If the analysis of bio-power permits or forces a reevaluation of the left opposition, it also leads to a reconceptualization of fascism. The transition between the system of alliances and juridico-discursive power, on the one side, and sexual surveillance and bio-power, on the other, is expressed in the ambiguous interaction of the analytics of sexuality and the symbolics of blood. "Beginning in the second half of the nineteenth century, the thematics of blood was sometimes called on to lend its entire weight toward revitalizing the type of political power that was exercised through the devices of sexuality. Racism took shape at this point (racism in the modern, 'biologizing,' statist form). . . . Nazism was doubtless the most cunning and most naive (and the former because of the latter) combination of the fantasies of blood and the paroxysms of disciplinary power."[32] This relationship might be simply expressed as blood over sex (blood > sex), hence the painfully predictable outcome of bathing the bio-political body in blood. The genocide of the Jews figures here as a malign eugenics, a purification of the racial blood more thoroughgoing and catastrophic than the forms of racism that operate within the relatively limiting framework of juridico-discursive power.

It is precisely at this point that an honorable, if ultimately unsatisfactory, role for psychoanalysis emerges. As we have seen, Foucault contends that psychoanalysis preserved, symbolically, the system of alliance within the emergent deployment of sexuality, enshrining and maintaining the juridico-discursive conception of power: "the law of alliance, tabooed consanguinity, and the Sovereign-Father." It brought the symbolics of blood under the aegis of the sexual law (sex > blood) and in this way opposed itself to racial eugenics. But, Foucault concludes, "this position of psychoanalysis was tied to a specific historical conjuncture." Once that moment has passed, conceiving of the sexual in terms of the law, blood, sovereignty, and so on, is a "historical 'retro-version.'" Ultimately, we "must conceptualize the deployment of sexuality on the basis of the techniques of power that are contemporary with it."[33] Which is to say, the psychoanalytic version of sexual power/knowledge has been historically superseded.

It is not Foucault's intent in the *History of Sexuality* to develop a systematic alternative to the left-Freudian emancipatory project. He does, however, draw one practical conclusion; rather than liberating sexuality, we need to liberate ourselves from sexuality:

> We must not think that by saying yes to sex, one says no to power; on the contrary, one tracks along the course laid out by the general deployment of sexuality. It is the agency of sex that we must break away from, if we aim—through a tactical reversal of the various mechanisms of sexuality—to counter the grips of power with the claims of bodies, pleasures, and knowledges, in their multiplicity and their possibilities of resistance. The rallying point for the counterattack against the deployment of sexuality ought not to be sex-desire, but bodies and pleasures.[34]

Breaking away from the idealism of sex does not carry with it the promise of human emancipation; but it might permit us to enjoy ourselves as embodied beings.

Psychoanalytic-Marxism against Foucault. Thus does Foucault provide us with a virtual mirror image of psychoanalytic-marxism and its objects of analysis. Instead of seeing the sexual drive as a determinant of social interaction, we see historically variable patterns of social interaction determining the conceptualization of sex. Instead of viewing placements of power (e.g., capitalist hegemony and resistances to capitalist power) from the perspective of interests (production) and affects (desire, sexual drives), we view placements of interest and affect from the perspective of power. And instead of perceiving sexual liberation as a vital aspect of human liberation, we recognize that it is vital to free ourselves from the project of sexual liberation.

How are we to respond to the Foucaldian critique? The prudent course would be to follow Plato's advice in the *Phaedo*. Supposing someone were to challenge a "supposition" in your argument, Plato has Socrates say, "You would let him be and would not answer, until you examined the consequences to see if they were in agreement or discord together." Only if the challenge could not be met by attacking the attacker would one turn from offense to defense: "And when you must give account of that supposition itself, you would do it . . . by supposing another supposition, whichever seemed best of the higher suppositions, until you came to something satisfactory."[35] If we were to play this dialectical game, we would first attempt to defend psychoanalytic-marxism by defeating Foucault. We would seek out the inadequacies in his critique of the left Freudians and in his own history of sexuality. If these were of a sufficient magnitude, we could rightly claim that the criticism didn't touch us. Only if Foucault survived the assault would we be forced to further clarify or reform our own positions.

The problem with proceeding in this fashion is that the desire to win can usurp the desire to know in such a way as to preclude further theoretic development. Everything turns into battles along the perimeter, and the central issues are never truly joined. Let's invert the discursive rule instead and say to Foucault: "If Marxism is identified with economic determinism, psychoanalysis with sexual reductionism, and psychoanalytic-marxism with the project of sexual liberation, then we, too, can see the necessity of going beyond these analytical modalities. But in fact, our own 'suppositions' or premises are quite different from those of the orthodox Marxists, orthodox Freudians, or left Freudians. These premises must be specified, if the debate between us is to be meaningful."[36]

Let's begin with the classical anthropological question: What do all human individuals have in common, by virtue of which they are characterized as human and distinguished from that which is not human? We must not ask this question naively. Recall Foucault's desire "to circumvent anthropological universals to the greatest possible extent, so as to interrogate them in their historical constitution." But, granting that we wish to interrogate such universals, is it necessary to circumvent them? And aren't some anthropological assumptions always embedded in social theory? Might it not be better to explicate these assumptions, if for no other reason than to make them available for interrogation? To put it another way, we are not so naive as to attempt to conceptualize "human nature as such." Rather, we aim to specify those minimal features of human beings that help us to understand the variable forms of human interaction with which we happen to be concerned. When it is appropriate, we can also investigate the "historical constitution" of these concerns and the ways in which they shape our "anthropological universals."

Four "suppositions," then: (1) human individuals are inherently interactive; (2) human interaction is structured by the interpenetrating modalities of sensuousness, work, desire, and consciousness; (3) the gateway between sensuousness and properly mental functioning, that is, the first stage of self-formation, is the oscillation between the paranoid-schizoid and depressive positions; and (4) normatively, girls and boys pass through this gateway—which is also the passageway to individuality—in different fashions.[37]

Human interaction. In the inner world as in the outer one, we always find more than one of us. The monad, the solitary individual, is a result of psychosocial processes, not their premise. Which is to say, the "individual as such," like "sex as such," is a fetish. We therefore begin with the interaction of two or more human individuals. Such interactions can be arranged along a continuum. At one extreme an individual or a group of individuals has absolute control over another. Resistance is futile, as the expression goes. At the other extreme power is absolutely equalized, with the consequence that it has no determining effect on the interaction. We will suppose that in the latter situation mutual recognition is possible, while in the former it isn't. Or, to vary the normative framework, in one case we have the possibility of freedom, in the other case the possibility of domination. Between these extremes, different kinds of interaction—variously cooperative, competitive, mutualizing, mutually resistant, antagonistic—are possible. Nothing in "human nature" can be assumed to determine a priori which types or patterns of interaction are going to predominate—except that for better or worse children, in their immaturity, are going to be subject to the power of adults.

Sensuousness, work/desire, consciousness. All human individuals, whatever their difference otherwise, are creatures of sensuousness, work, desire, and consciousness. Likewise, all their interactions can be characterized in terms of these interpenetrative modalities.

—Sensuousness: Human individuals are psychophysiological organisms who, as such, are oriented toward pleasure and away from pain. Let us call this the "determinacy of pleasure and pain." Because, at this elementary level, pleasurable experiences tend to be life-sustaining, painful ones (if sufficiently intense) life-threatening, the determinacy of pleasure and pain does not contradict the imperative of self-preservation. From the ontogenetic beginning, actual experience tends to mix pleasure and pain. Aggression may be understood as the force mobilized in human individuals when pain must be overcome to secure pleasure.

—Consciousness: The psychophysiological determinacy of pleasure and pain links us to other animate species. Our capacity for conscious mentation through the mediation of language differentiates us from them. With respect to those species nearest to us, the difference is not absolute, but it does meet the old dialectical criterion of a transformation of quantity into quality.

—Work/desire: Between sensuousness and consciousness two humanizing modalities of interaction can be specified. On the one hand, and as Marx emphasized, human beings learn to work in ways that distinguish us from other species. On the other, and as psychoanalysts emphasize, human desires (not just sexual desire) are distinctively polymorphous and displaceable. They lack the automatic fixity of purely animal instinct. Thus in both regards we are creatures of imagination. Human beings are, one might say, the nonliteral animals or, more precisely, the least literal animals.

Human values. No positive normative claims are built into this model. One could posit a value for human life itself, but this position turns in a well-known logical circle: the value of human life must be presupposed if human life is to be valued. One can, however, put forward a restricted negative claim: our anthropology provides no a priori basis for valuing one individual or collectivity over another. If an arbitrary valuing of life is combined with this restrictive claim, however, the substantive dimensions of the model then suggest four values: (1) reduction of unnecessary pain; (2) satisfaction of needs and creative work; (3) gratification of desire and fulfilling relationships; and (4) some version of mutual recognition. Yet what counts as unnecessary pain, for instance, is notoriously variable, so these values are thin, not thick, as well as existentially indeterminate.

Self-formation: paranoid-schizoid position ↔ depressive position. Let's picture an infant, female or male, in the early months of postnatal life. We'll assume its psychophysiological needs are to be satisfied through interaction with its mother, who has needs, desires, and a mind of her own. We know that she is not reducible to the performance of maternal functions, but this knowledge is not shared by her baby. The baby's life moves in a rhythmic, metabolic circle. At one extreme there is interaction with the mother, organized around alimentation. At the other extreme there is sleep. The rhythm of life is the movement from alimentation into sleep and from sleep into alimentation. The emergent meaning of this experience is subject to the determinacy of pleasure and pain.

Thus far the depiction is not particularly psychological, and certainly not psychoanalytic. The baby and its mother could figure in a variety of narratives, even Marxist and Foucaldian ones. When, however, we speculate on the ways in which the infant's external world shapes the formation of its internal world, we move into properly psychoanalytic territory. To begin with, the infant's inner world is not, strictly speaking, mental. It is not differentiated from the body, but rather permeated by sensations. These sensations are organized around the polarities of alimentation and somnolence. As they are mentalized, the inner world becomes structured by images of interaction, on the one side, and aloneness, on the other. Each side is also affectively colored, as are the processes that link and disjoin them.

The habitability of the emergent inner world depends upon the degree of pleasure to be found in the actual metabolic process. Pleasure is a function of the adequacy of care, and adequacy of care is a function of both the mother's capacity for caregiving and the infant's capacity to make use of caregiving. In optimal situations mother and infant find ways of cooperating in this momentous endeavor. The infant's experience is then relatively pleasurable, and the inner world is relatively easy to inhabit. But the more the actual process of mother–child interaction is experienced as painful and the more, therefore, aggressivity is mobilized, the more the inner-world polarity of interaction becomes paranoid and persecutory, and the more the inner-world polarity of aloneness becomes schizoid and withdrawn.

It should be added that pain and the expectation of pain are accompanied by both anger and anxiety. These affective states can interact in such a way as to be mutually amplifying. This adds to the need for paranoid-schizoid defenses, which may or may not be adequate to contain potentially explosive affective intensities. The greater the intensity, the more rigid the defenses, until the point is reached at which the paranoid-schizoid position breaks down and psychical chaos ensues.

The paranoid-schizoid position, characterized here in its emergence, is a variable attribute of human psychological experience, but a highly ubiquitous one. It lacks that primary moral criterion—concern for the well-being of others. It is not in this regard immoral, but rather premoral. According to Klein, a moral orientation begins to be formed during the first year of life in the emotional attitude she characterizes as the depressive position. The baby begins to experience the (m)other as a separate person and as someone who can be damaged by its hostile impulses. Complex patterns of guilt and reparation come into being, along with the experience of gratitude to the (m)other for maintaining her love and nurturing despite the emotional storminess of the situation. When all goes well, the infant emerges with a "capacity for concern."[38] Subsequently, the infant who becomes a child and the child who becomes an adult will oscillate between the ruthlessness of the paranoid-schizoid position and the concern for others of the depressive position, depending upon how well-established the depressive position is in the first instance, and upon the level of uncertainty, stress, anxiety, and deprivation to which the person is subjected in the second.

Individuation and gender differentiation. As noted above, the oscillating field established by the paranoid-schizoid and depressive positions is the gateway between sensuous and properly emotional experience. It is also the space in which individuality is constituted and the formation of gender begins. This is not to deny that the gendering of children by their parents can begin even before they are born, nor that the process of gender formation is prolonged, complex, and often unstable. Nor is it to claim that individual identity is constituted at once and for all time. It is to put forward the claim that the processes of emergence from sensuousness, individuation, and gender formation are interdependent and equally foundational.

In *Group Psychology and the Analysis of the Ego*, Freud distinguished between relationships of identification, in which one would like to "be" the other, and relationships of object choice, in which one would like to "have" the other.[39] Both terms are problematic in themselves and in any possible empirical application. But they will do to distinguish between a primary relationship, in which the infant does not clearly distinguish itself from its mother, and a secondary relationship, in which the infant is capable of making and (more or less) maintaining the distinction. At its simplest, this is all that is meant by "individuation."

Individuation does not mean becoming an individual in a monadic sense, nor for that matter in a mutualizing one. Either outcome is possible—or both, at different times. Which form of individuality emerges depends in part on the psychical position the person comes to occupy: insofar as individuality is a function of the paranoid-schizoid position, it is monadic (as well as predatory); insofar as it is a function of the depressive position, individuality tends to be empathic and mutualizing. Individuality can be maintained in the oscillation between the paranoid-schizoid and depressive positions. There is, however, a loss of individuality when the infant (or adult, for that matter) lapses back into the primary relationship of identity. The prospect of this loss is at once terrifying and compellingly seductive.

There is now a substantial body of research (both empirical and theoretical) suggesting that girls and boys negotiate the passage to individuality in different ways.[40] Briefly, for girls, the primary feminine/maternal identification is maintained. Individuation has to occur despite this gendered entanglement, with a third party or position required for individuation within same-sex gender identification. Archetypically, this party or position is masculine in a twofold respect: on the one hand, the little girl accepts her father (who is normatively the bearer of masculinity) as the object of erotic desire; on the other, she partially identifies with him, both to differentiate herself from her mother and to maintain her mother as an object of erotic desire. It is this latter component of feminine gender identity that is so often repressed in patriarchal cultures. When repression is successful, the girl who becomes a woman takes her assigned position within a perfectly binary (either/or) sexual order in which assertiveness, initiative, and desire for union with a woman are gendered masculine. For boys, the primary maternal identification is simultaneously rejected and devalued in the process of individuation. To be male is to be not-female; to be a boy is to be not-a-girl. Which is to say, the boy must not only repress but split off—rigorously separate himself from—the part of himself that is identified with his mother and her desire. He must identify instead with his father and his father's desire. The signifier of this twofold identification is the phallus (the magical, phantasied, or imaginary version of the penis). We see, then, that (normatively) masculine and feminine identity are alienated mirror images of each other. They are not, however, equivalents. The phallus signifies not only selfhood and desire but power—perhaps also, as Lacan would have it, the authority of the Law, the right of public speech, and so on. In this regard (and only in this regard), the girls who become women are the have-nots in the relationship.

At this juncture, a not unkindly critic might object that this depiction of self-formation, individuation, and gender differentiation goes well beyond the bounds of the anthropological. The introduction of normative conceptions of gender formation, especially, puts us in the realm of historical variation. I quite agree. Indeed, I would add that we have also begun to encounter the repressive mechanisms and familial drama of which Foucault was so skeptical. This proves, if proof were needed, that anthropological suppositions quickly slip back into the historical manifold from which they have been abstracted, revealing in the process the interests, desires, or will to power of their originator. But before breaking off our anthropological construction, we should note that at no point along the line did we arrive at the fetishistic "sex as such" which was the object of Foucault's analysis and criticism. Quite the contrary: insofar as he was a critic of psychoanalytic metaphysics—of psychical energy, disposable libido, and the like—we are Foucault's allies and not his opponents.

From anthropology to history. Even at the discursive level of anthropology, the identity of human individuals soon gives way to the differences between them—between one generation and another, one gender and the other, one sexual orientation and another, one individual and another. And when the distinction between individual and collectivity or between one collectivity and another inevitably emerges, we think of differences between races, ethnicities, nationalities, as well as those between social classes, patterns of belief, and so on.

It is just here that the most unproductive debate can occur, with one side insisting on what human beings have in common and the other on the ways in which we differ from each other. But just as we cannot think difference without identity or identity without difference in formal (or dialectical) logic, neither can human interactions empirically avoid fluctuating patterns of identity and difference. The more productive questions are not, therefore, essentialist (is *x* essentially the same as or different from *y*?), but rather situational and relational: When do differences make a difference? Is the difference or identity a good thing or a bad thing, by what standard, and for which party? When do identities mask differences and when do differences mask identities? In other words, if we put to one side the essentialism of *either* identity *or* difference, we can ask, more concretely: When is the relationship of identity and difference problematic?

There are various ways of answering this question. Referring back to our anthropological categories, I would say that the relationship becomes problematic when, as between any two parties, there are metabolic incompatibilities, oppositions of interest, disjunctive affects and opposed desires, and impediments to mutual understanding. These points of tension constitute the field of contestation between individuals and collectivities of individuals (or between collectivities and individuals). How the contest plays out depends, perhaps most importantly, upon (a) the degree and extent of antagonism structuring the field and (b) the power differentials active (or activated) within it. In fields of interaction with low levels of antagonism and relative equalization of power differentials, relationships of identity and difference are not especially problematic. Identity tends to be mutualizing, difference to be individuating. Differences, to put it another way, tend to be mutually enriching. But the greater the antagonism structuring the field, the more identity functions as constraint and difference as the basis of opposition. And the greater the power differential between individuals and/or collectivities in such circumstances, the more both identities and differences become the instrumentalities of domination.

When these antagonistic differences are specified to the historical integument of capitalism, we come to the political problems of domination and liberation that are at the center of psychoanalytic-marxist discourse. We cannot explore them further in the present context, but if psychoanalytic-marxism were found to contribute to their elucidation and/or their solution, then we could justify our general premises on these pragmatic grounds.

Where do we now stand with respect to psychoanalytic-marxism and Foucault? First, having joined Foucault in his critique of the sexual fetishism of the left Freudians, to that extent we have immunized psychoanalytic-marxism from his critique. To be sure, once gender differentiation is introduced, the interpretive nexus of the family and juridico-discursive power reemerges. But because our analysis of gender is more historical than anthropological, we can, like Foucault, study gender relationships in their situational specificity.

Second, our reformulated version of psychoanalytic-marxism permits the subsumption of the better part of Foucault's history of sexuality. Let's limit ourselves to his major thesis, namely, that the sexual sciences are instrumentalities of emergent bio-political relationships, replacing the system of blood and alliance that constituted the field of operation for juridico-discursive power. We'll leave to one side the possible objection that juridico-discursive power is not tied so tightly to the early modern system of alliance as Foucault seems to maintain—in other words, that its mechanisms continue to operate within the field of bio-power relations, perhaps with greater subtlety but with no loss of efficacy.[41] The point is rather that both forms of power can be analyzed from a psychoanalytic-marxist perspective. For example, using the anthropological notions outlined above, it is possible to conceptualize the way in which the capitalist mode of production permeates and disrupts even the sensuous or metabolic level of social interaction while simultaneously operating through structures of economic, sexual, and racial domination that resemble the Hegelian configuration of lordship and bondage.[42] Focusing on the sexual sciences as disciplinary and regulative forms of power linking the capitalist disruption of life processes to the more obtrusive macroformations of domination would enrich this interpretation, but it would not overthrow its premises.

Let these points and the preceding arguments stand as a defense of psychoanalytic-marxism. They do not amount to a critique of Foucault, except insofar as he is a critic of psychoanalytic-marxism. Hence, what, if any, critical or interpretive leverage do our anthropological suppositions provide, with respect to the substance of the analytics of power/knowledge? Note that this question does not initiate an internal critique of Foucault's position. Again, we depart from Plato's recommended strategy, not asking whether Foucault's data are adequate to his interpretations or if, for example, he must implicitly rely upon Marxist or psychoanalytic categories despite explicitly excluding their use. Nor will we attempt a critique through comparison, as might be done by analyzing specific empirical and/or pragmatic issues from Foucaldian and psychoanalytic-marxist perspectives. Instead, let's limit ourselves to an interpretation of Foucault's analytic orientation, one which might or might not be viewed as a criticism.

Simply put, Foucault conceptualizes power and knowledge from the perspective of the paranoid-schizoid position. A recurring theme of the *History of Sexuality* is the productivity of power, the objects of knowledge it creates rather than the ignorance it generates. At a minimum, power brings things into view—forces them to speak—hence the link between the (psychoanalytic) consulting room and the (church) confessional. In each instance sexuality must be brought to the surface and subjected to the gaze of the inquisitor, that is, the power which brings things to light is persecutory. Enlightenment is a stripping away of defenses, an overcoming of resistances, the establishment of universalizing patterns of surveillance, regulation, and discipline. Yet these patterns are established quite dispassionately, coldly. Not proceeding from the monarch's desire, they are not assertions of sovereignty or acts of revenge. They are not even adequately configured in the image of Bentham's panopticon—with its central point from which all the prisoners' actions and words can be monitored—but in terms of a decentered panopticism: "There is no need for arms, physical violence, material constraints. Just a gaze. An inspecting gaze, a gaze which each individual under its weight will end by interiorizing to the point that he is his own overseer, each individual thus exercising this surveillance over, and against, himself."[43] No wonder, then, that Foucault was discontent with the repressive hypothesis. Power in the paranoid-schizoid position shines its light ever more brightly; what appears to be repression is only resistance to enlightenment, an artifact of the productivity of power. While Foucault expressly wanted to prevent the reduction of power to this malign version (or vision) of enlightenment (insuring visibility's being only one of the strategies operative in modern society), it seems fair to assume that knowledge-as-surveillance was paradigmatic or exemplary for him. And, I am suggesting, the psychological basis for such a conception is the paranoid-schizoid position, in which the possibility of persecution is combined with impersonal coldness.

Given this interpretation, it is not difficult to understand either the recourse to Foucault by those who are interested in emancipatory struggles or the difficulty of using his ideas to justify such efforts. On the one hand, his perspective insinuates that Big Brother (or a host of little brothers) is watching—indeed, that being watched doesn't even require someone's watching; on the other, empathy and mutual recognition, guilt and reparation, are features of the depressive position or perspective. These values, vital for the moral or ethical grounding of political action, are simply absent in a paranoid-schizoid world. And if this world is the only world, then it follows that emancipatory efforts lack a justificatory basis. One can, to be sure, beg the question of justification. Society is a bio-political state of war in which the resistance of the other is always fair game. Because Foucault encourages us to see the operations of power at the microlevel, there is no difficulty in conceptualizing actions that oppose the extension of disciplinary power. But at best—that is, if successful—any such action can only reconfigure the distribution of forces; it cannot alter the nature of the game. This is made strikingly clear in Foucault's own attempt to articulate an emancipatory project, in which he proclaims, as we have already noted, that "the rallying point for the counterattack against the deployment of sexuality ought not to be sex-desire, but bodies and pleasures." Granting that sexual liberation is not the goal, rallying around the body and its pleasures is not liberating. Splitting body from mind in this fashion, which puts "the body" at the center of the struggle, is itself fetishistic, a thing-ification of the self and reduction of the whole (no matter how complex and multicentered) to a part. "The body," like "sex as such," is the product of affective distancing and dissociation, an artifact of paranoid-schizoid mentation. Panopticism creates the body as its object; it cannot be resisted on that basis.

Finally, when viewed from this angle, we can also see why Foucault would have minimized the emancipatory claims of psychoanalysis. As noted, the paranoid-schizoid position rules out mutual recognition. One does not share feelings with another or see things from the other's point of view. To that extent, clinical interaction is necessarily a power struggle, and one which the patient cannot win. To be sure, s/he can evade or thwart the analyst's will to know and thereby defeat the analysis, but these are schizoid and paranoid maneuvers that leave the psychical situation unchanged. Surveillance has not been extended, to be sure, but only because no analysis has taken place. The patient must be brought into the purview of the analyst's will to know, the disciplinary gaze must not be averted or subverted, and the analyst must be internalized if the analysis is to be successful. And in such a successful instance, yet another piece of psychical territory will have been assimilated to the "power domain" (as Nietzsche would put it) of enlightenment.

Various objections can be raised to this interpretation of Foucault's point of view. In my opinion, the most powerful criticism would be that the postulated paranoid-schizoid dynamics are simply in the eye of the beholder, that what we have here is yet another instance of the object to be known having been swallowed up by the knowing subject. Interpreting the *History of Sexuality* as a textualization of the paranoid-schizoid position is precisely an example of a power/knowledge relationship. Transparently, a psychoanalytic-marxist will to know aims at overcoming the resistance of Foucaldian social theory. To put it another way, the problem with my interpretation of Foucault is that it presupposes the validity of anthropological principles that he is entitled to call into question. He may not be positing an ontological will to power, but he is using the principle of overcoming resistance as his interpretive perspective. He is free to examine our premises, no less than those of the left Freudians, in this light. And he might well see them as normalizing and regulative, as part and parcel of the regime of bio-power, even if they do not center on the fetish of "sex as such."

Here we reach the end of our discursive line. Foucault is a neo-Nietzschean, not Nietzsche himself. Unlike his predecessor, he does not really push his arguments to their limits. There is, I think, a quite genuine modesty in this deference, but there is also a kind of evasiveness, an unwillingness to take responsibility for the implications of a given line of reasoning. In other words, Foucault gives himself the room to back away from his most extreme and provocative positions. Because he avoids ontological or foundational questions, he can always retreat to the position that power is just one perspective among many and is not to be privileged over interests and desires. This is a more reasonable (commonsensical) position, of course, but it does not constitute a fundamental challenge to psychoanalytic-marxism or other versions of hedonic and utilitarian social theory. Nietzsche, by contrast, challenges these very hedonic and utilitarian presuppositions—including the determinacy of pleasure and pain.[44] So we end, it is plain, on a question mark: What is the relationship between the will to power and the first principles of psychoanalytic-marxism?

Notes

1 Michel Foucault, *The History of Sexuality*, Vol. 1, trans. Robert Hurley (New York, 1990 [1976]).
2 Friedrich Nietzsche, *The Will to Power*, trans. Walter Kaufmann (New York, 1968 [1901]), 346. I attempt to work through the relationship between the will to power and basic psychoanalytic notions in my current book project on Nietzsche, psychoanalysis, and gender, from which this essay is derived.
3 And perhaps was—by Foucault himself; see Gérard Raulet, "Critical Theory/Intellectual History," trans. Jeremy Harding, in *Michel Foucault: Politics, Philosophy, Culture*, ed. Lawrence Kritzman (New York, 1988), 17–53, esp. 17. But cf. Michael Mahon, *Foucault's Nietzschean Genealogy* (Albany, 1992).
4 Foucault, *History of Sexuality*, 3.
5 Ibid., 6.
6 Ibid.
7 Ibid., 96, 114, 5.
8 Ibid., 36, 53, 81, 150ff. This last articulation of an opposing stance is more Lacanian than classically Freudian–Marxist, but for Foucault the differences between these positions are not critical.
9 Ibid., 11, 10.
10 Friedrich Nietzsche, *Thus Spoke Zarathustra*, in *The Portable Nietzsche*, ed. and trans. Walter Kaufmann (New York, 1954), 103–439; quotation from 227.
11 "Michel Foucault, 1926–," in *The Cambridge Companion to Foucault*, ed. Gary Gutting (New York, 1994), 317. On "Maurice Florence" as arguably Foucault himself, see Gutting's preface (viii).
12 Foucault, *History of Sexuality*, 17–18, 23, 35.
13 Ibid., 41–46.
14 Ibid., 65–67.
15 Ibid., 105.
16 Ibid., 82, 85.
17 Ibid., 90.
18 Ibid., 92–93.
19 Ibid.
20 Ibid., 114.
21 Ibid., 119–22.
22 Ibid., 123.
23 Ibid., 130.
24 Ibid., 113.
25 Ibid., 131.

26 Michel Foucault, "Two Lectures," in *Power/Knowledge: Selected Interviews and Other Writings, 1972–1977*, ed. Colin Gordon, trans. Colin Gordon, Leo Marshall, John Mepham, and Kate Soper (New York, 1980), 78–108; quotation from 88–89.

27 Foucault, *History of Sexuality*, 136–37.

28 Ibid., 147.

29 Ibid., 136, 143, 145.

30 Ibid., 151.

31 Ibid., 155.

32 Ibid., 149.

33 Ibid., 150.

34 Ibid., 157.

35 Plato, *Phaedo*, in *Great Dialogues of Plato*, ed. W. H. D. Rouse (New York, 1956), 505.

36 This is an extremely simplified and condensed representation of the propositions put forward in my *Psychoanalytic-Marxism: Groundwork* (New York, 1993), esp. chap. 6. I have also modified the following presentation so as to respond to some of the issues raised by Foucault.

37 As is well known, the paranoid-schizoid and depressive positions are basic elements in Melanie Klein's version of psychoanalytic theory. I have adapted these notions to fit within the story I am telling. See Melanie Klein, "Some Theoretical Conclusions Regarding the Emotional Life of the Infant" (1952), in *Envy and Gratitude* (New York, 1975), 61–93.

38 D. W. Winnicott, "The Development of the Capacity for Concern" (1963), in *The Maturational Processes and the Facilitating Environment* (New York, 1965), 73–82; quotation from 73.

39 Sigmund Freud, *Group Psychology and the Analysis of the Ego*, Vol. 18 of *The Standard Edition of the Complete Psychological Works of Sigmund Freud*, ed. and trans. James Strachey (London, 1953–74), 106.

40 This is not the place to review this literature, which in any case has become too rich and diverse for easy characterization. My own approach has been largely shaped by the object-relations stance of American psychoanalytic feminism; see Jessica Benjamin, "The Bonds of Love: Rational Violence and Erotic Domination," *Feminist Studies* 6 (1980): 144–74; *The Bonds of Love: Psychoanalysis, Feminism and the Problem of Domination* (New York, 1988); and *Like Subjects, Love Objects* (New Haven, 1995); Nancy Chodorow, *The Reproduction of Mothering* (Berkeley, 1978); *Feminism and Psychoanalytic Theory* (New Haven, 1989); and *Femininities, Masculinities, Sexualities* (Lexington, 1994); Dorothy Dinnerstein, *The Mermaid and the Minotaur* (New York, 1976); and Jane Flax, *Thinking Fragments* (Berkeley, 1990); and *Disputed Subjects* (New York, 1993).

41 Foucault is somewhat equivocal in this regard.

42 See Wolfenstein, *Psychoanalytic-Marxism*, chap. 8.

43 Foucault, *Power/Knowledge*, 155. See Martin Jay, *Downcast Eyes: The Denigration of Vision in Twentieth-Century French Thought* (Berkeley, 1993), for a delicate treatment of the problem of vision and the visible in Foucault.

44 Although this aspect of Nietzsche's philosophy has received insufficient attention, see

the excellent article by Ivan Soll, "Nietzsche on Cruelty, Asceticism, and the Failure of Hedonism," in *Nietzsche, Genealogy, Morality: Essays on Nietzsche's Genealogy of Morals*, ed. Richard Schacht (Berkeley, 1994), 168–92. Soll argues that the will to power successfully challenges hedonic and utilitarian forms of explanation with respect to cruelty and asceticism.

Kathleen McHugh

Women in Traffic: L.A. Autobiography

To be content with the easy pleasures of the feminine is to lose a fundamental opportunity: an opportunity to precisely use our material experiences to map out the changing relationships between identity, ideology and gender within the historical moment in which we live.
—Elsbeth Probyn, *Sexing the Self: Gendered Positions in Cultural Studies*

Identity-oriented approaches to film and to representation in general have been both necessary and problematic. Necessary as a corrective to an objective, exclusive, elitist critical stance, such approaches insist upon the importance of the critic's location, upon the place and power dynamics from within which s/he speaks. Yet to signify that place as *within* the self (as "identity"), however socially marked by gender, ethnicity, race, or sexuality, is to invoke the conventions of bourgeois subjectivity (interiority, authenticity, sentimentality) and to subsume those socially marked constructions within those conventions. Thus, in order to avoid issues of who I am or what the feminine is and to investigate instead how gender *works*, I take up Probyn's suggestion

The *South Atlantic Quarterly* 97:2, Spring 1998.

here and bring one aspect of my material experience—I live in L.A. and I commute—to bear upon another—my work in feminist film criticism. As the title indicates, my essay fashions elements of my autobiography (my gender, the city in which I live, and one of its most striking material conditions) to reconsider cinematic representations of women in relation to the trope of automobility.[1]

The sociogeographic particulars of any given location can provide provocative metaphors for the construction of an enigmatic and generative political self, a self whose evocation symbolically incorporates material experiences. Such invented selves obviate problematic universalist or essentialist assertions (such as those that trouble many varieties of identity politics), while also grounding theoretical explorations in a specific environment or situation. This approach can produce surprising and inventive models for thinking an environmentally and politically appropriate(d) self. To live and work in L.A. is to be in traffic; the fortuitous initials invoke both the city and femininity, coupling them at the intersection of autobiography and automobility. Here I use the automobile—a ubiquitous figure and feature of life in Southern California—to literalize and remotivate a metaphor intrinsic to theoretical discourse about women, but articulated most cogently in Gayle Rubin's watershed piece "The Traffic in Women." I make use of the actuality and the metaphor of women's automobility to contextualize and nuance the other dominant gender metaphor that rises out of L.A. and the film industry—women as objects of the gaze.

"Don't let her get away!" The research trope of "women in traffic" quickly pays off. In the 1975 article that inaugurated feminist psychoanalytic film theory, Laura Mulvey's "Visual Pleasure and Narrative Cinema," the films used to illustrate women's role in spectacle and narrative share another feature that Mulvey doesn't mention: they all depict and more or less depend upon women's movement, upon their self-motivated *traffic* through the diegesis.[2] While Josef von Sternberg's *Morocco* (1930) culminates in Amy Jolly's barefoot trek into the desert, the plot of *Dishonored* (1931) turns on Magda's travel behind enemy lines. In the more domestic *Blonde Venus* (1932), Helen Faraday's attempt to keep her son involves their cross-country travel in trains, by hay wagon, and on foot, chased by an army of private detectives and anonymous men out for reward money. The Hitch-

cock oeuvre shares the same insistent motif: in *Vertigo* (1958), Madeleine is tailed by Scottie as she drives aimlessly through the streets and environs of San Francisco; the protagonist of *Marnie* (1964) travels from city to city, changing her luggage, clothing, and hair color to evade detectives as she deceives one gullible mark after another; in *Psycho* (1960), Marion Crane, having stolen forty thousand dollars, hightails it out of town in her car, to be stopped and later followed by a suspicious police officer. In each narrative, women in traffic, in movement through the diegesis, stir up the interest of the law and its agents, who pursue, surveil, and attempt to stop them.

Mulvey chose her films well, avoiding more gender-specific genres such as the western, where the narratives concern men on the move, and the woman's melodrama, where the claustrophobic space of the home provides the compression necessary for plots that lack any significant geographic movement. Indeed, D. W. Griffith, whose name, films, and Victorian ideologies designate one cinematic beginning, distinguished between the genders precisely on the question of movement: "Man is a moving animal. It isn't so with women."[3] The adventure thrillers featured in "Visual Pleasure and Narrative Cinema" illustrate clearly the anxiety and the sadism instigated by violations of the Victorian binary *men move/women stay home*, by women's efforts to move, to travel, to fend for themselves, unattended and unprotected, outside the law. Thus the narratives that found the psychoanalytic theorization of gender and sexuality in the cinema actually constitute a liminal body of films unlike those genres—the western and the melodrama—whose narratives are clearly gendered according to a class-based status quo inherited, through Griffith, from nineteenth-century Victorianism. In such boy genres as the western, women are neither consistently specularized nor necessarily the objects of narrative sadism. As often as not, it is the gunfighter himself who is subjected to sadistic treatment (as in *The Man Who Shot Liberty Valance, One-Eyed Jacks, A Man Called Horse, Fistful of Dollars*, and *The Good, the Bad and the Ugly*), while the women in these films, if any, are often there just long enough for their frailty to motivate the plot. As regards women's genres, many feminist critics (e.g., Mary Ann Doane and Linda Williams) have commented on the insufficiency of Mulvey's model to address the narrative and specular dynamics of the melodrama.[4]

The films Mulvey chose render exceptional cases of women who move through the diegesis, working and attempting single motherhood (*Blonde*

Venus), struggling against class inequities (*Psycho*), making their way as career grifters (*Marnie*) or as spies (*Dishonored*), or, in the case of those women who have the time and the money, just cruising around (*Vertigo*). My précis exaggerate the women's economic situations to make the point that these films overtly raise *class* issues that are then mystified by their intensely Oedipalized gender narratives. Marnie, the daughter of a prostitute who caters to sailors, is routinely woken up and sent into the living room when the men in white uniforms come to the door; unlike her mother, however, Marnie grows up to prey on *rich* men, bankers and businessmen, to whom she never grants sexual favors. In *Vertigo*, the distinction between elegant, elusive Madeleine, who doesn't have to work, and cheap, sluttish Judy, a working-class shop girl, turns out to be both real and an "act," a sleight of hand accomplished by clothing and posture in the vertiginous dynamics of the film. This false false distinction is only enhanced by the girl in the middle—the middle-class professional woman, pragmatic and sexless Midge.[5] *Dishonored* and *Blonde Venus* both feature a woman who prostitutes herself for a good cause—nation and motherhood, respectively. The class angle in *Psycho* is simultaneously presented and mystified by its Oedipalized framing. In the first office scene, the wealthy Tom Cassidy leers at Marion Crane as he tells her he can ward off unhappiness, flipping in her face the forty thousand dollars he plans to use to buy his daughter a house for her wedding present.

These plots wed motifs of money, class, agency, and frequently *prostitution* to women's diegetic movement or transportation. Not altogether coincidentally, these apparently unrelated concerns are signified precisely by "traffic," a term whose meanings include prostitution (i.e., "the traffic in women") and all forms of pedestrian and vehicular movement. Originally referring to trade—buying, selling, dealing, communications, and business—an early (1561) usage of the word also connoted sexual trade. Not until the nineteenth century, with the many developments in transportation technologies, would "traffic" come to mean "the passing to and fro of persons, or of vehicles or vessels along a road, railway, canal, or other route of transport."[6] The term thereby references both bodies as property, objects of trade, and bodies as subjects capable of autonomous movement, whether self-propelled, vehicular, or both. The distinction between these kinds of bodies (as objects or subjects of movement) is obviously an *economic* one that informs the construction of differences in social identity—

racial, class, and gender. In terms of the possible relations among women's gender identity, the types of movement of which they are capable, and the socioeconomic aspects of gender construction, these form a matrix of relations that bears closer investigation in popular and independent films.

Mulvey's articulation of gender and sexuality as relating *exclusively* to castration ("the female form . . . speaks castration and *nothing else*") marks this formulation historically as class limited, in that class (labor, material relations) is what gender and sexual difference cannot speak; it is the "nothing else" besides castration, the structuring absence of modern sex/gender systems.[7] Significantly, Mulvey does not theorize women's movement or the economics of their movement in the films she examines. However, the films themselves crystallize another aspect of the cinematic representation of female sexuality: women's literal and social mobility as the impetus for the sadism directed at them. In these plots women are in traffic and the law is after them—to stop them and not let them get away.

From Objects of Exchange to Auto-Motivation. Published in 1975, the same year as Mulvey's article, Gayle Rubin's landmark essay, subtitled "Notes on the 'Political Economy' of Sex," engages exactly those issues precluded by Mulvey's psychoanalytic approach—sexuality and gender difference in relation to political economy.[8] Rubin's article, investigating the nature and genesis of women's oppression and social subordination from a more materialist and historical standpoint, summarizes the structure and evolution of this oppression as the "traffic in women." The source of women's subordination to men lies in those social relations which constitute a society's sex/gender system: "Every society has a sex/gender system—a set of arrangements by which the biological raw material of human sex and procreation is shaped by human, social intervention and satisfied in a conventional manner, no matter how bizarre some of the conventions may be."[9] The sex/gender system of kinship, based on the incest taboo and the exchange of or traffic in women, once organized all other social relations—political, economic, and educational. Now, Rubin observes, sex/gender systems organize and reproduce only themselves, as the development and evolution of the state has generally superseded kinship in organizing political and economic relations.[10] Thus sex/gender systems have come to *complement* economic systems, and this division is symptomatic of modern social organization in the West. While economic systems transform raw natural resources into objects for human consumption, sex/gender systems "take up females as raw materials and fashion domesticated women as products."[11] Seizing upon women's historically preeminent social functions as wives and mothers, Rubin underscores the exploitive character of those roles by conflating women's conventional social location ("the domestic sphere") with their invisible labor (as "domestics") and an oppressive relation (as "domesticated"). She also stresses the economic implications of women's domestication (noting the instance of housework), but while finding Engels's famous investigation of gender, sex, and labor provocative, Rubin ultimately deems it outdated and draws on Freud instead for her analysis of why it is women who do housework.[12]

The feature of Rubin's essay that provides for a reinterpretation of the films examined by Mulvey is an argument about women's static social location (the home) and the particular historical circumstances under which they moved through the socius via marriage and other forms of exchange between men. As Rubin observes, "The relations of such a system are such that women are in no position to realize the benefits of their own circulation."[13] This perception is further nuanced by two points implicit in Rubin's analysis: (1) the category "woman" and the modes of exchange that have distinguished the genders have never been homogeneous across cultures; and (2) the traffic in women that structured kinship systems has changed dramatically such that women in the West now have a relation to social exchange and movement quite different from what they had in kinship societies or in the eighteenth and nineteenth centuries. In historicizing sex/gender systems and insisting on their cultural specificity, Rubin has provided a frame by which the disparities between her own approach and Mulvey's can also be historicized. Our social organization is predicated on an illusory but persistent distinction between the economic and political systems (the public sphere) and the sex/gender system (the private sphere), a distinction that was itself frequently reproduced in feminist and other methodologies in the humanities and social sciences during the 1970s and 1980s.[14] Tending to emphasize either materialist or symbolic concerns, those methodologies produced two different and seemingly incompatible research objects: "real" women versus representations of "woman."

"Women in traffic" provides a trope; as both a literalization of and a metaphor for our historical moment, it registers the symbolic and material changes produced as certain women have begun to enter into social relations as agents rather than objects, that is, as they have acquired much more autonomy over their literal, social, and sexual mobility. This synthesis or trope can be implemented methodologically by comparing the history of the cinema to that of the automobile, by considering their distinct and interrelated effects on sex and gender constructions that are presumably classless.[15] Both are industries that create private space within the public sphere, a significant feature of their gendered function in relation to women of a certain class. Approaching gender construction outside its usual containment within identity and subjectivity, I want to look instead at its *industrial context*, bringing that context to bear on women in traffic *in* the cinema.

Moving Pictures, Moving Vehicles. As might be expected, the history of the automobile, from its speculative prehistory to its Fordist organization, has close parallels to that of the cinema. Roger Bacon dreamt in the thirteenth century, as did Leonardo da Vinci in the sixteenth, of self-propelled vehicles.[16] Both thinkers also speculated on the implications and the possibilities of the camera obscura.[17] As with the cinema, prototypes of the automobile were developed throughout the nineteenth century for sport, as curiosities, and (particularly in the latter case) as playthings for the wealthy. The technological advances that made the automobile possible were developed from machines analogous in function to the automobile, such as the bicycle and the locomotive, as well as from some that were not, such as the sewing machine and the electric cash register. As with the kinetograph, kinetoscope, and cinematograph, various formats (such as the gasoline, electric, and steam engines) vied for dominance of the automobile market once the product caught on and demand for it grew. The 1890s were crucial years for both the cinema and the automobile; the first public screening by the Lumières in December 1895 occurred during the same period when commercial production of the automobile began in Europe.[18] While U.S. and European cinematic technology developed in conjunction, the United States was ten years behind in the development of the automobile; after World War I, however, American production dominated both industries. Beyond the organizational, financial, and technological parallels between the cinema and the automobile, similar imbrications of class and gender interests also emerged as crucial to the "distinctly American achievement" of both.[19] Historians of these industries note that the success of each in the decade between 1905 and 1915 hinged on its appeal to middle- and upper-class women.

While film historians include among the complex factors leading to mass spectatorship the development of plots and venues appropriate to middle-class women,[20] the gender/class angle took a slightly different tack in the automobile industry. The electric and internal-combustion engines came to constitute the automotive terms of sex difference, with the industry marketing electric cars to women and those with internal-combustion engines to men. Electric cars had only a limited, local range; they were clean, quiet, and slow, and they didn't have to be crank-started. The same year that Henry Ford developed the Model T he bought an electric car for his wife, Clara; for travel over distance, she relied on her husband or her son, Edsel, to drive her in a car with a combustion engine.[21] Gasoline-fueled combustion engines were powerful, complicated, fast, and capable of long-distance runs. They were also dirty and loud, and their crank-starter mechanisms were notoriously difficult to operate. As John Rae observes, "The electric starter . . . was a major factor in promoting widespread use of the gasoline automobile, particularly because it made the operation of gasoline engines more attractive to women."[22]

The development of the electric starter signaled the end of the electric car and its gendered marketing, but the presumed appeal to women on which its marketing was based indicates the social and economic concerns that were wrapped up in gendered marketing strategies for automobiles. For instance, a December 1910 *Motor* ad stated: "To the well-bred woman, the Detroit electric has a particular appeal. In it she can preserve her toilet immaculate, her coiffure intact. She can drive it with all desired privacy, yet safely—in constant touch with traffic conditions all about her."[23] To be "well-bred," a woman had to maintain both her appearance and a certain degree of privacy, gender values that were widely purveyed in nineteenth-century America by the cult of domesticity. The cult had introduced an ideal of femininity predicated on an array of class-exclusive markers, among which were a delicate, fragile, *unlabored* appearance; the restriction of social movement to the home and other appropriate private environs by rigid moral codes; and a related moral sensibility characterized by excessive modesty and a need for privacy. While working-class women did not have the economic means to adhere to any of these strictures (to appear fragile, stay home, or observe strict conventions of privacy), they were nevertheless held to the same morally sanctioned, middle-class modes of dress, deportment, and social behavior. For example, in 1895, a working-class woman in New York City, who was attempting to find her sister's house after dark, asked two men for directions. She was subsequently arrested and convicted of disorderly conduct, the presumption being that any woman out alone at that hour was a "public woman," or prostitute. (She was released from the workhouse only after a doctor's examination proved her to be a "good" girl.)[24]

The Victorian ideology of separate spheres fostered a generalized, yet tacitly class-based, anxiety about women's venturing beyond the private sphere, either literally or figuratively. Public transportation in the early twentieth century was unreliable, inconvenient, sometimes dangerous, and utterly lacking in privacy. Virginia Scharff describes the turn-of-the-century social outcry and political action that focused on the problem of protecting female virtue in the context of mass transit: "Beneath the welter of political conflicts, there lurked the idea that the very character of mass transit set it on a collision course with bourgeois ladyhood."[25] The automobile saved the day, providing the well-bred American woman with an initially limited, privatized mode of transportation that would enable her to fulfill her increasingly important cultural role as a consumer while safeguarding her immaculate toilet and coiffure. Thus the automobile protected a feminine appearance standard and code of behavior vested with explicitly moral and tacitly class-based distinctions.

Although many histories of the American automobile point to its role in ameliorating class differences, such analyses are usually related to men.[26] The relationship of women, specifically upper- and middle-class women, to public transportation in the early twentieth century casts the automobile and its relation to the period's gender and class concerns in a very different light. While automobility threatened nineteenth-century America's preeminent gender distinction—men move and women stay home—the needs of the economy demanded a more mobile female consumer. The automobile preserved the class-exclusivity of a feminine ideal instituted by a social order that had used gender since the nineteenth century to privatize and mystify class inequity. Unlike public transportation, with its threats to a woman's "well-bred appearance" and privacy, the automobile (once the problems with the combustion engine were solved) allowed middle-class women to be auto/mobile without ever having to rub shoulders, or any other body parts, with strangers on the subway, the trolley, or the train.

The Gaze, the Girls, and the Drive. Given its complicated and cathected functions involving money, class, agency, gender, social geography, and the mercurial demands of late capitalism, the highly charged relationship between women and automobiles is hardly surprising. The stereotype of the bad woman driver, persisting despite actuarial statistics that show women in all age groups to be much better drivers than men, indicates the ambivalence toward women's automotive agency, that at stake is their ability to move freely through public space. In midcentury American films, this type of contradiction surfaced in a slightly different way. Although often focused on domesticity, the private sphere, and emotions, these films contain very few representations of women engaged in domestic labor.[27] Instead, their domesticity is often narratively secured by way of contrast to "bad" women in traffic. In *Notorious* (1946), for example, Ingrid Bergman's reckless drunken driving and impetuous agency at the beginning is contrasted by her romanticized helplessness at the end, when Cary Grant literally carries her, near death, out of the house where she has been operating as a spy. In *Written on the Wind* (1956), Dorothy Malone, as Marilee Hadley, drives her own sports car and picks up men, "fast" behavior that is set against the demure domesticity of Lauren Bacall, who lets the men drive and gets Rock Hudson. Women are variously struck down, blinded, or blown up by or in automobiles in *Suspicion* (1941), *Postman Always Rings Twice* (1946, 1981), *The Big Heat* (1953), *Magnificent Obsession* (1954), and *The Godfather* (1972), each narrative using the car to threaten or destroy romance, domesticity, or reproduction.

As these examples and those cited earlier suggest, Mulvey's attempt to anchor gender representation in the gaze is not wrong but her focus interiorizes gender distinctions while the films themselves locate this interiority within narratives that both literalize women's movement and endeavor to contain it. As the century has progressed and the demands of the economy have produced more middle-class working women, gender representations, as might be expected, have been increasingly destabilized. Given the role of the automobile in negotiating between an apparently nonmaterialist feminine gender identity and the economic realities of late capitalism, it would seem that many "insecure" cinematic representations of femininity must rely heavily on the motif of women in traffic—on their autonomous movement—a motif that would occur in some tension with the (class-based) appearance standard that generally subtends representations of women. And an array of recent films has, in fact, presented "brave new girls" in narratives where concerns with appearance and the gaze coincide with and are sometimes overridden by representations of women's automobility and agency. Setting aside such obvious examples as *Tank Girl, Basic Instinct,* and *Bound,* I want to focus on four films, variously typed as sci-fi, action, or independent, each of which formally and narratively foregrounds the relationship between the gaze and the drive[28] in either apparently liberatory or more knowingly complex and self-reflexive representations of contemporary women.

James Cameron's *Terminator* (1984) was a breakthrough film in several ways. It made Arnold Schwarzenegger a star. Following Ridley Scott's *Alien* (1979) and *Blade Runner* (1982), it completed the rebirth of science fiction film inaugurated by *Star Wars* (1977). Unlike their blockbuster predecessors, *Blade Runner* and *The Terminator* have *sexualized* Oedipal narratives. *The Terminator,* however (like *Alien*), has a female protagonist, who ultimately triumphs over the cyborg monster programmed to track her down and kill her.[29] The story is actually her story, a literal and psychical odyssey that converts teenage waitress into futurist warrior–mother. She enters the film on a scooter and leaves it in a jeep, having learned in between to make and throw bombs and to drive get-away cars. In the elegant time-loop narrative that structures this sci-fi action thriller, Sarah Connor becomes a warrior to save her unborn child and, by inference, the future of the human race.

While *The Terminator* emphatically severs maternity from domesticity, in its closing scene the importance of the woman's image is reasserted even as this particular woman, armed and visibly pregnant, heads for safety in Mexico, her german shepherd at her side. At a gas station just across the border, a young boy, praising her beauty, takes a snapshot of Sarah and then sells it to her. Within a film that is all about a naive young woman's becoming a superhero, it is finally this still, this image, upon which the narrative depends. Kyle Reese, the unknowing father, receives the image from John Connor, his (unborn) son, and travels through time because of it, his desire insinuated in the two types of reproduction—photographic and biologic—it represents. The time-loop narrative inverts the logical relationship between the two, the reproductive bodies retrospectively following the path of the image. Our own entry point into this temporally regressive narrative is marked specifically by the reproductive imperative—by the reproductive value of Sarah Connor's body and the danger in which her autonomy and agency places her and, by implication, the whole human race. Kyle subdues her and curtails her independence, convincing her, with ample support from the Terminator, that she needs him. It is not until after her body has been inseminated that she begins to fight and to take charge. (This same equation between maternity and physical prowess structures the *Alien* trilogy, more insistently with each sequel, as, of course, it also informs Sarah's characterization in *Terminator 2: Judgment Day* [1991]).[30]

Ultimately, it is Sarah's photograph, not her agency and mobility, that seals the ideological relationship between present and future, one in which an apocalyptic vision of mass destruction is contained and subsumed within the brief but intense romance between her and Kyle. As Sarah drives off at the end, *The Terminator* leaves us not with the future that she and the rest of us face, but rather with the tragic loop of love, desire, and loss figured in the snapshot, in that still, frozen image of a woman with which the narrative begins and ends. The dynamism of the film and the kinetic prowess of Sarah Connor—who, even after being severely wounded, destroys the Terminator, announcing, "You're terminated, fucker"—suggest that we are in a whole new realm of cinematic gender construction. Here the still, which formally and narratively equates Sarah's and the film's reproductivity, also serves to contain Sarah in a more conventional femininity, with her strength, her autonomous movement through the diegesis, and her motivation finally subject to the reproductive logics of her body and her image.

A film of a quite different genre, Ridley Scott's *Thelma and Louise* (1991) nevertheless develops a similar relationship between the narrative movement of its protagonists and the images of them produced within and finally *as* the diegesis. Several critics have pointed out that this narrative of two women in traffic unfolds between two stills: the snapshot that Louise takes when she and Thelma set out on their vacation, and the freeze frame that ends the film—women and automobility suspended between the law behind them and a very hard place beyond.[31] The photograph documents the women's frivolity in "setting off," their faces made-up, femmed-up, to-be-looked-at in conventional terms. But their idyll in Louise's Thunderbird convertible and the terms of their getaway are utterly transformed when Louise kills a man who attempts to rape Thelma. Further down the road, a good-time boy pleasures Thelma and then steals Louise's stash, leading Thelma to take up armed robbery as the solution to their economic woes. For Thelma and Louise must have money if they are to keep moving and not have to go back to their stultifying lives. As some feminist critics have indicated, the film explicitly connects mobility, money, and the conventional containments of gender, especially conventions of appearance. As the narrative progresses, as their flight becomes more and more determined, Thelma and Louise shed their lipstick and other accoutrements of conventional femininity. And far from sentimentalizing their actions with a romantic or maternal angle, the film points instead to male aggression, economic limitations, and the constraints of their respective feminine roles (wife and waitress) as their motivation to "keep on goin'."[32] When the police chase the pair to the Grand Canyon, where they are faced with going back or going forward together, Thelma and Louise drive off the cliff. The diegesis freezes, the Thunderbird in flight.

Unlike the grim tourist photo on which *The Terminator* ends or the cheerier one with which the odyssey of *Thelma and Louise* begins, the freeze frame at the end of the latter denotes another kind of travel. The narrative reaches a limit, having nowhere else to go; as far as feminine gender construction goes, it has exhausted all its options. In relinquishing the usual affective and narrative tropes that define and confine femininity, either at rest (spectacle) or in motion (romance or maternity), the film seems to push the association between women and cars beyond its conventional subjective anchors by refusing to name or resolve the social contradictions it has invoked, as exemplified by the freeze frame. Yet just before the car lifts off, we get a shot of the photograph that documents the beginning of the women's journey as it blows out of the backseat. Then, immediately after the freeze frame, the film begins running again, recycling an array of glamorous clips of Thelma and Louise before takeoff. In a move formally parallel to the end of *The Terminator*, the photograph blowing out of the car seals *Thelma and Louise*'s time-loop, one articulated solely in terms of images, still and moving, of the women. The final moments of the film thus refer its lack of resolution back to its own reproductive capacities—the images are preserved and can be *rerun*. Thelma and Louise, seemingly gender outlaws par excellence, become myth once again to be looked at.

In both *The Terminator* and, to a much greater degree, *Thelma and Louise*, narrative and iconographic tensions between feminine appearance and automobility organize class and gender issues such that class differences *disappear* within those of gender. Sarah Connor, like Louise Sawyer a waitress in a cheap restaurant, is transformed from a service worker into the mother–savior of the human race. In *Thelma and Louise* the two protagonists are both working-class women: Louise waits tables in a diner, while Thelma keeps house in a dismal tract home for her car-salesman husband. Their lack of mobility and the stultifying quality of their lives have as much to do with money as with men. However, by placing the emphasis on men, the film keeps gender issues "in the family," in the private sphere, and out of the socioeconomic arena of class and opportunity. The material constraints and claustrophobic spaces that limit the lives of Thelma and Louise melt away as they take to the road, their working-class accents and tastes dispersed into a country-western regionalism. Thus the film partakes of a myth that is archetypally American, male, and White: in the wide-open spaces of the territories, the West, the frontier, a man can escape any social barrier or constraint—domestic/familial, class, or criminal—any social marking (except race or gender), any dead end. The automobile, made for this myth, modernizes the fantasy of "lightin' out for the territories."[33] Adjusting the road movie to accommodate female protagonists, Scott uses a convertible to feminize the story, pitting spectacle against mobility. Throughout the women's journey, ample use is made of Geena Davis's and Susan Sarandon's beauty, of their hair, cheekbones, and bodies, with their faces sculpted in the rust-red hues and shadows of the panoramic landscapes that provide the locations for the second half of the film. Scott's camera consistently frames the women with or within the car, either stopped or in motion, often through the windshield. The car becomes a prop for their bodies, which assume an array of compelling poses (thus evoking and inverting the conceit of the car show). The women's automobility is ultimately subordinated to their appearance.

While *The Terminator* and *Thelma and Louise* make welcome and important changes in gender representation, the more dramatic and threatening implications of female agency—those that have to do with economic autonomy and the role of traditional femininity in mystifying class in America—are raised and defused in the films' symptomatic play between mobility and spectacle. F. Gary Gray's *Set It Off* (1996), on the other hand, tells the story that these earlier films cannot tell, realigning femininity, romance, maternity, and spectacle in relation to money, mobility, and opportunity. This film both elicits and alters the generic elements of the road/outlaw movie, as well as those of the gangster film, the female-friendship film, and the 'hood flick, by explicitly or implicitly referencing *Thelma and Louise, Bonnie and Clyde* (1967), *The Godfather, Body Heat* (1981), *Point Break* (1991), and *Boyz N the Hood* (1991). In alluding to these films via dialogue, gesture, mise-en-scène, and/or dramatic situation, *Set It Off* adjusts and corrects their genres as well, most notably for race and gender, but most insistently for class. Described by critics as a "Girlz in the Hood" or a "black *Thelma and Louise*," *Set It Off* tells the story of four African American women who, out of anger, desperation, or inspired frustration, decide to rob banks. Cleo (Queen Latifah), Stony (Jada Pinkett), Frankie (Vivica A. Fox), and Tisean (Kimberly Elise) "go way back together," and all save Cleo have strong motivations for striking back at the system: Stony's brother, Stevie, whom she has protected and nurtured since their parents died in a car accident, is killed by the police, who mistake him for someone else; the managers of the bank where Frankie works fire her after a violent robbery solely because she happens to know one of the gunmen from the projects; and Tisean's son is taken from her by social services after an accident at her workplace, where she has brought him because she can't afford childcare.

Cleo's motives are less melodramatic and more unequivocally self-interested and economic—she wants money and a cool lowrider. She has a dead-end janitorial job, an abusive and incompetent boss to whom she is clearly superior, and a girlfriend whom she keeps on a pager. Unlike the characters in most female-friendship or lesbian films, Cleo is played, with relish and without apology, as a convincing and compelling butch—the rarest sexual creature in contemporary American cinema.[34] She is also the narrative's "real" outlaw (and real hero), the one who does it for fun.

The film's director and writers (Kate Lanier and Takashi Bufford) avoided transforming class issues into gender issues by avoiding the conventions with which this transformation is typically accomplished. *Set It Off* does not use the iconography of either wide-open spaces or female spectacle, nor does it rely on a romance plot to resolve the thorny issues of women in relation to race, money, and opportunity that it raises. This outlaw "road" movie set in Los Angeles never leaves the city. Its heroines, save one, never get out of town; in fact, they have never even been out of town. The claustrophobic, rundown, urban 'hood (with its industrial skyline, projects, small, cramped apartments) contrasts sharply with the expansive luxury of the workplaces where the heroines clerk and clean (an upscale bank, plush corporate headquarters, an enormous private home). Gray focuses on the women's labor, setting many scenes in workplaces, garages, and the streets, as opposed to their homes. In fact, Stony's home is the only one of the four we see, and then just briefly.[35] The automobility of these women is similarly fettered. Only Cleo owns a car, and stolen cars are always used for the robberies. When Tisean becomes separated from the other three after their first bank heist, she takes a bus back to the projects; and, as the women are making their getaway after their last job has gone horribly awry, Cleo's car breaks down. Stony finally gets out of town on a tour bus. These instances of constrained automobility exist in tension with the film's representation of the women's femininity, sexuality, and relationships, all of which are subsumed by their economic situations. It is noteworthy that the only one of the four who has a successful romance is Cleo. The other women are each personally cathected to a "troubled" Black masculinity—Stony's dead brother, Frankie's 'hood friend-turned-bank robber, and Tisean's vulnerable son—while their jobs expose them to verbally and sexually abusive employers. *Set It Off* suggests that the only relationships working-class Black women can have with Black men are political and economic. Conventional romance, predicated on leisure and a protected, delicate femininity, is available only to the economically privileged.

These points are emphatically made in a subplot involving Stony's romantic pursuit by a bank executive. As Stony cases the first bank the women intend to rob, its handsome new manager, Keith Weston (Blair Underwood), approaches her, wanting her phone number. She plays along, gets his number, and their romance, brief but intense, is marked by her understanding and insistence that the relationship between them will never work because of their different class backgrounds. On their first date, Stony arranges to meet Keith at his condo. As he shows her into the spacious, elegant, and richly appointed loft, saying, "It's not much, but it's home," we wince with her at his utterly distorted frame of reference and the dramatic contrast between his space and those in which she lives and moves. Stony and the film itself refuse to endorse Keith's liberal-humanist racial solidarity. While he would like to believe that his upper-class, Harvard-educated background is compatible with her own, Stony acerbically mocks his illusions, pointing out that the humanist perspective is itself always privileged—only people who have money can pretend that it really doesn't make a difference. This subplot is skillfully deployed to extend *Set It Off*'s engagement with economic issues beyond a racialized dichotomy, ultimately providing an astute critique of the fairy tale romance of class rise. Before Keith takes Stony to a formal bank function, he directs their limo driver to a fancy boutique where he buys her a beautiful dress, since her own party clothes would be unsuitable. Stony then spends an idyllic evening with Keith; she loves him, but she does not buy the Cinderella story in which he obviously believes and that informs classical cinematic romance narrative. A *Chicago Tribune* review of the film makes this point cogently, if unwittingly: "When Stony begins dating a suave bank executive . . . who buys her pricey dinners and clothing, you hope she'll ask whether he has three friends so the women can lay off the gunplay."[36] Beyond the fact that this critic apparently misread Cleo's sexuality, the notion that romance can solve any woman's economic woes is precisely the myth that *Set It Off* brilliantly exposes. Indeed, many reviewers of the film missed its economic themes, some even criticizing the dramatically different mise-en-scènes of Stony's world and Keith's as a flawed production design, unrealistic and jarring.[37]

What really jars, though, is what the film lacks—spectacular representations of the women that would have elided all the class differences. While all four women are stunning, across butch/femme registers, their beauty never becomes the iconographic or narrative axis whereby their auto/mobility might be reassuringly transformed into feminine spectacle. Photographic images of the women do figure in this film's plot, as in those of *The Terminator* and *Thelma and Louise*, but in *Set It Off* these images are not, significantly, personal snapshots, nor do they ever achieve metanarrative status—two related features of the earlier films by which spectacle and nostalgia override the political aspects of their plots. Rather, the images in *Set It Off* are mug shots and surveillance photos, used by Detective Strode to prove that the four women know each other, that they are collaborators in crime. In addition, the film's ending makes its avoidance of feminine spectacle particularly apparent, for Cleo's death functions as a spectacle of another kind—a masculine one—whereby, grossly outnumbered and outgunned, she briefly becomes unstoppable, larger than her inevitable mortality. Cleo's death contrasts dramatically with Stony's survival and escape on a humble bus, her mobility utterly functional and unspectacular.[38]

In the film's closing moments, we see Stony in a cheap motel room, cutting off her dreds, packing her money in a backpack, and remembering her friends. Unlike the clips at the end of *Thelma and Louise*, the scenes of the four women rerun here are clearly anchored to Stony's subjectivity and to her bonds with her friends. Signifying memory rather than spectacle, they do not serve to reproduce the four protagonists as spectacular, enticing images.

Following in the tradition of *Body Heat*, *Set It Off*'s last scene places Stony in a tropical milieu, pulling off the road to make a brief phone call to Keith. She doesn't speak, but he knows it's her. He tells her he's glad she's safe. She says, "Thank you," then hangs up and takes off in her red jeep down a mountain road toward the surf below. Unlike the ending of *Body Heat*, where the femme fatale sips a piña colada, waited on by polite and crisply uniformed locals, Stony ends up with rustic independence, her tropical paradise one of dusty roads and thatched roofs. *Set It Off*'s concluding fantasy does not have anything to do with luxury and conspicuous consumption, with indulged and pampered femininity, but rather with freedom and autonomy. The film completely undercuts any formulaic, if foundational, representation of White, middle-class femininity, knowing that what even begins to make this possible is a racialized class representation that cannot be reduced to or subsumed by gender.

And what of good girls whose automobility never exceeds the bounds of appropriate middle-class femininity? Todd Haynes's *Safe* (1995), an entirely different take on women and cars, addresses this question within the more claustral, interiorized gender dynamics of melodrama. A film that works in a much more self-reflexive and knowing way than either *The Terminator* or *Thelma and Louise*, *Safe* also approaches women and their automobility from a different generic perspective than *Set It Off*. While the heroines of *The Terminator* and *Thelma and Louise* finally function allegorically as universalized gender types, *Safe*'s aptly named protagonist, Carol White, represents a particularized race and class of women. Thus *Safe* shares with *Set It Off* a cultural, social, and economic specificity that limits their audience appeal. Mainstream cinema's need for mass identification has led to an insistent and pervasive use of gender to universalize characters, to maximize their potential for mass appeal. What the very different women in *Set It Off* and *Safe* indicate quite clearly is that class and race produce significantly different variants of "femininity," differences that mainstream culture works hard to efface. Haynes's film takes on an upper-middle-class White housewife who could be a suitable subject for melodrama were her socioeconomic contours not so painstakingly drawn.

Carol White lives in the Valley; she always speaks softly and wears pastels. She is a very nice person. Her house, her friends, her children, and her lifestyle are relentlessly insipid. One day, after a lunch date, a workout, and a trip to the dry cleaners, Carol has a breakdown in traffic. With all these errands to run, her own automobility proves too much for her. Carol White becomes overwhelmed by the public exposure that even her hermetically sealed lifestyle demands. Seeing exhaust fumes pouring out of the truck ahead of her, she starts to cough. She raises the windows of her luxury car and turns on the air conditioner, her panic rising, her coughing growing ever more hysterical. Frantically driving into a parking garage, her screeching tires an apt objective correlative for her panic, Carol stops the car, collapsing out of it, panting and gasping for breath.

Carol's breakdown takes the form of a radical sensitivity to the environment—specifically to commercial, urban spaces—which she takes increasingly extreme measures to control. She completely withdraws from her social world; she sees doctors and therapists who cannot help her before ending up at a retreat in the desert, living in an antiseptic igloo and going through recovery. Having very carefully plotted its course through the lifestyle and concerns of a leisured, privileged L.A. housewife, the film ends by savagely documenting the symbolic outcome of an affluent, White femininity whose only standards are appearances. In *Safe*'s final moments, Carol sits in her igloo, inhaling deeply from an oxygen tank. She gets up and approaches a mirror on the wall. In the reverse shot that ends the film, Carol White looks into the mirror/camera, faces her own image, and says, "I love you. I really love you." That outcome? A wounded and anemic narcissism whose self-focused interiority ultimately arrests all movement.

Notes

I would like to thank Lisa Duggan, David James, Katherine Kinney, Vivian Sobchack, and especially Chon Noriega for their generous insights and thoughtful feedback, all of which greatly enhanced this paper.

1 I take inspiration from Gregory Ulmer's method of "mystory," laid out in *Teletheory: Grammatology in the Age of Video* (New York and London, 1989), 82–112; and from my own experience teaching autobiography, where I have students abstract some aspects of their identities as research tropes. Identity is thus directed not toward programmatic or fixed ideological positions or problems, but rather toward the more properly epistemological—that which is not yet known—without, however, leaving it bereft of political grounding. Such research tropes as "women in traffic" frequently necessitate interdisciplinary work, disciplines being another way of fixing knowledge programmatically within identity.

2 Laura Mulvey, "Visual Pleasure and Narrative Cinema," *Screen* 16 (1975): 6–18.

3 Quoted in Michael Rogin, "'The Sword Became a Flashing Vision': D. W. Griffith's *The Birth of a Nation*," *Representations* 9 (1985): 150–95; quotation from 185.

4 See Mary Ann Doane, *The Desire to Desire* (Bloomington, 1987); and Linda Williams, "Something Else Besides a Mother," in *Issues in Feminist Film Criticism*, ed. Patricia Erens (Bloomington, 1990), 137–62.

5 See Virginia Wright Wexman's discussion of *Vertigo* relative to class and race in "The Critic as Consumer: Film Study in the University, *Vertigo*, and the Film Canon," *Film Quarterly* 39 (1996): 32–41.

6 Virginia Scharff, *Taking the Wheel: Women and the Coming of the Motor Age* (New York, 1991), 3–4.

7 Mulvey, "Visual Pleasure and Narrative Cinema," 8. Such an assertion is warranted historically. In Europe and the United States, gender distinctions permeate all economic strata at the same time that class differences become mystified by the public/private split, although in the United States this mystification was fundamental to the nation's (ostensible) resistance to aristocratic privilege and, as such, has been much more pervasive; see Nancy Armstrong, *Desire and Domestic Fiction* (New York and Oxford, 1987), 3–27; and Kathleen McHugh, "Making Home, Making Nation," in *American Domesticity's Invisible Style: Pedagogy, Hollywood Melodrama, Avant-Garde* (New York and Oxford: Oxford University Press, forthcoming).

8 Gayle Rubin, "The Traffic in Women: Notes on the 'Political Economy' of Sex," in *Toward an Anthropology of Women*, ed. Rayna Reiter [Rapp] (New York, 1975), 157–210.

9 Ibid., 199.

10 Ibid., 165.

11 Ibid., 158.

12 Ibid., 163–64. See also Friedrich Engels, *The Origin of the Family, Private Property and the State* (1884), trans. Alick West (New York, 1972 [1942]), 94–147.

13 Rubin, "Traffic in Women," 174.

14 Economic hierarchy certainly pervades households that include maids, nannies, and other domestic employees. Yet mainstream cultural narratives continually serve up an

image of the domestic as the best friend, confidante, and advisor to the woman of the house or, in such negative portrayals as *The Hand that Rocks the Cradle*, as a sexual or maternal competitor, while the economic relation is generally not articulated.

15 Kristen Ross discusses the very different history of French culture and the automobile, focusing on the clash between traditional and modern social organizations precipitated by the automobile and other industrial developments in France after World War II; see *Fast Cars, Clean Bodies: Decolonization and the Reordering of French Culture* (Cambridge, MA, 1996). Although Ross's book stops short of May '68, it nevertheless provides a congent context for this strike that brought down a government. France, like other European countries, differs from the United States in that gender construction there has never functioned as much to obfuscate and mystify class relations.

16 See John B. Rae, *The American Automobile* (Chicago, 1965), 1.

17 See Jonathan Crary, "Modernizing Vision," in *Viewing Positions: Ways of Seeing Film*, ed. Linda Williams (New Brunswick, 1995), 23–35, esp. 24.

18 See Rae, *American Automobile*, 8.

19 Ibid., 1.

20 See Lary May, *Screening Out the Past* (Chicago, 1980), 43–96; and, for more nuanced accounts of how this process related to morality, class, and spectatorship, see Tom Gunning, *D. W. Griffith and the Origins of American Narrative Film* (Urbana, 1991), 85–187; and Miriam Hansen, *Babel and Babylon: Spectatorship in American Silent Film* (Cambridge, MA, 1991), 23–89.

21 See Virginia Scharff, "Gender, Electricity, and Automobility," in *The Car and The City*, ed. Martin Wachs and Margaret Crawford (Ann Arbor, 1991), 75–85, esp. 77.

22 Rae, *American Automobile*, 47–48. The electric starting device was invented by Henry M. Leland and Charles F. Kettering; Leland's efforts were prompted by the death from gangrene of a friend, Byron Carter, whose jaw had been broken in a cranking accident that occurred when Carter tried to help a woman start her car.

23 Quoted in Scharff, "Gender, Electricity, and Automobility," 77.

24 See Glenna Matthews, *The Rise of Public Woman* (New York and Oxford, 1992), 3.

25 Scharff, *Taking the Wheel*, 6–7.

26 See David Gartman, *Auto Opium: A Social History of American Automobile Design* (New York and London, 1994), xiii–xvi; and Rae, *American Automobile*, 1–15.

27 The erasure of domestic labor provides for a "neat" binary between public and private spheres wherein both (middle-class) home and housewife unproblematically signify leisure. Her body should never be marred by traces of hard work, her femininity thus representing and mystifying class distinctions within what simply appear to be gender differences. For an extended discussion in relation to Hollywood melodrama, see "Housekeeping in Hollywood," in my *American Domesticity's Invisible Style*.

28 Among the many puns that shape or haunt this article, the "drive" is one of the more substantive, a topic in its own right; an altogether different version of this essay could pursue questions of gender, trauma, fatality, the gaze, and automobility in relation to the drive. For an excellent collection of essays on the pun—its implications and applications—see *On Puns*, ed. Jonathan Culler (New York, 1988).

29 Vivian Sobchack has discussed the regressive, patriarchal, and problematic qualities of

films like *The Terminator* and the threat that women pose in science fiction cinema (a threat "acted out" in a film like *Alien*); see "Child/Alien/Father: Patriarchal Crisis and Generic Exchange," in *Close Encounters: Film, Feminism and Science Fiction*, ed. Constance Penley, Elizabeth Lyon, Lynn Spigel, and Janet Bergstrom (Minneapolis, 1991), 3–30; and "The Virginity of Astronauts: Sex and the Science Fiction Film," in *Alien Zone: Cultural Theory and Contemporary Science Fiction Cinema*, ed. Annette Kuhn (London and New York, 1990), 101–14.

30 On the use of maternal affect in *The Terminator* and *Alien(s)*, see Constance Penley, "Time Travel, Primal Scene and the Critical Dystopia," in *The Future of an Illusion: Film, Feminism and Psychoanalysis* (Minneapolis, 1989), 121–39, esp. 130–33.

31 See, for example, Jack Boozer, "Seduction and Betrayal in the Heartland: *Thelma and Louise*," *Film Literature Quarterly* 23 (1995): 188–96, esp. 192; and Sharon Willis, "Hardware and Hardbodies, What Do Women Want?: A Reading of *Thelma and Louise*," in *Film Theory Goes to the Movies*, ed. Jim Collins, Hilary Radner, and Ava Collins (New York, 1993), 120–28, esp. 124.

32 See Cathy Griggers, "*Thelma and Louise* and the Cultural Generation of the New Butch-Femme," in Collins et al., eds., *Film Theory Goes to the Movies*, 129–41, for an inspired account of the relationship that the film develops between sexual preference and material and social conditions.

33 The phrase, like many of the connections to American literature made here, is drawn from Leslie Fiedler, *Love and Death in the American Novel* (New York, 1975), chap. 12.

34 More rare now than in the classical cinema, as Judith Halberstam observes in her comprehensive and insightful "Looking Butch: A Rough Guide to Butches on Film," in *Female Masculinities* (Durham: Duke University Press, forthcoming), where she also discusses Cleo.

35 Cleo lives in a garage—her car is her life—and she cannot imagine living anywhere but the 'hood. To Stony's repeated injunctions that they should leave town, Cleo says, "Can you imagine me in Thousand Oaks or Hollywood?" For her, getting out of town will never involve leaving L.A.

36 Mark Caro, "Alarming Failure," *Chicago Tribune*, 6 November 1996, 5: 1, 7.

37 Vicky Allan, "*Set It Off*," *Sight and Sound* (March 1997): 62.

38 Frankie's death is imbricated with Stony's escape as well, since it prompts Detective Strode's guilt. Kneeling over Frankie's body, he looks up to see Stony in the bus window—and he lets her get away.

Stathis Gourgouris

A Lucid Drunkenness (Genet's Poetics of Revolution)

It has already become customary to infuse the end of the twentieth century with a forward-looking gaze to some abyssal, unknown, but nonetheless impending end (of "history," of "ideology"). Repressed in the allure of this abyssal gaze is the knowledge that the end is measured by a precisely delineated historical past which shadows it completely. While rushing to peer over the other side, we forget that the ground on which we stand is continually slipping along with us. This ground is history's great shadow, animated by the twentieth century's revolutionary foundations, whether we understand them in terms of the explosive legacy of modernism in arts and letters, of microphysics in the world of science, or, most significantly (considering its lasting *aesthetic* power), of the 1917 proletarian revolution in Russia. Although recently bantered about as a category of nostalgia, revolution has become endemic to the twentieth century as much by virtue of historical fact as by virtue of a

The *South Atlantic Quarterly* 97:2, Spring 1998.
Material in this article is forthcoming from Stanford University Press in *Literature as Theory (for an Antimythical Era)* by Stathis Gourgouris and appears here by permission of the publisher. No portion of the text may be reproduced without permission from Stanford University Press.

certain historical pride. Witness to the twentieth century's claim to be the century of revolution, of revolutionary magnitude, is the extensive refiguration of the so-called Age of Revolution (the late eighteenth century) into its immediate progenitor. Be it agent of salvation or of destruction, the presence of the Enlightenment in the twentieth century has emerged, via an extraordinary accumulation of research and contemplation, as the *Ursprung* of modernity.

But the matter is burdened with a peculiar subversion of standard calendrical time by history itself. Although the end of this century is now aggravated by millenarian obsessions (the most amusing manifestation in a forest of sinister visions being Washington's recent pleas for a "Millennium Bug Czar" to take the kinks of the *oo* out of the federal computing system), its actual meaning is indelibly marked by the event and outcome that cut across its midpoint: the Second World War. This extraordinary occurrence, obviously rooted in the century's revolutionary origins but also raising against them the formidable presence of a monster child, launched a series of events that rapidly cascaded on each other's radical signification. The new technology of mass extermination (death camps, hydrogen bomb) posed the global dilemma of "socialism or barbarism" more desperately and concretely than the slogan's revolutionary genealogy (political and aesthetic), which harked back to the century's infancy. Against the century's revolutionary foundations, global history since the late 1940s has been directed toward an ever more expansive manifestation of the epistemic power of revolution, which, as Hannah Arendt readily recognized some thirty-five years ago, has exceeded and outlived every one of its various ideological justifications.[1] Under the logic of mass extermination, the world exploded and steadily overturned the terminology of order on all fronts, identifiable in turn by a multitude of names: decolonization, national liberation, civil disobedience, anti-imperialism, youth culture, cultural revolution, antiwar movement, racial and sexual liberation, urban warfare, ecological resistance.

Probably nothing since the era of New World discovery can compare with the geographic and geopolitical upheaval that characterized the postwar era. Nor was there ever such an extensive social and cultural rearrangement as has occurred in the last fifty years. National borders and cultural boundaries have been drawn, redrawn, and erased with a stunning range of violence, analogous in fact to internal lines of sociocultural definition being challenged, destroyed, and reconstructed. In a peculiar sense, the twentieth century actually begins at its halfway point, which means it must be measured in terms of its half-life (oddly appropriate considering that one of its exclusive contributions to history is the irreversible impact of the so-called atomic age). Or, more accurately, the twentieth century begins twice: first as a categorically revolutionary era, then again as an era of annihilation. There is a double origin at work, with all the paradoxical consequences that implies. A second origin by definition cannot claim the total authority of origin as such. It can neither be nor erase the source of its significance—in this case, the mark of a social (and cultural) order authorized and often actually achieved by revolutionary action.

On the other hand, a second origin implies a weakness in the first, a literal lack of determination. By the very interruption it incurs, a second origin draws the limit space of the first, a finite space that comes about if only by virtue of establishing a sequence of numbers. In this respect, the second origin assumes a determinant force simultaneously cast backward and forward in history, which is to say that it takes over the reins of signification in all directions, for what has been and what has to be. With its revolutionary foundations thus unerasable, the twentieth century reemerged at its halfway point with all the elements of an other. The epistemic effect of World War II consists in its having inserted next to the legacy of revolution the real experience of annihilation, which was, moreover, concretely recognized as a global reality.[2] From that point on, revolution and annihilation, as antagonistic epistemic agents implying each other's coherence, would permeate global reality in an unprecedented way. And the twentieth century, cut in half and reconstituted as a radiating half-life, finally came to be as a disturbance of life's relation to time: the legacy of a double origin and, consequently, of the simultaneous circularity and termination that contaminates both origin and telos. What distinguishes this century is the enormous political and epistemological radiation from events that, though long concluded, remain curiously alive, feeding on a frenetically unfolding present that allegedly erases them.

To speak, therefore, of the late twentieth century as an already present condition of the future is to fail to engage its historical essence. It is not only to impose an end on a historical condition that renders all teleology problematic, but also to commit the grave error of exorcising the ambiguous presence of a determinant double past by rhetorically invoking an insubordinate late development. Often, "late twentieth century" bears an affinity to "late capitalism," which describes the current state of a global economics (as a departure from the industrial capitalism that preceded it) whose own historical existence more or less testifies to a post–World War II phenomenon. In this respect, "late capitalism" denotes the particular economic condition of the twentieth century as such, not its alleged late phase. Thus in terms of both global history and global economics, "late twentieth century" is a shadowy term, suggesting a phantom era in mourning for a time that has not actually taken place. Any insistence on holding the "late twentieth century" in place, in order to study it beyond mere rhetorical usefulness, is frustrated by its affinity with the decaying body of time it is leaving behind: a so-called twentieth century whose origin and duration are themselves unstable notions.

In any case, no credible argument can be made against the generative role that revolution has played in the century's imaginary, whether it spans five or ten decades. One of the lessons of the twentieth century is that the symbolic universe of revolution seems bound to outlive its history. Whatever erasure was signified by countless statues of Lenin being torn down along with the Berlin Wall was matched by the recent exhumation of Che Guevara's bones that brought his disembodied symbolic presence back into history. Those who have pronounced *revolution* a dead word in our time are nevertheless bound to perceive the recent flurry of worldwide media reports on Che (both image and history having been recounted with relish and in detail) as one more commercial exercise in postmodern nostalgia. Such pronouncements may even serve genuine political ends, but they are predicated on maintaining a belief in politics as a domain of instrumental efficacy by repressing the knowledge of politics as a boundless arena of antagonistic imaginaries whose historical terms may be precisely documented, but whose resolution remains largely unpredictable and open to historical accident.

The epistemic significance of revolution belongs to the second domain. If revolution has any meaning at all—if those countless lives lost in its name do leave behind a demand on history that cannot be outmaneuvered—it is because revolution makes palpable, often against the grain of reality, humanity's capacity to alter its own destiny, its own understanding of itself. The revolutionary project is profoundly a matter of cognition, of gaining knowledge into self and other, often at the price of death. Perhaps this is why the degree of symbolic weight borne by the Marxist tradition in the twentieth century is matched by that of psychoanalytic theory and practice. If nothing else, the coinciding of the century's entrance into the stream of time and a theory of the human imagination's opening itself up to the world of the unconscious (i.e., the 1900 publication of Freud's *Interpretation of Dreams*) is uncannily emblematic. And although Freud's own life and testament covers the entire period before the century's definitive occurrence (in my terms), the psychoanalytic project generated a fallout of such magnitude as to become the means of detecting the parameters of this century's half-life. Certainly, Freud's last major works aspire to make psychoanalysis accountable to the work of culture itself, to lend the psychoanalytic project a broader epistemological foundation that would ultimately direct its insight into the unconscious mind toward society's drives of collective perversion, self-destructive totemism, failed sublimation.

The grand overturning of order that signifies the twentieth century in my view occurred in the most extreme terms possible—those of a death culture springing from the name of Culture, consistent with Freud's warnings in *Civilization and Its Discontents*, though inordinately greater than his most unconscious fears (if only because this overturning exposed the death drive of Culture as residing in the most refined folds of the European tradition). The psychoanalytic project entered the domain of "social science" at the point when the historical workings of death culture (whether the decade-long, systematic buildup of the Holocaust and the Gulag or the instant of the flash over Hiroshima) exceeded all "scientific" explanation as social phenomena. Thus, while not linked directly to the imaginary of revolution (like, say, Marxist epistemology), psychoanalysis remains central, for it engages with the knowledge of disorder and hence with humanity's prospects for dissolution and alteration. It does so despite the profound ethnographic prejudices incorporated in its legacy by virtue of Freud's extraordinary narcissistic daring in putting his own dreams and fantasies under the scope of a "scientific" inquiry with universalist aspirations. Indeed, nothing demonstrates the revolutionary potential of psychoanalysis more than the plasticity of its terminology, which has remained foregrounded in even the most radical theorizations that put the narcissistic and prejudicial fantasies of psychoanalysis into question.

And yet the actuality of revolution—the concrete sense of reality that becomes perceptible in the overwhelming dream-life of everyone who experiences a revolutionary situation—is simply beyond the cognitive realm of either Marxist or psychoanalytic epistemology in a strict sense. In its sublime turbulence and transience, the revolutionary moment consists of one's encounter with society's radical imagination: the abyssal domain from which humanity's creative/destructive capacities are unleashed, beyond logic and intention, prudence and fear—beyond the recognized limits of self. From this perspective, all (possibly profound) insights into a revolutionary situation according to Marxist or psychoanalytic categories of explication are essentially retroactive constructions. They cannot be otherwise because, in order to do justice to the radical creative/destructive imaginary inherent in a revolutionary experience, they must encounter it with the same radical capacity to create an object anew. This must literally be a *poetic* encounter. If the revolutionary project is a matter of cognition—in the (blank) face of annihilation and the indeterminate violence of self-alteration—then it is a matter of *poetic cognition*, of a synthetic and not analytic, an allusive and not demonstrable, understanding. In the final instance, societies control their destinies to the extent that they recognize the effects of their own mythopoetic production. This task is as much a matter of political action as it is a matter of a culture's capacity for self-reflection.

Let me submit these elliptical remarks as an overture to my perhaps contestable choice to address the significance of Marxism and psychoanalysis in the late twentieth century by way of a man who engaged revolutionary experience, without apology, as a fundamentally poetic experience—indeed, as a poetic project. My underlying assumption here is that a poetic sensibility is essential to any radical enterprise that seeks, without compromise, to topple a recognized order of self and other. Because a revolutionary project must mobilize, by definition, a highly inventive and unpredictable process of *self-propelled othering*, a radiating poetic force must always burn at the heart of such a project, even if not entirely understood, even if not (as is most often the case) entirely under control. Regardless of a given revolutionary project's particular social-historical parameters, political objectives, and ideological demands—all of which are both fundamental and outmaneuverable—a poetic praxis operates at its core, whether modern history's "professional" revolutionaries acknowledge it or not.

This is not to say that poets make revolution, let alone that poets make stalwart revolutionaries; simply invoking history's memory of Rimbaud should put the matter to rest. But it is to say, against the grain of our tendency to subject the puzzling moments of social disorder to the calming order of "scientific" analysis, that a poetic apprehension of the world should be given precedence when it comes to the (perhaps puzzling) enterprise of revolution. Marx himself, honest enough to recognize the primacy of Balzac in the enterprise of social analysis, was often given to poetic methods in his own work, of which the *Eighteenth Brumaire of Louis Bonaparte* remains a superlative instance. Such poetic engagement with history signifies a necessary understanding of society's mythological nucleus behind every concrete historical action. It concerns and addresses society's *mythistorical* foundations, and therefore, as a matter of method and not vocation, it is not the sole privilege of poets.[3] One can argue that Dostoyevsky's *Crime and Punishment* or *The Possessed* provides the most articulate and synthetic insight into what accounted for the eventual outbreak of the Russian Revolution or, by the same token, that Jules Michelet's grand story of the French Revolution (or of France in general) is equally animated by a spirit of inventive (poetic) understanding. Coming to terms with society's radical imagination (the creative/destructive force of self-alteration) demands that mythistorical knowledge be accessed, and it requires poetic thought, irrespective of any ongoing ideological manipulations.

It may sound paradoxical, but considering that the revolutionary legacy of the twentieth century was not fully realized until it encountered the silencing power of annihilation, this actually echoes Theodor Adorno's famous warning that poetry after Auschwitz is barbarism. The echo is negative yet in this sense consistent with Adorno's terms. In *Negative Dialectics,* he will revise and dramatize his thought by recognizing "the right of the tortured man to scream," thereby attributing to poetry the defiance of all syntax. Of course, his invective against the ongoing legitimacy of lyric plenitude once annihilation has been itself legitimized remains intact. Yet, in this double conception, Adorno's thought contains the grammar of history brushing it against the grain. As history tells it, the privilege of the world of the lyric subject is annihilated, but its relation to the radical imagination is not abolished. Rather, it is reconfigured so as to open itself up to what is most radically external, beyond all syntax, to whatever does not speak. After Auschwitz comes poetry's second origin. And in this respect, next to Paul Celan stands Jean Genet.

Obviously, Genet problematizes the figure of the witness exemplified by Celan's poetics, which takes Adorno's doubt at its most literal and thus opens it up to its full extent. Genet is a quintessentially vagrant figure whose passage through the terrain of the twentieth century effects a strange amalgamated testimony to both survival and mutation. He makes for a case study in survival against all odds as well as a story of profound asociality: the trajectory of a voyage against society itself. If this figure has any consistency at all, it is as a witness to displacement and mutability—social, political, sexual, geographical. Bastard, thief, homosexual, and vagabond are Genet's avowed personae, never to be domesticated or socialized, who testify to society's disappearance. Few artists recognized so radically that their authority was first and foremost a construction by an other, conferred upon them by the enemy (social convention), but in this respect usable as a weapon for killing the authorized self along with the entire domain of values that made it possible. Countless times in countless interviews, Genet repeated that he became a writer in order to get out of prison and that his literary authority was a sham, unworthy of conversation yet useful to those who had no voice to expose the sham they were actually living. Even his "sainthood," invented by Jean-Paul Sartre, who made him famous and therefore powerful, was something that Genet rejected and unmasked by showing the world sainthood's fundamental debilitation: he stopped writing literature for nearly thirty years. Genet was fond of simultaneously showing the real impotence of power together with its capacity for annihilation. A rare witness to the twentieth century's core antagonism between revolution and annihilation, he was all the more rare for knowing no guilt and seeking no artistic redemption.

But Genet also epitomizes the twentieth century's double life. By virtue of being abandoned to the public domain shortly after his birth in 1910, Genet became committed to a life on the margins, where subsocieties, always tenuous and artificially kept together (often with force), challenge the very legitimacy that society provides by perpetuating their institution. Orphanage, foster care, reform school, prison, the army: all defined Genet's communal experience up through adulthood—the institutional safeguards against the dangers of excess that Enlightenment society must identify, name, and circumscribe in order to control the means of producing boundaries of legality. Genet's particular trajectory through these socially constructed outsides was aggravated by his intransigent and guiltless homosexuality, which became the basis for his lifelong pursuit of an intuitive philosophical conceptualization of criminality. Genet's explicit theorization of the consubstantial nature of writer and criminal, beyond the codified romantic attributes of *le poète maudit*, is the key to deciphering both the glorious negation of his early work and the surrealistic affirmation of his late work, where the revolutionary replaces the criminal.

The nearly thirty-year chasm between early and late work, which not only proves insurmountable to his biographers and critics, but also explodes the category of mature work beyond recognition, suggests that Genet, like the twentieth century he so oddly shadowed, is marked by a double origin. In the first phase, essentially ending in 1949 with his official pardon by the State, we see a thief who became a master of the French language (though a school dropout at twelve) and an auteur of the first order in a process that remained utterly mysterious and incomprehensible to the very end.[4] What is so stunning about this period is the five prose works produced in rapid succession (as well as the debut of poems in the tradition of François Villon) that scandalized the intellectual and artistic community of Paris (Cocteau and Sartre, notably) not merely by their unabashed *criminal* nature (the lives of prisoners, prostitutes, thieves, murderers, and queers), but by their extraordinary literariness—all the more shocking and eloquent as the voice of criminality itself.[5] With these texts, the criminal became an author by taking command of the panoply of culture, which had condemned him to a life of crime, in order to transform that life into an object of culture: "The language I know best . . . is the one in which I was condemned. The tribunals pronounced my condemnation speaking French."[6] Genet recognized the paradoxical truth that in a society founded on the rights of man—of man sanctioned by law—the language of culture conquered territories beyond the reach of the language of law, the language of what is right. So, when he fashioned his criminal life into a work of art without shame, the underside of the law was suddenly graced with the emancipatory language of literary scandal.

Genet's legal emancipation and initial literary recognition coincided with the oddity of his proclaimed "sainthood," which Sartre predicated on the choice of a criminal life that society had granted him. There is a certain truth to this existentialist formulation, but the secret of Genet's making himself into something already conceived by the enemy was much more theatrical than existential—a matter of maquillage, not morality. Impersonation was one of his fundamental principles; an intrinsically decentered and performative sense of self lent itself to exploiting social roles by embodying them in an externalizing gesture. This author originated in self-copying from life to "stage"—a process that exploded both the original copying mold (the process of reproduction) and the framework of exhibition. Thus did Genet the bastard/thief/homosexual/vagabond become a literary figure. But literary status entailed a new life of legality (citizenship) that made the literary enterprise difficult by making it irrelevant. Genet's achievement of the social legitimacy that art assures deprived him of the *paranomic* legitimacy (criminality) of writing. The result was a decade of confusion and an occasional sense of impotence during which he nevertheless sealed his extraordinary literary presence with a dynamic, if continually self-subverting, foray into the theater. This poetic outburst against and beyond the mythification of his person was the last flash of the criminal imagination against symbolic authority, the concentrated dregs of excess. But it also buried Genet deeper, under a heavier weight of legitimacy: art's legitimate subversion of social order, which he, a criminal, recognized as a glorious sham. During the 1950s, just when the twentieth century was reconstituting itself under the logic of annihilation, Genet set out to annihilate his literary persona, initially by producing a stylized meta-theater that short-circuited the aesthetic alibi of theatricality itself, then by reducing himself to the silence he thought he (and his work) deserved. He thereby denounced in no uncertain terms the fraudulent status of his legend, which produced no gravity of art but only the novelty of an illicit show, no proper readers but merely scandalized voyeurs:

> I don't have readers but thousands of voyeurs who spy on me from the window that gives onto the stage of my personal life. . . . And I'm sickened by this interest that is awakened by the scandalous person I used to be. I wish that people would leave me alone. I want to start something entirely new. I do not want people to talk about me, nor do I want newspapers to publish things about my work. I want to be finished with this legend.[7]

Out of this explicit self-annihilation emerged another Genet: the extinguished poet who would grant his legendary name and the legitimacy of his illegitimate past life to those who criminalized themselves in the act of fashioning a revolutionary language from the social void, deterritorialized or simply groundless. The death of Abdallah, arguably Genet's dearest lover, marked the turning point, beginning with a failed act of self-annihilation (Genet's suicide attempt in 1967). The coincidental sense of personal void and radical overthrow of reality that prevailed during the late 1960s was one which Genet, existing entirely outside the bounds of his generation, could embrace with genuine clarity and passion. At this point of utter personal emptiness, of zero-degree self-reference, he achieved the selflessness required to grant one's signature to the voice of another, which culminated in his return to the authority of literature in his last work, the last remnant of his life, *Un Captif amoureux*. Published a month after Genet's death in 1986, it is nominally a chronicle/memoir of his voyage to an avowedly alien terrain and resurrection from self-annihilation (a revivification that began with the animating events of May '68). Genet experienced life again in the Black Panther community during a two-month period of illegal residence in the United States (spring 1970) and then in the company of Palestinian fedayeen at Jordanian camps where he made several visits over approximately fifteen months between 1970 and 1972.[8]

At first glance, *Un Captif amoureux* is an amalgam of memories of an eccentric involvement in two communities conceived on the basis of—and committed to—the precarious existence of revolutionary thought and action, an existence haunted by the imminence of death. This project had a deep ontological dimension, due not least to Genet's knowledge that he was dying of throat cancer. To understand the ontological stake, we need to consider the particular conditions of the text's historical genesis, namely, what made Genet return to literature after deliberately cultivating self-erasure.

While his experiences with the Black Panthers and the Palestinians profoundly affected Genet and spearheaded a long-term devotion to the political essay as the only "legitimate" mode of writing (due to its immediate use-value in the political arena),[9] they failed to coalesce into any artistic expression, even in the limit-sense of the term, despite Genet's often agonizing desire and the copious notes he made. The turning point this time was his accidentally witnessing the immediate aftermath of the Sabra and Shatila massacres in September 1982; "Quatre heures à Chatila," a celebrated piece that strips history bare with stunning lyricism and the passion of immediacy, appeared about four months after these events.[10] This extraordinary experience of annihilation, dramatized by the historical accident of his presence in nearby Beirut, which brought Genet's personal wanderings into perfect coincidence with history's merciless dismantling of the limits of the personal, produced a poetic encounter with the violence of the world, his first in decades. Yet another encounter with Adorno's aporia of poetry's (or life's) possibility after Auschwitz, Genet's response to history's inarticulate pain amidst the heaps of ruined bodies in Shatila must have included responding to his own puzzlement over his daring to act as history's mythopoetic agent without succumbing to the narcissism of the poet–revolutionary.

Within two years, the long-envisioned book about his Palestinian experiences had been composed entirely from scratch—from those shards of memory that the experience of massacred life had rekindled. The palpable presence of annihilation sparked a poetic invocation of revolutionary life dormant in the cells of memory as a powerful love experience. What makes *Un Captif amoureux* formidable from the outset—before we even get drawn into the great mythistorical intricacies of the writing—is its being at once a work of love-affirmed life (of love for and by the world's constructed others) and a work of mourning (for the death of those named in its pages and the nameless multitude massacred in Shatila, for the death by cancer that was to finalize the trajectory of Jean Genet, the witness).[11]

Genet's first literary publication in twenty years, affirming life and glorifying finitude in the same gesture, proved to be animated by the same explicit desire to disrupt the public's complacency that had characterized his work throughout. Against the backdrop of the voyeuristic devouring of his scandalous name, the text's force—its annihilation of the fetish "Genet"—derives from binding the authorial persona into a love encounter with otherness in the process of signifying itself, that is, in a process of revolution, itself an encounter between the historical and the mythological. Genet had become a celebrity by self-consciously cultivating the criminal persona that would animate the mythological world of his fiction; he could even be said to have fictionalized "Genet," who then became real in his novels. He articulated this principle in describing the *Thief's Journal* as a work "meant to indicate what I am today, as I write it. It is not a quest of time gone by [*une recherche du temps passé*], but a work of art whose pretext–subtext is my former life."[12] The obvious Proustian reference ought to resound against the split of one's life before and after fictionalization (or pre- and post-authorized existence, from the viewpoint of the criminal). Proust realized that one's life must be brought to an end if life is to be achieved in fiction or, even more, if fiction is to be given life in the most concrete sense. His fiction, therefore, became a chronicle of and memorial to this double death-and-life process, much as his corklined room became a space of self-entombment (or what would be self-imprisonment in Genet's terms) that enabled the generation of life in fiction, the birth of authorial vocation. Like Proust, to whose genius he explicitly aspired, Genet put into practice the risk of knowing language's incapacity to bring the moment of experience back to life, of language's marking, if anything, the death-moment of experience signified by what we call memory. He understood from Proust that the time of autobiography is always present-time and that this memorial service for a life long gone whose void energizes the creation of life anew is a veritable act of poiesis during which the authorial persona erases itself in being reinvented as the subject of mythical history, as legend. The *Thief's Journal* is probably the most explicitly Proustian of Genet's works, similarly involved in a poetic *sur-vie,* the legendary overstepping of life as fiction-in-the-making.

Writing against the name of his prison novels, Genet understood his last work as a continuation nonetheless of the project begun with the *Thief's Journal,* where the reality of an already legendary existence reaches its poetic culmination in the always present tense of being read: "I refuse to live for any other end than the very one which I found to contain the first misfortune: that my life must be a legend, in other words, legible, and that the reading of it must give birth to a certain new emotion I call poetry." The thief-become-poet here declares, "I am no longer anything, only a pretext."[13] Desiring to foster a poetic experience with his last work, Genet revisited his signature rhetorical figures and staging techniques (impersonation, betrayal, gesture, masquerade, transsexuality, chance), except that the *autography* composed here is not limited to some sort of theatrical identicide but dares the full range of a cultural mythography.[14] In the end, a radical and undeconstructible difference between Genet's previous work and this one makes *Un Captif amoureux* a prism through which his life-work can be assessed. If Genet's life was once the self-avowed pretext for writing himself out of prison, the writing of his last work was the gift of life to Jean Genet, thief no longer, who had to steal once more—from death. (As he said himself, "I've never helped the Palestinians. They've helped me to live."[15]) *Un Captif amoureux* was literally a matter of life for Genet, of affirming life in the knowledge of imminent death—not merely life "within" the singularity of the body, however, but life out there in the world: collective, amorphous, ephemeral.

This love of worldly life coalesced into a poetic core in the face of the dramatic finality of Shatila, when Genet realized that what had kept him alive since his suicide attempt was being held captive by a love that circumvented the usual identitary mirroring. The English translation of the title, *Prisoner of Love*,[16] misses the multiple nuances of the French: not only a prisoner of love but also a prisoner *in* love, this prisoner is both captured and captivated by love. The thief who fashioned himself as scandalous poetic myth in order to extricate himself from prison and then courageously acknowledged the irrelevance of his art in a "free life" here discovers, at the point of death, a way to reassume the value and art of poetic creation by fashioning a self-determined captivity in the deterritorialized or groundless domain of society's others. What makes his discovery possible is an element that permeates all of Genet's work, not unlike a thread weaving together his double origin: the polemical attitude he never abandoned even at his most despondent, even when he abandoned literature. Indeed, that very abandonment of literature, drawn in and held to particular circumstances (never as a matter of abstract principle, ethical or aesthetic), was polemical: "I don't know why Rimbaud chose silence. I said that he had understood why he had no choice but silence. As for me, since all my books were written in prison, it seems I have written them in order to get out of prison. Outside of prison, writing had no more reason to be. My books did get me out of the slammer, but afterwards, what is there to say?" But this is not a casual matter, despite the tone. On the contrary, Genet's application to the writing of literature was total, tirelessly driven by a rare obsessional energy, yet equally meticulous, his extraordinary mastery of the literary language being a conscious stratagem: "to make sure that those whom I call 'my torturers' understand me."[17]

If the reason for writing was to get out of prison, the purpose of writing was to address the social institution that made prison possible, not out of any desire for mercy, vindication, or even confession (as "autography" precludes the credibility of confession, for it exposes its inherent performativity). Genet succeeded in making classical French the language of scandalous matter as a polemical gesture. More than a case of the subaltern taking on the master's language, it was a gesture of simply speaking to the master in his own language, the reality of his language. It made no difference that, as Genet hastened to add, "the real torturers don't read me . . . they don't give a fuck," for his aim was wider and more ambitious. When this aesthetically correct language was subjected to syntactical unpredictability, which turned the rules of logical or moral subordination inside out, the trivial and perverse was made to bear its full glory. Criminal literature would force the dominant culture to encounter its own lawless underside in its own exalted language. "Perhaps," suggested Genet, "writing is what's left to you when you've been chased off from your given language [*la parole donnée*]"[18]—which is also to say, when you have been deprived of whatever authority enables you to give your word. The outcome, in effect, is that you become literary when you are no longer able to be credible. Discredited by reality, you cannot survive except by becoming a legend—or legible by other means.

Genet never lost that sense of being socially discredited even when he knew he had accumulated considerable artistic capital and could extend his credit to the world's disenfranchised. His nomadic existence, moving from hotel to hotel—his refusal to own property or allow himself a domestic life, a permanent home—was symptomatic of the sense of homelessness and asociality he felt he had inherited from birth. But it was also a chosen condition of "social irresponsibility" that enabled his "immediate social engagement."[19] This clearly anomalous pairing of social irresponsibility and engagement defies all ethical categorization, at least in terms of any post-Enlightenment ethics, but it is the key to understanding Genet's power. This radical provisionality (the other side of immediacy), as Edward Said has argued, characterizes Genet's words in all contexts due to "his unceasing search for the freedom of the negative identity that reduces all language to empty posturing, all action to the theatrics of a society he abhors."[20] The provisional word, taking the place of the given word, discredits the discourse of promise (foundational to both Kantian ethics and bourgeois liberal politics), a position that Genet would eventually come to hold in full consciousness of its risks and consequences.

On this basis, Genet found love in the ranks of communities that were socially and politically deprived of promise or, more accurately, communities with a long history of being at the wrong end of society's promises, having been broken by promises, and, if I may indulge, robbed of a promised land. If there is a central impetus to *Un Captif amoureux*, a book without a center in an unprecedented sense, it would have to be Genet's desire to approach, through literary language, the imaginary terrain of a people without territory—not exactly a desire to approach the territory of the Other (as a politically correct reading of Genet would inevitably conclude) but to poetically chronicle the plenitude of the (collective) self of the Other as it arises from the experience of social groundlessness or deterritorialization. (Parenthetically, the paradoxical notion of a *poetic chronicle* suggests both historical account and historical invention, and it cannot be otherwise: the history of the Other cannot be written as truth, but only as poetry.) One of the first things Genet realized about the Palestinians was that their territorial dispossession had mobilized a national imaginary where none had been necessary before, a self-representation as an autonomous entity in a phantasmatic world of plenitude and poetic pleasure manifested as revolutionary force.[21] Autonomy in the domain of fantasy—the national imaginary—is dramatically achieved without national territory. Indeed, it is the prerequisite for gaining an autonomous territory, although it guarantees neither that territorial acquisition nor any actual autonomy upon its acquisition, upon nationhood.[22]

In a much-discussed passage of *Un Captif amoureux*, Genet describes witnessing a group of Palestinian fedayeen playing a card game with an uncanny degree of formality, with the dreary ceremony of a tennis match. In the course of his meticulous description, he refers to the Japanese ceremony of *Obon*, in which the dead are treated to a taste of the world of the living via an entire community's acting out their clumsy encounters with the bodily complexity of life. The ceremony culminates in tenderly mocking laughter by the living, who, with irony and affection, have briefly brought those immobile skeletal features to life. Genet then goes on casually to inform the astonished reader: "The game of cards, which only existed because of the scandalously realistic gestures of the fedayeen—they'd played at playing, without any cards, without aces or knaves, clubs or spades, kings or queens—reminded me that all the Palestinians' activities were like the *Obon* feast, where the only thing missing, exacting such solemnity in a smile, was whatever must not become apparent."[23] Here, reality meets its match in a performance of the imaginary that casts lack as the vehicle of affirmation, of self-representation, without ever shadowing, in this perfect masquerade, the actuality of lack.

Genet considers this incident emblematic of the experience of dispossession and its consubstantiation with the fantasy of autonomy that doubly exemplifies the revolutionary's ghostly daily life at the border of death. There are immediate destructive consequences to such disembodying, "for to play only with gestures when your hands ought to be holding . . . all the symbols of power makes you feel a fraud, and brings you close to schizophrenia. Playing cards without cards every night is a kind of dry masturbation."[24] The ritual magnification of territorial dispossession and deprivation of symbolic power in a conspiratorial collective show of empty gestures becomes a vacant exercise in self-reference, without pleasure, when not accompanied by any actual reversal of the real conditions of lack and dispossession—hence Genet's fundamental differentiation between the realms of art and revolution (to which we shall return). While charmed by this performance (for he values such theatrics of gesture highly), Genet also recognizes its cost—absorption into abyssal nonexistence. "The cards were neither present nor absent. For me they were like God: they didn't exist. . . . The end of the game was its beginning: nothing at the start and nothing at the finish. . . . Their gestures were in danger of becoming useless according to the law of the theater: they were substituting the rehearsal for the performance. . . . Absence was in their hands just as it was under their feet."[25] Everything infuses such a disembodied existence, in which even the most objective materiality is absence (of land, of nation, of victory, of reception, of play, of object), a fully incorporated absence that permeates the entire horizon of life. And yet, this extraordinary image of death rehearsal preoccupies Genet because it also exemplifies, to an almost theoretic degree, the fact that a politics of dispossession and deterritorialization is a theatrical politics, specifically, a politics of impersonation.

Impersonation is a crucial principle in Genet's work, operating both as performative device and as ontological exigency. From his earliest stage of self-consciousness, he recognized that he inhabited—indeed, embodied—a falsity according to bourgeois society's standard measures of truth. Bearing the matrilineal name left the father not merely absent and unknown, but unsignified. The name of the father is a literally empty sign, not just devoid of power but a voided identification, making Genet a man without heritage, without proper law (and, of course, without property). Signified by a negative Oedipal naming, Genet bore the mother's name as his legal identity in a society that organized its laws of identity and property around the father's name.[26] Moreover, his already disjointed genealogy was further ruptured when the original bearer of his name promptly abandoned him to a terrifying singularity. This man without proper law, this false son, was then reborn into the law of the State, a foundling registered with the Assistance publique, and from then on consistently encumbered with false origins, a false family, a false village.

Many years later he would declare himself "a Black in white or pink skin color, but a Black nonetheless. I do not know my family."[27] A man whose lineage has been appropriated and erased like that of African slaves may recognize the contingent authority of skin color, but this isn't to imply any failure to understand that his privileged recognition by the world at large (particularly White America) was not for being White, especially given Genet's exploitation of his privileged status to support the Black Panthers. What enabled him to answer the Panthers' call without hesitation was his sense of the permeable boundaries of self as abolishing the condition of mirroring from the encounter with the Other and exposing the "mysteries" of identification. In the absence of prescribed boundaries, the encounter must be staged anew each time—a theatrical experience of the other that defined Genet's life and work. Unconstrained by pressures of identification, he could abandon himself to the Black Panther family like a child: "What did it mean, my pink and white presence among them? This: for two months I was to be David's son. I had a Black father thirty years younger than myself. . . . He was very careful with me, as if my weakness had somehow made me dear."[28] It is impossible not to recognize in this self-amused narration the genuine pleasure of being fathered—and in the most appropriate fashion: a Black father for a child with a black past, now a world-worn man well into his sixties turning to the innocent selflessness of a thirty-year-old utopian whose experience of the world had been a strictly enforced one of the margin. Not to make too much of it, but Genet was quite conscious of the theatrical play of identities in this case, not least the particular inflection his homosexuality gave to this paternal projection onto a man who was inevitably locked into the Panthers' collective production of images of virile masculinity: David Hilliard, the party's national chief of staff, who served as Genet's personal guide. Prior to articulating this recognition of being fathered, Genet jokes about Hilliard as his mother (referring to the tender care he once gave the flu-ridden visitor)—to the great amusement of the Panthers, which prompts an astonishing passage:

> They often amused themselves by mixing up the sexes and catching grammar out in sexism, but their whole block and tackle, perfectly molded, was much in evidence through their trousers. It was a long time before the sculpture was exploited. I mean as power. The Blacks'

> natural, though to the Whites excessive, virility was perceived as exhibitionism, but was aimed at none other than the exhibitionist profusion of White bosoms at parties given for the Panthers. . . . In any event, trousers were cut in an almost Florentine style, and the doctrine was expounded in an ostentatious manner. Logically enough, the Blacks had moved on from line engraving to sculpture in the round.[29]

The earlier invocation of Hilliard as "mother," while operating in several discursive registers, does not abolish his fatherly function; on the contrary, Genet, a resolute orphan, would seek to reconstitute the symbolic presence of both parental figures, while the Oedipal antagonism between them would be quite useless to him at this stage. (In view of Genet's noting the diffusion of sexual signifiers at play among the Panthers in their daily modes of address and self-identification, we can surmise the amusing overtones evoked by association with the exclamatory use of "mother" in Black slang.) The passage quoted above reveals Genet's astute perception of the gender-bending play in Black Panther language as arising from a masculinist confidence, a theatrical alienation-effect that tempers, in the luxury of in-house relations, the rigorous exigencies of performative virility in the White world. This sort of arguably innocent linguistic transvestism (innocent because it does not go far enough and cannot bear the full burden of its assumptions, understandably, given the social-historical conditions of its enunciation) points nonetheless to the explosive and unceasing performativity of the Black Panther community. Although Genet gives away his political preferences by slipping into naturalist terminology, he still manages to convey a sense of the plasticity of this collective language. So-called Panther rhetoric, a notorious kind of word-mongering that wreaked havoc in the discursive marketplace, was essentially an imagistic device, sharing in the general symbolic havoc that the Panthers performed with evident relish. But what Genet unveils, with delicate irony, is a discourse that has historically drawn the most formidable and inviolable lines of battle—straight lines of difference—while also pursuing internally a sensual roundness: in clichéd terms, a phallic geography aimed at the enemy that marks a terrain of borderless inclusion for its own.

The political logic behind this dichotomy was the necessity for a Black revolution to disrupt the age-old mastery over the signification of *Black* and *White*, the manifest racial antagonism of which had always been specifically sexualized. The major battlefield for the Panthers was precisely this terrain of symbolic signification, which Genet recognized right off, perhaps against the grain of the Panthers' own image as revolutionaries aspiring to speak less with their symbolic presence than with their guns. The revolutionary work was entirely theatrical: the appropriation of the master's idiom to serve the spectacular manipulation of meaning by which war is waged at the level of the image. The Panthers' campaign was particularly shocking to bourgeois America because these extravagant, otherworldly Black men with guns were a step ahead of the media age; they were too big, too excessive, for a 1970s mass-media frame designed to appropriate and neutralize challenges to the symbolic system (which was why the Panthers were more or less picked off one by one, as single targets containable only within the frame of a gun barrel). Their spectacular intervention in the more general spectacle was a tragic product of despair, heightened by the real and constant threat of death, of extinction.

Where the Panthers did succeed was in abolishing the canonic invisibility of Blackness in America. As Genet perceived, the Panthers attacked first and foremost by sight. Their major achievement was a theatrically exercised subversion of the historical invisibility of Black Americans by means of an "extravagant but elegant" self-fashioning in such concrete terms (those of dressing reality in a defining way) that their traces remain visible even today. Surely, the aesthetic legacy of "Black is Beautiful," to which the Panthers' performance contributed radical (and thus lasting) features, was not limited to the wide acceptance of Black images of self-representation in popular culture throughout the 1970s, but is also evident in their elaborate revival during the 1990s. At the same time, however, the proliferation of those self-images signaled the disarmament and appropriation of Black radical culture—in effect, its political erasure. Genet's own theatricality enabled him to deconstruct the relation between the Panthers' semiotics of action and the symbolic field that determined their reception. A theatrical performance in the real world provides no safeguard for excess. Reality is unforgiving.[30]

Genet's most dramatic example of reality's harshness toward the symbolic is Hilliard's reluctance to join him at Stonybrook for a lecture on behalf of the Panther cause, obliquely expressed as fear of the local landscape: "There are still too many trees." The oddity of the comment sends Genet down a path of decipherment that goes to the heart of the Black/White divide in America, to the different conceptualizations of the world (or of the social imaginary, we could say) whose original traces are concretely and indelibly historical. For a Black "the sight of a tree revived a terror that was not quite a thing of the past, which left the mouth dry and the vocal chords impotent. . . . What separates us from the Blacks today is not so much the color of our skin or the type of our hair as the phantom-ridden psyche we never see except when a Black, in simultaneously humorous and secretive fashion, drops a phrase that seems to us enigmatic. It not only seems enigmatic; it is so."[31] The enigmatic terrain itself serves as concrete evidence of the radical historical difference marking the two sides in America's race war, with even the most seemingly innocent objects symbolically embodying this historical difference. Symbolic content leaves real traces, and real innocence is overwritten with traces of real guilt. This hard reality is precisely why the Panthers' theatricality had as real an impact as a bullet from a gun ("the Panthers can be said to have overcome through poetry"[32]), but it is also why that proved to be their undoing.

The Panthers were victimized by the materiality of their own phantasms, the same phantasms that gave them their sense of radical difference and, by extension, their revolutionary fearlessness. It is a paradoxical and tragic condition, as most formidable theatrical expressions of society have been through the ages. Genet describes the Panthers as "haunted by fears and fantasies I'd never know except in ironical translation"; "haunted by negatives—'anti'-forces—a rejection of every kind of marginality striving with an equally strong attraction to marginality and its strange ecstasies"; "haunted by the idea of death, which they translated into looting."[33] One recalls Frantz Fanon's realization that "a Negro is forever in combat with his own image,"[34] that is, at some level his image, regardless of the self-fashioning, is not his own. Much of what the Black movements of the 1960s were about involved this agonizing attempt to gain mastery over the production of their own image, ultimately a task of the most radical social imagination—the revolutionary task par excellence. At the level of revolutionary signification, Malcolm's act of X-ing his name is of the same order as the National Assembly proclaiming 1792 "Year One of the Revolution" and abolishing the Christian calendar. The Panthers, however, took to this production of new self-images with such indefatigable, obsessive energy that they were outrun, outperformed, by their own invention. Driven by a reality-theater gone out of control—one which, moreover, aimed to consume the very boundaries of staging—the Panthers caved in under an overproduction of images that exceeded any capacity for self-reflection, as if propelled by an astronomical metabolism that burned the organism's cellular structure to a crisp.

Genet was particularly attuned to this annihilating force of symbols, having already witnessed it on a smaller scale in Paris during the events of May '68 amidst his genuine joy at seeing France dismantled, even briefly. Invigorated perhaps by this joyful revolutionary experience, Genet committed himself to the movement during his two-month sojourn with the Panthers (later staging various solidarity events in Paris as well) with a resolute equanimity in the face of violent confrontation that the Panthers had surely never seen in a White man before. There are two ways of accounting for this: on the basis of (1) Genet's sense of himself as a criminal, and (2) his sense of autonomy due to his uncompromising homosexuality. For the Panthers, Genet's criminality must have endowed him with a palpable credibility. Given their image of rather inflexible sexual politics, however, his homosexuality would likely have been a source of puzzlement. Yet nowhere in Genet's reflections is there the slightest hint of discomfort on either side. His homosexuality figures as unproblematically as his Whiteness, much as it did for Genet in any other context—self-evident, unworthy of discussion. Knowing Genet, there is nothing astonishing in this, nor in his uncensored descriptions of the Panthers' obvious eroticism or their poetic powers, inherent in Black culture (which from another mouth would sound alarming, to say the least). Edmund White devotes some thoughtful pages of his biography to this issue, reporting that Genet never hid his erotic desires and even danced in a pink negligee for Hilliard and other Panthers one night after taking a heavier than usual dose of Nembutal (he was a longtime regular user). The Panthers considered this impromptu performance (unusual, even for Genet) a highly theatrical expression of the flexibility of sexual identity, a position then echoed in Huey Newton's famous paper from prison, arguing for greater sensitivity to the gay and women's liberation movements and for the party's solidarity with their positions on the common ground of revolutionary action. Genet, with a characteristic lack of self-importance, considered the Panthers to have much more urgent concerns than his sexual preferences. It is worth noting, however, that the Panthers later invited him to write an article about homosexuality on their behalf, as they considered him the appropriate voice for their position.[35]

The point is not that Genet changed the views of the Black Panthers on the nature and history of sexuality, but that his sense (and performance) of homosexuality—together with his sense of criminality—converged with the performative politics of revolutionizing identity as practiced by both the Black Panthers and the Palestinians. He repeatedly argued that his being a criminal was interwoven with his being a homosexual, and his attitude toward both was absolutely guiltless. The current activist notion of "homosexual culture" would seem absurd to Genet, for he conceived homosexual life as one of continual subversion and alienation, a criminal practice by definition. He saw his own homosexuality as the common language (or vitalizing spinal cord) that informed the criminal trajectory of his life from "bastardhood [to] treason, [to] the refusal of society and finally [to] writing, that is to say, a return to society by other means."[36] As the language of criminality, homosexuality bore the unique pedagogical burden of articulating society's contradictions as well as the means of subverting society's capacity to assimilate contradictions. Homosexuality implied an existential *paranomia* for Genet—not merely a transgression of the law but an existence beside (and besides) the law, a kind of affirmative lawlessness: "The rules are not preexistent in [any] interrogating conscience, nor [written] on some Tablets of the Law. The rules must be invented each time. They are more aesthetic than moral, and it is because they are uncertain that one discovers them—or one invents them. The rules which guide me and that I invent are against rules, I mean against the law."[37]

Any serious study of Genet's sexual politics nowadays would have to come to terms with the apparent contradiction between his astonishing production of avant-garde homosexual literature beginning in the late 1940s and his resolute resistance to engaging in "gay-affirmative" politics, despite a deep generosity toward "antibourgeois" politics all over the globe. I say "apparent contradiction" because in reality there is none. Genet's resistance to the domestication of his sensibility, his militant and unmitigated commitment to articulating the negation of all identity, went hand in hand with his uncompromising homosexuality and has major implications for the discussion of identity politics today. In an extraordinary letter to Sartre (probably from about 1952, when Genet was trying to theorize for himself the irrelevance of writing literature in the context of his freedom and legality), he attempts to articulate a theory of homosexuality, including homosexual imagination in relation to social order.[38] Genet's basic assumption is that homosexuality develops out of the diffuse sexuality of childhood in response to the traumatic realization of death and the existential crisis that arises with adolescence. This crisis gets sublimated not as the pursuit of self-preservation by other means (chiefly biological reproduction, hence heterosexual desire), but rather as the pursuit of endless pleasure on the inevitable way to death, with desire then channeled into funereal representations—rituals of degeneration—that, insofar as they become actions in reality, cannot but provoke society's wrath. "The significance of homosexuality is a refusal to continue the world" and "to alter sexuality" by "struggling against" the world's "useless manliness." Transvestism, Genet argues, does not involve "nostalgia about the idea of the woman one might have been, which [now] feminizes; rather, it's the bitter need to mock virility" by becoming a woman who embodies the incapacity to continue life. In pederastic love, the beloved is invested with desire because (or insofar as) he will have the fate of the lover—a certain death. "The beloved becomes the object ordained to 'represent' *death* (the lover) in life." In this respect, the beloved becomes a double, a reproduced self and bearer of self-reproduction (without an other) who, as Genet repeats throughout this letter, is essentially sterile, hence *antisocial* in a fundamental sense. Insofar as this funereal imaginary does not translate into any concrete action whereby death would become actual (suicide or murder), it is activated as pure imagination, at once erotic and poetic. "The sudden refusal of the responsibility to live" breathes life into either an erotic creation of oneself (whereby "my pleasure will be *endless*") or a poetic creation of this eroticism in language. "A poem is only the *activity* of a funereal theme. It is (definitely) its socialization, a struggle against death. The themes of life propose action and forbid the poem." In other words, poetry obeys the same imaginary of desire as homosexuality, which is against the virility of life and society (in the straight sense of both words) and thus gains—or even generates—a life that society criminalizes and ultimately seeks to destroy. The poetic/erotic imaginary of homosexuality derives from death, but, insofar as it is actualized, provokes a lethal response from society, which then becomes an agent or bearer of death.

What emerges from this improvised theoretization (beyond the sexualizing of death which feminists have theorized as a particularly male obsession) is homosexuality conceived as a bearer of nonidentity and poetic destruction. The former involves a peculiar sidestepping of the self–other determinant relation by an endless nomadic condition of impersonation, the latter a paradoxical act of altering (*othering*) the order of reality by elevating antisocial activities to myth. The two presuppose each other and are in effect intertwined. Genet's work consistently demonstrates that impersonation is the initial act of homosexual love, which is constituted not as a reciprocal relation with the other but as a theatrical staging of the other in oneself. To this extent all of Genet's work is theatrical in the ancient performative sense of poetic activity, as witness the fact that he considered himself a poet (when he did not call himself a thief), never a novelist, a playwright, or an intellectual, culminating in his frequent references to *Un Captif amoureux* as a Homeric work on the model of the *Iliad*. Poetry and homosexuality are ultimately linked by a mutual performativity that presupposes a radical externalization of the imaginary well beyond any identitary concerns. Homosexuality thus yields a poetics of nonidentity—in essence, a poetics against the law, or poetics of criminality—perfectly encapsulated by the two terms with which Said describes Genet's intentions in his play *The Screens*: "gestural impropriety" and "poetic deflagration."[39] Genet's performativity is always improper and incendiary, not in the banal terms of offending bourgeois morality but in undoing the very terms of that morality, its configuration of identity. What the poet performs is always a skewed representation of the world because the world is never settled to begin with; that the world itself is in a continual process of performance is the deepest meaning of its intrinsically conflictual (i.e., political) nature.

If poetry is involved in an impersonation of the real, an attempt to transcribe history's theatricality, it is involved in the imitation of imitation (for Genet, a notion entirely free of the problematics of authenticity). An illustrative incident described in *Un Captif amoureux* shows Genet himself being impersonated by Mubarak, a Black Sudanese officer in the Palestinian corps who serves as an intellectual deflection of Genet's presence in the camps (as well as an implicit link to his experience with the Panthers). A larger-than-life outsider who, unlike Genet, is really on the inside, Mubarak can speak of revolution and Spinoza or of God and dance in a single phrase. Responding to a gesture made by Genet in a mocking imitation of him, Mubarak declares, "Now I'll imitate Jean imitating me," prompting this reaction from the author:

> Seeing yourself in the glass, once you realize the left is on the right, is nothing. Nothing next to seeing yourself there under the trees, with-

> out a mirror, talking and walking about, so cruelly depicted by the voice of the Sudanese, the gestures of his arms, his thighs, his neck, the movements of his whole body. . . . He imitated me [*il me représenta*] going up and down some steps of muddy earth. Thanks to him I saw before me a gigantic figure outlined against an almost black sky, descending in the distance, though nearby, a bit stooped with the weariness of age and from marching up and down hills—a march that became fabulous before me, as high as the clouds over Nablus—limping at the end of the day. The limp was simplified and exaggerated, but just like the way I walked [*fidèle à ma démarche habituelle*]. I realized I was looking at myself for the first time not in the so-called mirror of the psyche but through an eye or eyes that had found me out, not only hill by hill but step by step, stooped over, descending a staircase cut in stone. Everyone had seen me and reconstituted me.[40]

Genet describes his experience of this performance with mixed feelings of cruelty and admiration. The staging forbids any kind of authentic or realistic representation; Mubarak imitates Jean imitating him, thereby impersonating himself through another. Genet may be the object of representation here, embodied in Mubarak's gestures, but he is not an object of reflection; he is effectively a mediating object, a pretext (as he would say on another occasion) for Mubarak's poetic performance. On the other hand, Genet does recognize himself in this mediation, but what he recognizes is a representation, a gestural poem that reconstitutes him in a fabular setting, a supernatural theater. His limp, at once "simplified" and "exaggerated," represents through precisely this untenable simultaneity not only his way of walking but, indeed, his way of being in the world, his *démarche*. Although Genet notes the audience's laughter, he denies any parodic element in the performance. Mubarak's impersonation is described with the reverence accorded a theatrical interpretation (in the sense of *hermēneia*: dramatic presentation), which reflects on the abilities of this gigantic actor to render the elderly, limping Genet as a mythic figure (not unlike an Oedipus approaching Colonus).

Nothing in this impersonation inspires identification (the "mirror of the psyche") by either the actor or the one acted, which may be why Genet acknowledges feeling a hint of cruelty. If there is something disturbing in the experience, it is due not to an encounter with one's deeper, perhaps even repressed, identity but to the encounter with one's image externalized beyond its identitary boundaries. It constitutes an externalization for Mubarak as well, an exorcism of one who has possessed his inner being. This possession is explained when Genet recalls what had spurred his own mocking imitation of Mubarak and led the Sudanese to improvise a Genet act for the troops: a private scene, accidentally witnessed by Genet, of Mubarak dancing near his car to a Rolling Stones song blasting out from the car stereo across the Jordanian desert, circa 1971—"barefoot and wearing only his trousers, the elderly Black, with his greying fuzzy hair, strumming at a nonexistent guitar, his right hand working where you pluck the strings, his left coming and going on an imaginary neck."[41] Mubarak never forgives this violation of a private ritual (which Genet terms "catching him dancing as if in Africa"), but for the latter it is another instance of the performative as the hyperreal (the "air-guitar" reminding him of the cardless card game). Together, these incidents amount to an object lesson on how the poetics of impersonation exceeds the boundaries of identification, which has formidable implications for both the politics of self-fashioning (including the prospects for self-alteration) and the politics of addressing (and indeed dressing) the other.[42]

Genet describes another scene in which the operations of a poetics of impersonation are hardly innocent. Six male Israeli agents in blonde wigs, posing as three queer couples, get near enough to three PLO officers in Beirut to kill them and escape, unharmed and undiscovered. Genet handles the entire incident as a legend to be unmapped, tracing its moments of rehearsal as moments of potential transformation beyond the boundaries of the specific act. What concerns him is what happened not within the time frame of the incident as such (when they "suddenly switched from acting to action") but within the temporal continuum interrupted by the event: the gradual process of dressing up for their parts (rehearsals for reality) and the subsequent rapid process of undressing, of reconquering the Edenic reality of their identity:

> Six curly blonde wigs, a bit of red on the lips and black around the eyes, are not much to have brought such unsuspected dismay to the streets of Beirut. The inward laughter of transvestites who never ceased feeling like men may have echoed the terror of real transvestites, afraid of being found out through their prattling voices (not quite like women's) and their old gestures, though using all their efforts to disguise them. But the six curly-haired Israelis couldn't afford to for-

> get for an instant that they were men, trained to kill and with muscles meant for fighting. The strangeness of their situation lay in the gentle feminine delicacy of their movements, and their transformation from one moment to the next into the precise gestures of murderers—not murderesses. They knew how to kiss tongue on tongue, heads on one side, and penis on penis; but all that was facile and came easily to mind. What was more difficult and took longer to learn was how to lift a hair very lightly off the beloved's brow, or flick a ladybug off his shoulder. The rehearsals, in a street in Israel, must have taken some time. The youths had to be able to arrange the fold of a scarf and give a high-pitched laugh, then whip off the glad rags and become warriors whose one object was to kill. Really kill. Not as in the last act of a play, to applause, but for real, with dead bodies. I wonder if it isn't comparatively easy and pleasant to slip into tender femininity, and hard to throw it off to commit a crime.[43]

Literature's astonishing capacity to theorize the world to which it gives voice makes any interpretive commentary on this passage cumbersome. Genet has captured the entire terrain of speculative understanding by giving us the secret history that poses all those questions erased with such finality by the historical event. He knows that the irreversible event—the final act of killing—assures that the impersonation will exceed identification, whereby the immediate implication is that, as a result of this poetic excess, the other gets killed. (A couple of pages later, Genet warns that the Palestinians should beware of "Israel's poetry and charm.") Yet he also knows that the success of the mission (not merely to kill but to maintain the identitary boundaries in order to kill) paradoxically presupposes a successful identification in the act of impersonation—a transvestism that creates its own reality qua transvestism—a reality convincing enough to be shared, even if only for a microsecond, by the intended victims. How, then, does this vested transvestism (transient as it is, though achieved with long and rigorous rehearsal) become derealized? How does the transvestite reality get undressed in the aftermath? Who assumes the responsibility for (re)creating the bare reality of (generic) man—the man whose identity is never in doubt? The answer must lie in the irreversible act of murder, when (self-)identity returns because the other has been annihilated. A residue remains nonetheless in the doubt toward which Genet so subtly gestures at the end of the passage: the memory of the difficulty of "undressing" at the moment of necessity, of becoming man again in order to kill—the moment that, as future anterior, will have been justifying the transvestite experience, a travesty of identity from which one cannot escape uncontaminated, whatever the historical result. This residue acts as a corrosive agent against a history that covers its tracks.

There is thus no innocence in transvestism, no possibility of divestment, as it were, even in cases where the transvestite act is a pretext for an action designed to betray it. There is no question of identifying with the other in this act of impersonation, for it entails the othering of one's own identity (even in that ephemeral, perhaps momentary, *in-vestment* of the other), which occupies (in the sense of Freud's *Besetzung*) the space of oneself and leaves on it the traces of a question. No identity survives, in this respect, for one is nothing but a potentially endless stream of appearances in a boundless shadow play instantly brought to life on different occasions, at different points in time, according to the particulars that dress the shadows with meaning and thus make it possible to identify them. The ultimate implication is that the very notion of identity (including the logic that covers up its phantom existence) is marked by a condition of *transversality*,[44] that is, a nomadic proliferation of (self-)images at the core that open one to a multiple and multifigured existence from which there is no escape and no return, for behind lies the void.

Such a conception of the self derails any sort of politics (or ethics) based on the other, any sort of action that presupposes an antithetical relation from which to draw conclusions of power (for the dominant) or of justice (for the dominated). This is the most crucial political implication of Genet's entire corpus, linked as it is to his most troubling articulation: the poetic evocation of betrayal. In a provocative attempt to think precisely through this obstacle, Leo Bersani recognizes in Genet, as a fundamental *archē* (point of departure and point of governance), the "ambitious intention of imagining a form of revolt with no citational relation whatsoever to the laws, categories, and values it would contest and, ideally, destroy." Genet's fundamental principle of revolt ignores the dominant terms that give meaning (indeed, identity) to revolt, eschewing any attempt at opposition (even parody) in any sense that would acknowledge their existence. If Genet makes use of culture's dominant terms at all, Bersani argues, he does so in order "to exploit their potential for erasing cultural relationality itself (that is, the very precondition for subversive repositionings and defiant repetitions)," [45] thereby outmaneuvering the privileged status of transgression that enables revolt to be categorized as an ethical standard and fosters the catastrophic (for Genet) condition of (re)cementing the privilege of identity. For transgression eventually becomes an alibi for the moral upper hand, as well as an occasion to recede into the comfort of redemption, both of which, according to Genet's intransigent paranomia, constitute the most reprehensible agencies of bourgeois communal identity. Even more, the identitary ethics of transgression ensures that the memory of having once been oppressed will continue to determine one's actions after liberation, while (as Bersani argues in his reading of *The Maids*) genuine revolt is possible only when one's subjectivity has been truly *altered* and can no longer be related to (identified as) an oppressed subjectivity.

Genet's entire work, like his very way of life, was conducted as a great onslaught on the metaphysics of community, which for him amounted to the gravest deception of the logic of identity. His profound political generosity and commitment in the last twenty years of his life was an attempt to practice a politics that explored a different sort of association: the revolutionary collective as a society held together by the coarticulation of fantasy, not by the community of law. The prototype remained the anticommunal society of criminals, where, contrary to our romantic visions of underworld loyalty, betrayal was the safeguard against moral convention—criminal society's immediate undoing. At this level, to betray one's comrade was paradoxically to safeguard his status as a criminal—in essence, *not to betray him*. Not just paradox but an exemplary case of the logic of nonidentity (i.e., paradoxical only from the standpoint of identitary logic), this mode of thought and action points to an epistemological framework that is continuously othering the terms of analysis and calculation. An identity based on betrayal is entirely incalculable; it defies the means of determination. Since it can hardly be identified, it can hardly be called an identity at all. A way of being that entails continual mutation, its geographic principle is not simply nomadic but *groundless*.

Such groundlessness makes Genet truly puzzling—if not downright disturbing—to even the most sympathetic interpreters who seek to characterize him in the face of such acts as his stealing a painting from Giacometti's studio, from the man he considered worthier than any other he had ever encountered. But Genet's compulsion to subvert even relations of friendship—relations of the greatest value to him and so (in Bersani's terms) the value of relationality itself—evinces his paradoxical sense of loyalty to his own defiance of social order and its powers of rehabilitation and appropriation. Obsessed with evading detection from the outset of his (criminal) career, Genet consistently falsified data about himself and his life. All juridical decisions and psychiatric profiles pertaining to him should be taken as discourses contaminated a priori by the logic of the subject they profess to know objectively, as Genet took pride in fictionalizing his feats of robbery and vagabondage to the experts who judged him. Falsification as betrayal of the self in resistance to its appropriation by the purveyors of truth amounts to just another instance of impersonation—a theatrical alienation-effect staged against oneself. It means a staging of identity that reveals identity as a matter of staging; hence Genet's explicit commitment to all those who would derealize their identities and expose them as colonized sites, stages of imperialist power. In Said's disarmingly succinct terms, "Imperialism is the export of identity."[46]

Genet's "fierce antinomianism" (another Said characterization) ascribes an explicit eroticism to what becomes in fact a poetics of betrayal: "Anyone who has not known the ecstasy of betrayal [*trahison*] knows nothing about ecstasy at all."[47] At one level, such ecstasy may be specifically linked to a homosexual erotics that takes exchange out of the sexual encounter and thus violates the traditionally understood self/other relation. This would be Bersani's reading, in accordance with "the antirelationality inherent in all homoness" and underpinned by Genet's undeconstructible position of utter solitude as the only possible access/way to truth, which disappears in the moment of dialogue or confession, since the disloyalty of language itself leads to truth's betrayal by the very encounter with the other, betrayal by communication.[48] And yet the passage that concludes with this erotic exaltation of betrayal sketches it as based not merely on the encounter with the other, but on the *translation of the enemy* (Genet's terms) such that each position becomes the other's shadow, with even their dreams being difficult to disentangle. To configure one's enemy as one's shadow hardly suggests a symbiosis, for if nothing else, there are no longer any bodies left; they have vanished in the translation, the betrayal of their own terms. The ecstasy of betrayal is literally due to being catapulted outside one's body and taking form at the point of groundlessness, of/as shadow.

In other words, Genet does dissolve the substance of relationality embodied in the self/other encounter, but he does it precisely by employing an essential gesture of *othering* (translation) in order to articulate a dissolution of the self/other relation in the act of betrayal. By the same token, Genet's late work demands that we amend such an exclusively homosexual discursive framing of the problem as Bersani's (which isn't to say that a homosexual imaginary is no longer at work). Genet's evocation of betrayal as ecstasy occurs at the outset of a work organized around his captivity in a love extending beyond sexual practice (including its domain of fantasy) to a kind of total love experience that allows individual bodies to retain their palpable sensuality but to remain indiscriminate and divested of specific sexual interest. Such was Genet's avowed experience of both the Palestinians and the Black Panthers, a total commitment to being captive and in love that, in such contexts, further aggravates the already disruptive notion of the ecstasy of betrayal. And betrayal of the Palestinians in particular is explicitly entertained by Genet: "The day the Palestinians become institutionalized, I will no longer be on their side. The day the Palestinians become a nation like other nations, I will no longer be there. . . . I think that it's there that I will betray them. They don't know."[49] Is this the same notion of betrayal? If so, it would suggest that at the point of national institution the Palestinians would also be at the epitome of their friendship with Genet, were we to literally follow his script of originary betrayal in the criminal world. But this would cancel out the possibility of reading Genet's betrayal as directed against institutionalization itself—a foolish reading given everything to which Genet's life attests. A closer reading reveals a stunning consistency of positions, despite the second one's appearing more conventional. Just as betraying friends in the criminal world safeguards their criminal integrity, so would betraying revolutionaries at the height of their political achievement safeguard their revolutionary integrity. Institutionalization is the betrayal of revolution, for it turns revolution over to ritual, Genet says; hence only a betrayal of this betrayal could sustain the undomesticated energy that makes revolution possible. Genet's evident anarchism reveals the true epistemic *co-incidence* of Trotsky's famous rival phrases: revolution betrayed opens the way for permanent revolution.

In addition, however, *Un Captif amoureux* encapsulates a poetics of betrayal that embraces the totality of that term's various political significations and confirms the "nonrelational betrayal" of the homosexual imagination (according to Bersani) by exceeding both the homological and the heterological framework. The major question emerging with Genet's avowed love for the Panthers and the Palestinians is that of a possibly residual Orientalism at work, which would combine the traditional elements of the discourse with the various other paraphernalia that usually clutters the exoticism of revolution. Here, I believe, Genet's poetics of betrayal becomes most politically trenchant. There is no doubt that *Un Captif amoureux* was written as a tribute to those unexpected life sources Genet encountered when his own life had reached the void, sources whose reverberations continued to animate him when the actual void of death had locked onto him. The love for the Other (to be blunt, perhaps even vulgar, for the sake of the issue's seriousness) was total, genuine, selfless, and without guilt. Yet Genet's stance over the last twenty years of his life against all those irrevocably *other* suggests that "to betray them is not to abandon them exactly, but to retain for himself the right not to belong, not to be accountable, not to be tied down," as Said notes, in a unique critical recognition of betrayal in Genet as an act that abolishes the possibility of "going native," of laying claim to the other's territory even out of genuine love for the other.[50] Such betrayal ensures that one's love for the other is not actually an unconscious and veiled love of oneself against the other.

The complete picture is paradoxical at the core: betrayal as both translating the terms of your enemy/other to the point of mutually entangled dreams and refusing to take the terms of your friend/other as your own to the extent of becoming one and the same. The two sides of the paradox reveal the deep-seated ambivalence of translation itself, an epistemic ambivalence that makes it, in the last instance, practically untenable. What Genet himself adds to this string of ambivalent figures, whose transversal logic organizes his poetic and political imaginary, is the figure of the transsexual:

> As the old sex fades and, he hopes, finally drops off useless, he'll be possessed of a joy close to madness when he refers to himself as "she" instead of "he," and realizes that grammar also has divided into two, and the feminine half has turned a somersault so that it applies to him, whereas the other half used to be forced on him. The transition to the non-hairy part must be both delightful and terrible. . . . "Farewell to half of me—I die to myself." To leave behind the hated but familiar masculine ways is like forsaking the world and going into the monastery or a leper house. To quit the world of trousers for the world

> of the brassière is a kind of death, expected but feared. And isn't it also comparable to suicide with choirs singing the "Tuba mirum"? . . . A transsexual is a sort of monster and hero combined.[51]

Genet latches onto the figure of the transsexual in the context of discussing the hero's odd epistemological status: boundless joy of life in the face of death's certainty and imminence. The initial cause of reflection is the experience of listening to Mozart's *Requiem* in a Beirut hotel room (hence the reference in the passage above), which he describes as an apotheosis of ambivalence, the lament for death colliding with its life-giving glorification in a heroic encounter that wrests from death the joy of life. This same life-and-death play operates at the foundations of the transsexual experience—for Genet, a bona fide heroic position in our strictly gendered identitarian world. The transsexual betrays the identity of sex itself, taking "sexual identity" to the very limit of the notion, as real as the world and yet beyond the world: "Escape from the world at last! Changing sex doesn't consist merely in subjecting one's body to a few surgical adjustments: it means teaching the whole world, forcing upon it a change of syntax. . . . (The adjectives describing you ought henceforth be feminine.) Your still unadjusted right hand will move to hide an erection no longer possible."[52] The transsexual embodies a history of permanent translation from one to an other, poised between two deaths: the bones of one identity exhumed and translated into the ossuary of the other, and so on, an infinite palindrome wherein the literal and the allegorical are put into mutual question. Such transversal logic characterizes both betrayal and transsexuality and consists in a permanent externalization of self, making of oneself a gift to the other, yet a gift of a self that vanishes; neither penetrating nor swallowed by the other, the identity of both giver and receiver is rendered null and void.[53]

The request by the Palestinian fighters that after Genet's death his bones be distributed among them and scattered over the Dead Sea bears the full symbolic weight of his own project of infinite externalization, the translation of his words and bones alike. His non-identitarian understanding enables him to perceive and describe the evanescence of life in a revolutionary situation, a twilight existence (*entre chien et loup*) the sheer space-time ambivalence of which endows it with an always imminent capacity for metamorphosis. *Un Captif amoureux* is rife with references to the Palestinians' ghostly existence, a condition forged from both the reality of death in their daily lives and the imaginary vision that gave reality to their project, but also reinforced by Genet's phantasmic presence among them—by the uncanny reality of Jean Genet, the famous French author who chose to share their moment in history without the slightest hint of self-interest.

He was perfectly aware of the power of this condition, a power marked, like everything else, by profound ambivalence. On the one hand, the Palestinians drew a great, mythological power from their shadowy existence such that "the very real State of Israel finds itself shadowed by a ghostly survival," in the sense that all permanence is haunted by the durability of evanescence, by what can reappear from the void and overcome (*sur-vie*) the permanence of any existence. Indeed, the phrase in French is even more revealing. "L'État bien réel d'Israël se connaît doublé d'une survie fantomatique" suggests that Israel, insofar as it has achieved the hard reality of institutionalization, is now open to a sort of cinematic dubbing in another language that splits (doubles) its national-imaginary institution.[54] On the other hand, Genet wonders whether his own ghostly status as witness (tainted all the more by his chronicle's formal affinity with death) may drag the Palestinians into a stream of shadowy existence, retroactively animated by a ventriloquist, a puppet master, a "shadow-showman." This would involve a certain materiality of death in the very act of animation, since shadow-theater figures realize a palpable representation of death, a death dressed as life (*travestied*) by the ubiquitous but invisible puppeteer who dares to speak their many voices. Genet's long reflection, as the book draws to a close, on his task as shadow master (a task he equates with the animation—not the fulfillment—of prophecy) dwells on the necessary betrayal of history for the sake of mythistorical creation: "The transformations of a fact into words, signs, and series of words and signs become other facts that can never reconstitute the original that generated my transcription." This inadvertent *betrayal of facts* (Genet's terms) is the inevitable result of an encounter between the poetic imagination and the mythological inventory of society, an encounter between two dreamworlds that coincide within one another:

> What I recount may well be what I experienced, but it was different in that the disparateness of my own existence had merged into the continuity of Palestinian life, though still leaving me with traces, glimpses of, sometimes severances from, my former life. . . . Sometimes I wonder whether I didn't live that life especially so that I might arrange its episodes in the same seeming disorder as the images in a dream. All

> these words to say, *this is my Palestinian revolution,* recited in my own chosen order. . . . Trying to think the revolution is like waking up and trying to see the logic in a dream. There is no point, in the middle of a drought, in inventing the necessary gestures for crossing the river when the bridge has been swept away.[55]

Genet's poetics of disappearance, converging with his portrayal of revolutionary existence,[56] suggests that for every act of erasure in history—the revolutionary moment par excellence—another concrete historical manifestation is generated; historical eclipse and poetic naming are intertwined. Genet says at one point that "eclipse is a word full of meaning," and that meaning, literally sliding right over any attempt to shed permanent light on it, eclipses representation. What hovers behind this sort of obsessive metaphorizing is Genet's unequivocal position on the relationship between art and revolution or, if you will, between the dreamworlds of poetic imagination and of social-historical creation. In both realms, a palpable dream logic is at work, the common root of humanity's capacity to imagine new forms, to alter its self-conception and thus its destiny in the world. And although both dreamworlds are real, "we know that one can act on [one's own poetic] dreams in a practically unlimited fashion. One cannot act on the real in an unlimited fashion. A different discipline is needed, which is not a grammatical discipline."[57]

These impermeable limits of the real forbid the artist's delusion of being master of historical creation. Even the greatest innovations in art, Genet argues repeatedly, do not precede but follow events of historical transformation, for "no genuine revolutionary action can be based on precedents; revolutionary actions have the freshness of the beginning of the world."[58] In this respect, the artist is no revolutionary and should resist any narcissistic fantasy that he might be, for in revolution the integrity of one's body is at stake, in art one's reputation.[59] This reconfiguration of narcissism is one of the main tasks undertaken in *Un Captif amoureux,* where Genet might be said to recuperate his consistently failed sublimation in life by enacting a sublimation beyond the exercise of personal poetic fantasy—the writing of a daydream, as he often characterized his early work—so as to produce a writing suited to the revolutionary imaginary and the peculiar sublimation that *it* involves.

At the same time, Genet has learned history's lesson well: revolutions are ephemeral entities and, once institutionalized, turn against the artists and intellectuals who supported them with antithetical energy. This is inevitable and indeed desirable, for it ensures that art will never submit to the instrumental demands of revolution, just as revolution will never depend on art for realization. Art and revolution may enter into an alliance determined by the same historical contingency that coordinates their antithetical relation. Genet identifies two strains in artistic work between which "there must be no question of preference. On the one hand there is the work which serves the revolution; this is constructive in the sense that it destroys bourgeois values. Then there is another kind of artistic work, essentially violent and inflammatory, in the sense that it refuses to submit to any value or to any authority. It disputes even the existence of man." Because revolution demands attention to practical matters, Genet goes on to argue, the revolutionary capacity of art (its second strain) is useless, perhaps even detrimental, which is why so many artists have met with their destruction before revolutionary tribunals. But by virtue of the same anarchist nature, art pursues revolution against its ensuing domestication. Genet concludes that "it is the duty of revolution to encourage its adversaries: works of art. This is because artistic work, which is the product of the struggle of the artist in isolation, tends to contemplation, which, in the long run, may turn into the destruction of all values, bourgeois or otherwise, and their replacement by something else that will more and more come to resemble what we call freedom. . . . Finally, the definition of a work of art could be the following: an object that is really of no *use*."[60]

Literature is of no use in a conventional sense because it is a protean entity that can never be pinned down except as "a barricade to hide the void" of reality, as Genet tentatively describes *Un Captif amoureux*. Yet in this process of dissimulation, of one sentence overwriting the space of another and all consistently overwriting the blank page of reality, the poetic imagination registers its own void, the void that enables radical self-alteration, creation ex nihilo. In this respect literature, as a specifically mythographic enterprise, manifests the void of history instead of erasing it. *Un Captif amoureux* begins with an exemplary meditation on the paradoxical transparency of written signs, which may not give meaning to (which is also to say, erase) the blankness of the page that embodies history. The legibility of history, Genet implies, may be due less to its being written than to its being read, with reading understood not as an interpretive task (reading between the lines) but as an act of poetic invention, of writing against the already written: "Reading between the lines is a level art; reading between the words a precipitous one. . . . Another way of putting it: the space between the words contains more reality than the time it takes to read them."[61] The political implications of this poetics of history are immediately apparent to Genet. Disavowing his famous 1970s comment that "the Blacks were the characters on the white page of America," he makes the writing of this book a demonstration that revolutionary history manifests itself by having died on the page, as if the blood from its numberless anonymous deaths has seeped through all the cracks and become not signs and margins, black ink and blank spaces, but sheer texture:

> The black words on the white American page are sometimes crossed out or erased. The best disappear, but it's they that give form to the poem, or rather the poem of the poem. If the Whites are the page, the Blacks are the writing that conveys a meaning—not of the page, or not of the page alone. The abundance of Whites is what the writing is set down on, and it forms the margin too. But the poem is composed by the absent Blacks—the dead, if you like—the nameless absent Blacks who wrote the poem whose meaning escapes me but not its reality. Let the absence of invisibility of the Blacks we call dead be well understood. They are still active. Radioactive.[62]

Here, the meaning of poetry may be entirely elusive to anyone not residing inside it, not dead and nameless to history along with it. The poem's reality, however, the palpable *sense* of the poetic imagination (society's imaginary) bleeding through the textures of the real, is perfectly comprehensible. This applies not only to the Blacks in White America but to the Palestinians occupied by the Zionist dream, or perhaps more accurately, as Genet himself might have put it, the Palestinians participating unwittingly in another's dream, one in which they come to be the blank shadows as the dream space is invoked as *tabula rasa* and written over with a new, naturalized ancestry.[63] Genet's radical skepticism cannot but drive him to interrogate his presence among both the Panthers and the Palestinians as "the dreamer inside a dream, a factor of unreality in both movements, the European saying to a dream, 'You are a dream—don't wake the sleeper!'"[64] Nevertheless, trusting that the blood reality of history's poem will permeate all the signs and blankness, he can close with daring: "This last page of my book is transparent."

Such trust in the human capacity to alter (*other*) itself without limit and without guarantee as to enable someone of Genet's meticulous antinomianism to conclude by subscribing to a transparency of the real speaks of an extraordinary lucidity. I daresay this lucidity comes from an intoxicating love of life and a total equanimity before mortality, precisely as Genet perceived the Homeric universe, exemplified not by the modernist Odysseus but by the tragic Achilles, whose short poetic life, beyond ritual and sacrament, became the mythistorical model for all the characters in *Un Captif amoureux*. What made such lucidity possible was the total absence of any transcendental desires and anxieties in Genet's life and work—a consistency and a passion that have to be rare. Genet's poetic and political imaginary is pagan through and through. It is terribly misguided to call him "a mystical atheist," as Edmund White has done on several occasions; even Genet's most ostentatious sketches of Catholic fantasies are pagan elaborations, not unlike those stunning depictions of hell in Italian Renaissance painting. An atheist, he says, is hardly dangerous, for he approaches the underside of Christian moralism, while "paganism puts the unbeliever back amid the so-called 'mists of time,' when God didn't yet exist. A sort of intoxication and magnanimity allows a pagan to approach everything, himself included, with equal respect and without undue humility."[65] This sort of intoxication is hardly "the destructive, panicked drunkenness" that all revolution eventually ritualizes (as *potlatch*); it is rather, as Cornelius Castoriadis put it, the "lucid drunkenness" of society's poetic praxis, of what establishes the freedom to create and explore new forms of social life.[66] This capacity is infinite, though limited by death, precisely because it does not limit the reality of death by means of some transcendental afterlife. Having dedramatized death, as he was fond of saying, Genet brought his mortality to full realization while correcting the final proofs of *Un Captif amoureux* and beginning to draft its unrealized sequel.

Notes

This essay is dedicated to Edward Said.

Translations from the French are mine unless otherwise indicated.

1 Hannah Arendt, *On Revolution* (New York, 1963).

2 The Second World War, a truly global affair, was the first of a kind that the Great War, despite its ambitious label, never was—testifying instead, like much else that surrounded it, to a still-prevailing nineteenth-century order that had exceeded its strict temporal limits. That the Great War essentially brought about the death of this order, as Proust demonstrates inimitably, does not mean that it instituted a new order as such. The his-

torical puzzlement over the interwar period, particularly evident in political and cultural history, points to the suspended nature of an epoch that did not know what to make of its failed revolutionary legacy.

3 *Mythistorēma* is Greek for the novel, or fiction more generally. My use of it here extends the term's literal meaning to cover the intersection between the myths societies create (and recreate incessantly) to represent themselves and their others and the historical contingencies of myth's generation. Myth is always contemporary, though given readily to transhistorical narratives. To speak of society's "mythistorical foundations" is thus to speak of a continually shifting ground—which, like the course of a river, is explicable yet unpredictable—since history and the social imagination are both limited by their *event* yet infinite in their project.

4 William Burroughs quoted Genet as having said, "There was the French language and there was me. I put myself inside the other, then the work was done"; see Edmund White, *Genet, a Biography* (New York, 1993), 510. We will return to the conceptualization revealed in this phrasing, including its unavoidable sexual staging.

5 Jean Genet, *Notre-Dame-des-Fleurs* (Monte Carlo, 1944); *Miracle de la rose* (Lyon, 1946); *Querelle de Brest* (Paris, 1946); *Pompes funèbres* (Paris, 1948); *Poèmes* (Paris, 1948); *Journal du voleur* (Paris, 1949).

6 Jean Genet, "Entretien avec Hubert Fichte" (December 1975), in *L'ennemi déclaré: Textes et entretiens*, ed. Albert Dichy, Vol. 6 of *Oeuvres complètes de Jean Genet* (Paris, 1991), 141–76; quotation from 165.

7 Interview with Saadalah Wannous from the 1970s published in *Al Karmil* (in Arabic) in 1986; quoted in translation by White, *Genet*, 347.

8 See Jean Genet, *Un Captif amoureux* (Paris, 1986); all page references given in subsequent notes are to the 1986 folio/paperback edition published by Gallimard. See also Jean Genet, "Affirmation of Existence through Rebellion," *Journal of Palestine Studies* 16 (1987): 64–84, where he says, "The books I wrote previously were all part of a dream, of a daydream. And since I outlived this dream, this daydream, I had to take action in order to achieve a sort of fullness of life" (67).

9 The political articles, speeches, and interviews posthumously collected in *L'ennemi déclaré* must be read in juxtaposition with *Un Captif amoureux*, for it is as if these two volumes are each other's shadow, as if bringing the enemy out into the open finally allowed Genet to return to an imprisoned condition (the experience of love), which made art again possible.

10 Jean Genet, "Quatre heures à Chatila" (1982), in Dichy, ed., *L'ennemi déclaré*, 241–64.

11 On the consubstantial nature of massacre and cancer as catalytic for the realization of *Un Captif amoureux*, see also Patrice Bougon, "Politique et autobiographie," *Magazine littéraire* (September 1993): 67–70, esp. 68.

12 Jean Genet, *The Thief's Journal*, trans. Bernard Frechtman (New York, 1964 [1949]), 71.

13 Ibid., 119.

14 *Autography* is David Lloyd's term, his way of distinguishing Genet's practice of eradicating the source of subjectivity (narrating and narrated) from *autobiography*, which retains it intact; see "Genet's Genealogy: European Minorities and the Ends of the Canon," in *The Nature and Context of Minority Discourse*, ed. Abdul R. JanMohamed and David Lloyd

(Oxford, 1990), 369–93, esp. 384. I would contest, however, Lloyd's differentiation between Genet and Proust in these terms. Their differences are many (language, style, representation of homosexuality, etc.), but their points of departure coincide.

15 In an unpublished note quoted by White, *Genet*, 523.

16 Jean Genet, *Prisoner of Love*, trans. Barbara Bray (Middletown, CT, 1992 [1986]).

17 Jean Genet, "Entretien avec Bertrand Poirot-Delpech" (January 1982), in Dichy, ed., *L'ennemi déclaré*, 227–41; quotations from 230. Of course, "the torturers" are all those representatives of dominant bourgeois morality who were Genet's preferred readers, not "homosexuals and writers," but rather "Catholic bankers, or . . . policemen or *concierges*" (quoted in White, *Genet*, 207).

18 Jean Genet, "Entretien avec Antoine Bourseiller" (summer 1981), in Dichy, ed., *L'ennemi déclaré*, 217–26; quotation from 226.

19 Genet, "Entretien avec Fichte," 142.

20 Edward Said, "On Jean Genet's Late Works," *Grant Street* 36 (1990): 27–42; quotation from 32.

21 See Jean Genet, "The Palestinians," trans. Meric Dobson, *Journal of Palestine Studies* 3 (1973): 3–34: "The Palestinians became conscious of themselves as an autonomous nation . . . only when the nation was deprived of its territory. . . . The Palestinian nation, unable to remain in a land where it might, indeed, have lost its flavour, is obliged to find in fantasy rules which it observes rigorously as a means of saving itself from fading away in dreams and idealism. . . . This independence, this peculiar autonomy, it owes to its revolutionary spirit" (5).

22 For a detailed discussion of national fantasy and the national imaginary, see Stathis Gourgouris, *Dream Nation: Enlightenment, Colonization, and the Institution of Modern Greece* (Stanford, 1996), esp. 10–46. My use of "the imaginary" here, as in *Dream Nation*, has little to do with the specular narcissistic figuration of otherness that most Lacanian criticism (Slavoj Žižek's being a notable exception) associates with the term, often ignoring Lacan's own rearticulation in his *R.S.I. Séminaire* (Paris, 1975). It refers, rather, to the magma of radical significations by which society conceptualizes, identifies, and institutes itself (often as other) in conjunction with history's particular demands, as developed in the work of Cornelius Castoriadis; see, especially, *The Imaginary Institution of Society*, trans. Kathleen Blamey (Cambridge, MA, 1987 [1975]).

23 Genet, *Un Captif amoureux*, 47; *Prisoner of Love*, 25; translation modified.

24 *Prisoner of Love*, 28; *Un Captif amoureux*, 52.

25 *Un Captif amoureux*, 178–79; *Prisoner of Love*, 107–8; translation modified.

26 His matrilineal name was all the more important because it signified another singular aspect of Genet's life: his mother was the only woman with whom he ever had intimate contact. In an unpublished manuscript from around 1973, Genet describes himself as being "strong from never having passed through a woman except at the moment of birth, when I was still blind, mute, and doubtless drowned" (quoted in White, *Genet*, 517). The whole ensemble of psychic antagonisms entailed here explains the symbolic prominence of Hamza and *his* mother in *Un Captif amoureux*, which concludes with an allusion to this pair as a pietà figure that constitutes the book's principle. This issue has been widely and interestingly discussed, but I want to avail myself of Genet's own

theatrical principles to dedramatize this pretext figure and leave it in the wings here, unstaged and undiscussed.

27 Genet, "Entretien avec Fichte," 149.

28 Genet, *Prisoner of Love*, 261; *Un Captif amoureux*, 427.

29 *Un Captif amoureux*, 426; *Prisoner of Love*, 260; translation modified.

30 "If the Panthers acted, they didn't do so on stage. . . . It would be wrong to expect that an ideal curtain could be brought down on their performances. Excess in display, in words and in attitude, swept the Panthers to ever new and greater excess" (*Un Captif amoureux*, 141; *Prisoner of Love*, 85; translation modified). See Gisèle Child-Olmsted, "Black on White: Language and Revolution in Genet's Political Writings," *L'Esprit créateur* 35 (1995): 61–69.

31 Genet, *Un Captif amoureux*, 69; *Prisoner of Love*, 46; translation modified. In an earlier work, Genet had made the same point from the opposite angle: "White hatred in America is such that I wonder whether every White man in this country, when he plants a tree, does not see *Negroes* hanging from its branches"; "Introduction à *Les Frères de Soledad*" (1970), in Dichy, ed., *L'ennemi déclaré*, 63–70; quotation from 69.

32 Genet, "Les Frères," 69.

33 Genet, *Prisoner of Love*, 259; *Un Captif amoureux*, 424.

34 Frantz Fanon, *Black Skin, White Masks*, trans. Charles Lam Markmann (New York, 1967 [1952]), 194.

35 For an insightful discussion and framing of this issue, see White, *Genet*, 526–31.

36 Jean Genet, "Interview with Madeleine Gobeil" (January 1964), in *The Selected Writings of Jean Genet*, ed. Edmund White (New York, 1993), 447–60; quotation from 457.

37 Genet, "Entretien avec Bourseiller" (notes de travail), 398. For a detailed discussion of paranomia, see Stathis Gourgouris, "Enlightenment and Paranomia," in *Violence, Identity and Self-Determination*, ed. Hent de Vries and Samuel Weber (Stanford, 1997), 119–49.

38 See White, *Genet*, 383–86.

39 Said, "Genet's Late Works," 36. See also Genet's image of the symbiotic coincidence of poetic inspiration and poetic history as two matches that, ignited together, become one in their simultaneous immolation (*Prisoner of Love*, 318; *Un Captif amoureux*, 520).

40 Genet, *Un Captif amoureux*, 348–49; *Prisoner of Love*, 211–12; translation modified.

41 *Prisoner of Love*, 212; *Un Captif amoureux*, 349.

42 For an exceptional argument concerning this same disruption of the impersonation/identification equation in Fanon's work—a resourceful feminist critique that also elicits the most revolutionary aspects of his psychoanalytic figuring of sexuality and colonialism—see Diana Fuss, "Interior Colonies: Frantz Fanon and the Politics of Identification," *diacritics* 24 (1994): 20–42. (Parenthetically, many aspects of Fanon's and Genet's work can be aligned as well as juxtaposed, in addition to their common endowment of assimilationist prefaces by Sartre, particularly in the intersecting domains of violence and poetry, sexuality and revolution.)

43 Genet, *Un Captif amoureux*, 266–67; *Prisoner of Love*, 160–61; translation modified.

44 The term, from Félix Guattari, *Psychanalyse et transversalité* (Paris, 1972), is also specifi-

cally applied to Genet by Guattari in "Genet retrouvé," in *Cartographies schizoanalytiques* (Paris, 1981), 269–90, esp. 276.

45 Leo Bersani, "The Gay Outlaw," *diacritics* 24 (1994): 5–18; quotations from 5 and 6.

46 Said, "Genet's Late Works," 38.

47 Genet, *Prisoner of Love*, 59; *Un Captif amoureux*, 101. *Trahison* applies to a range of related notions in English (*betrayal, treachery, treason*) and is also linked, by root, to *translation* (as in the famous Italian phrase *tradittore traduttore*). For Genet, the term is epistemically informed by a great deal of active power, an *askesis* at the level of life itself. See Paule Thévenin, "La trahison comme ascèse," *Magazine littéraire* (September 1993): 35–36.

48 Bersani, "Gay Outlaw," 10. See also Genet, "Entretien avec Fichte," 176; and "Affirmation of Existence through Rebellion," 78. Bersani goes on to say that solitude is "not a betrayal defined by its opposition to loyalty. It is betrayal of that opposition, a betrayal opposed to nothing because it consists merely in a movement out of everything" ("Gay Outlaw," 12).

49 Genet, "Affirmation of Existence through Rebellion," 77.

50 Said, "Genet's Late Works," 33.

51 Genet, *Prisoner of Love*, 52–53; *Un Captif amoureux*, 90–91. Note the impossibility of adequately rendering in English the rich interplay of gendered pronouns in the French:

> surtout à mesure que le sexe ancien se fanera, espérant qu'il tombât, définitivement inutilisable, une joie proche peut-être de la démence quand, parlant de soi il ne dira plus "il" mais "elle," comprenant alors que la grammaire aussi se partage en deux et que, tournant sur elle-même, une moitié s'applique à lui, la féminine, alors qu'on imposait l'autre du langage. Le passage de l'une à la moitié non velue doit être délicieux et terrible. . . . "Adieu chère moitié, je meurs à moi-même. . . ." Quitter la démarche virile abhorrée mais connue, c'est laisser le monde pour le carmel ou la léproserie, quitter l'univers du pantalon pour celui du soutien-gorge, c'est l'équivalent de la mort attendue mais redoutée et n'est-ce pas comparable au suicide afin que les choeurs y chantent le *Tuba mirum*? Le transsexuel sera donc un monstre et un héros.

52 *Prisoner of Love*, 150; *Un Captif amoureux*, 249–50. The mistranslation here (resulting in the parenthetical phrase) is quite inventive, given the quandary of genderless English: "Enfin être hors du monde! Changer de sexe ne consiste pas seulement à subir sur le corps quelques corrections chirurgicales, c'est enseigner au monde entier, afin qu'il vous désigne, un obligatoire détournement syntaxique . . . et vous en resterez pantois car je ne connais pas de féminin à ce mot; encore mal éduquée votre main droite se portera là afin de dissimuler une érection impossible puisqu'il ne vous restera plus de quoi bander."

53 Genet's view of transsexuality clearly proceeds from an exclusively male imagination; the ambivalence begins with the turning of a "he" into a "she" and not the other way around. In a psychoanalytic sense, however, this is not a real issue because, for one thing, the transsexual exemplifies the epistemic dissociation between sex and gender and thus renders the masculinist schema of self/other irrelevant. More importantly, no matter which way the sexual translation goes, it is always, according to Catherine Millot, "the woman

as Name-of-the-Father [that] marks the limit to the mortifying exigency of the Other"; *Horsexe: Essay on Transsexuality*, trans. Kenneth Hylton (Brooklyn, 1990 [1983]), 59.

54 Genet, *Un Captif amoureux*, 496; *Prisoner of Love*, 304.

55 *Un Captif amoureux*, 504–5; *Prisoner of Love*, 308–9; translation modified.

56 As Scott Durham observes, "Genet feels compelled to include the subject's disappearance in the portrait itself. It is as if the content of the portrait were momentarily invaded by the photographic negative which will henceforth be its only ground"; "Genet's Shadow Theatre: Memory and Utopian Fantasy in *Un Captif amoureux*," *L'Esprit créateur* 35 (1995): 50–59; quotation from 55. See also Guattari, "Genet retrouvé," 274; and Patrice Bougon, "Le cliché, la métaphore et la digression," *L'Esprit créateur* 35 (1995): 70–77.

57 Genet, "Affirmation of Resistance through Rebellion," 72.

58 Jean Genet, "Entretien avec Michèle Manceaux" (May 1970), in Dichy, ed., *L'ennemi déclaré*, 55–62; quotation from 57.

59 See Genet, "Entretien avec Fichte," 147.

60 Genet, "The Palestinians," 32–33. In this impassioned argument for the irreducibility of both art and revolution in the course of their mutual, undeconstructible antagonism, Genet sounds much like Adorno, despite their obvious differences in manner. Said alone has recognized this rather peculiar but convincing affinity, which deserves some serious elaboration; see "Genet's Late Works," 39–40.

61 Genet, *Prisoner of Love*, 3; *Un Captif amoureux*, 11–12.

62 *Un Captif amoureux*, 358; *Prisoner of Love*, 218; translation modified.

63 This point is elaborated in an exemplary way, fully commensurate with Genet's (down to the very terminology of dreams and naturalized spaces) by Uri Eisenzweig in "An Imaginary Territory: The Problematic of Space in Zionist Discourse," trans. Debra Bendel, *Dialectical Anthropology* 5 (1981): 261–85.

64 Genet, *Prisoner of Love*, 149; *Un Captif amoureux*, 248.

65 *Prisoner of Love*, 35; *Un Captif amoureux*, 62.

66 Cornelius Castoriadis, "Culture in a Democratic Society," in *The Castoriadis Reader*, ed. and trans. David Ames Curtis (Oxford, 1997), 338–48; quotation from 345. See also Genet, "Entretien avec Fichte," 162.

Catherine Liu

Conspiracy (Theories)

Psycho-Marxism is a new name for a necessary madness, a madness that has to do with thinking psychoanalysis and Marxism at the *same time.* If there is a particular urgency in the call for a reconciliation of these two theoretic systems, it might have to do with the resurgence of historicism in literary and cultural studies. This new form of historical criticism would like to leverage hostile takeovers of other enterprises still in operation within the sectors of literary and cultural criticism. What it promises is no less than a return to and a consolidation of Enlightenment values which the institutions of Greater Academia find unquestionably more reassuring and definitely more profitable. It embraces a kind of interdisciplinary approach that, while appearing intellectually innovative, is most responsive to the changes taking place in the economic reorganization of the University itself. Its regime, for we already live and work under it, does not tolerate dissension or discussion; dismissing theoretic terms as "jargon," it seeks nothing less than a monopoly on academic production. What has become increasingly evident is that, while theoretic discourses can accept and even

The *South Atlantic Quarterly* 97:2, Spring 1998.

incorporate historicizing methodologies and approaches, historicism remains completely resistant to theoretic interventions.

Historical criticism sees its compatibility with journalism as a sign of its superiority.[1] Under such circumstances, it would be highly advisable to contemplate a merger—psycho-Marxism—that might stave off external attempts at hostile takeover. The new consolidated body would have to reorganize and redistribute its assets in order to produce and reproduce more effectively, in the name of theory, a libidinization of thinking and a critique of simpleminded historicism at the *same time*—not an easy thing to accomplish. We should not underestimate the differences between psychoanalysis and Marxism. Assessing their incompatibilities is the only way we can engineer a successful and lasting merger. What is at stake here is the survival of resistant strains of independent and critical thinking. One recent attempt to merge psychoanalysis with Marxism along Lacanian lines was visible in the titling of a conference organized by the newly established Association for the Psychoanalysis of Culture and Society "Psychoanalysis and Social Change."[2] This title marks one way of joining psychoanalysis and Marxism—by a conjunction. Here, psychoanalysis is supplemented by the Marxist slogan of changing the social. In the case of "psycho-Marxism," the hyphen offers another interesting joint or patch. While the name of Freud disappears into the prefix *psycho-*, historical materialism and leftist political economy are still designated by the name of Marx. The psychoanalytic theory to which most thinkers of psychoanalysis-with-Marxism have recourse, however, is firmly based on the work of Lacan, in which a return to Freud via a reading of the Saussurean signifier at once acts out and defers group-psychological formations by presenting itself as the ultimate "update." Those four words, "Psychoanalysis and Social Change," also partake of an attempt to stay tuned to the changing times, which could explain why this title begs to be read as a kind of epistle posted to a superegoic addressee who calls for a strategic merging of psychoanalysis and the social. Such a title implies that psychoanalysis is on the side of change for the better, that it is already hailed as a promulgator of a teleological force behind change, theorizing change and perhaps even enacting it. This is, unfortunately, very difficult to justify, given the way in which psychoanalytic theory since Freud has conceived of both the "social" and "change." It is not at all clear that psychoanalysis would allow for a conception of progressive social change at all. Freud does not seem to have described the possibility of collective progress or cure, but in his later writings he does seem very concerned with certain stubborn, unchanging group-psychological structures that shape the formation of the social entity.

In *Civilization and Its Discontents,* Freud offers a very complicated and ironic view of the efficacy of psychoanalytic intervention in the realm of the social. If civilization is the process by which human beings learned to coexist more or less peaceably with one another despite a constitutive aggression, Freud never ceases to remind us of the ruinous price paid for such a renunciation of aggression. His own skepticism about mastering aggression, exploitation, and violence by means of an equitable distribution of property is nowhere more evident than in his allusion to the Communist revolution in Russia:

> The communists believe that they have found the path to deliverance from our evils. According to them, man is wholly good and is well-disposed to his neighbor, but the institution of private property has corrupted his nature. . . . I have no concern with any economic criticisms of the communist system; I cannot enquire into whether the abolition of private property is expedient or advantageous. But I am able to recognize that the psychological premisses on which the system is based are an untenable illusion. In abolishing private property we deprive the human love of aggression of one of its instruments . . . but we have in no way altered the differences in power and influence which are misused by aggressiveness, nor have we altered anything in its nature.[3]

For Freud, the constitutive aggressive instincts of the human subject make for the most ambivalent sorts of relations in social or intersubjective life, but in psychoanalytic terms intrapsychic life is also conditioned by the aggressive and destructive impulses that one part of the psychic apparatus directs at another. Psychoanalytic theory, then, is about the thinking through of intersubjective aggressiveness in terms of or alongside intrapsychic aggressiveness. What this forces is a reevaluation of social history altogether, which Marxists might indeed find quietist, complicitous, and even reactionary. In another sense, however, class struggle can be understood in terms of this constitutive aggression: the gap between the classes is formed by resentment, on the one hand, and will to power, on the other. It is possible that Ernesto Laclau had this kind of analysis in mind when he discussed the Marxist break with the Enlightenment in terms of these two points: "(a) the affirmation of the central character of negativity—struggle and antagonism—in the structure of any collective identity; and (b) the affirmation of the opaqueness of the social—the ideological nature of collective representations—which establishes a permanent gap between the real and the manifest senses of individual and social group actions."[4] This class struggle and antagonism understood in terms of a constitutive aggression can then allow for an analysis of the regressive aspect of all "social group actions." The tenacity of various forms of totalitarian rule can be understood in terms of group-psychological identifications founded on the love of a strong leader and the suppression of all intragroup dissension. The regressive aspects of revolution and revolutionary action would have to be analyzed from such a point of view in a way that orthodox Marxism could not tolerate. Laclau's analysis of the "revolution of our time" is founded on an optimistic analogy that he constructs between the "hegemonic subject" and the "subject of the signifier." This take on the relationship between "revolution" and "our time" is more pessimistic. My time is different from Laclau's time: the problem is perhaps the impossibility of sharing this first-person plural possessive pronoun.

Psychoanalysis has been accused of being out of time, of ignoring time, but Freud's most important insights disrupted any linear conception of the time line of individual experience. There is no reason to think that social time—"our" time as opposed to "my" time—is safe from such disruption. *Civilization and Its Discontents* offers two major theoretic insights into the nature of changes in social formations. The first has to do with the relationship of the group to the primal horde structure,[5] and the second with the tensions created by the impossible Christian imperative to love one's neighbor as oneself. It is also in this work, however, that Freud refuses the role of prophet, thereby depriving us of the comforts offered by religious injunctions. His refusal is scandalous and produces a kind of transferential discontent that continues to bear the fruit of a tenacious resistance because he offers nothing that might make us feel good about doing good or being virtuous. "Thus I have not the courage to rise up before my fellow-men as a prophet, and I bow to their reproach that I can offer them no consolation: for at bottom that is what they are all demanding—the wildest revolutionaries no less passionately than the most virtuous believers."[6] What Freud implies is that psychoanalysis has in a certain sense renounced the idea of history as the history of progress and (home- as well as self-) improvement(s),[7] while at the *same time* it has given up on the moral superiority of preserving traditional virtues. Doing good by agitating for revolution and being good by preserving religious virtues are activities that aim at procuring the kind of comfort Freud refused to offer.

In the intellectual climate of the academy today, our eating-disordered reception of psychoanalysis manifests as a large appetite for different forms of consolation, for feeling good (about ourselves). Any discourse that refuses to satisfy this desire for good feeling has to bear the full weight of violent repudiation and passive forgetting. The incorporation of psychoanalytic terms such as *subject, identification, narcissism, regression, repression,* and so on, by politically driven disciplines allows for a kind of terminal forgetting or strategic nonreading of, and reflexive gagging on, psychoanalysis itself. This forgetful nonreading is most often justified on the grounds of "high" theory's alleged political irresponsibility and ineffectiveness. But let us not throw too much blame on the Anglo-American Marxists running cultural studies with organs like *Social Text.* Psychoanalytic theory seems to contain its own self-destruct mechanism, or, we could say, theory is that which effectively produces the most tenacious forms of resistance to itself. For instance, "Psychoanalysis and Social Change," as a title or proper name, indicates how eager psychoanalytically engaged theorists are to defuse the most scandalous aspects of psychoanalysis. Psychoanalytic theory, once swallowed too quickly, thereafter becomes resistance to theory. There are carnivorous, all-devouring apprenticeships the very zealousness of which leads to the indigestion of amnesia, a condition brought on us by a man who had not the courage to be a prophet, but who predicted with uncanny insight the fate of his own teachings.[8] There may be a conspiracy against psychoanalytic theory, but then again there may not be; what psychoanalysis permits, however, is a theorization of the structure of conspiracies themselves.

Conspiracy theories in general and the particular conspiracy theories that have arisen around John F. Kennedy's assassination can be read as popular attempts at theoretic production which are nevertheless uncannily remote-controlled by Frankfurt-school imperatives to forge a critique that would include psychoanalytic theory and ideological critique at the *same time.* This notion of simultaneity, of being faithful or accountable at once to Marxism and to psychoanalysis, is perhaps an impossible one, but the impossibility produces some fascinating symptoms. Conspiracy theory can be considered a popular, if not populist, effort to produce theory in an extra-academic setting; insofar as their production is symptomatic and notoriously obsessional, such theories point toward a failed and unconscious attempt to resolve contradictions, namely, those contradictions that continue to nag an unhappy marriage of convenience—one that is always on the rocks—between psychoanalysis and Marxism.

The conspiracy theories about Kennedy's assassination cover the ground between Marxism and psychoanalysis because they include (1) vulgar Marxist interpretation: JFK was the victim of a conspiracy between the Mafia and anti-Castro paramilitary forces, with the Cubans representing an antirevolutionary formation and the Mafia an extreme case of capitalist hegemony with respect to Cuba; and (2) vulgar Freudian analysis: JFK was the victim of intense Oedipal jealousy on the part of Lyndon B. Johnson and J. Edgar Hoover, who, representing the complicity of sexual and class resentment, had to engineer the president's death in order to accede to power. It seems that the trauma of the JFK assassination can only be "understood" or assimilated in an affectively satisfying way by producing conspiracy theories that actually take account of both Marxist and psychoanalytic structures of analysis.

The paranoia of conspiracy theorists can be understood in terms of a symptomatic overinterpretation. That is, if interpretation always already falls into overinterpretation, so that one can always be accused of "reading too much into" anything, then the theorist, as a mutation of the philosopher, might take a kind of perverse pleasure in the Freudian claim that "the delusions of paranoiacs have an unpalatable external similarity and internal kinship to the systems of our philosophers."[9] Every text is a conspiracy. The primal conspiracy by which we are haunted, according to Freud, is the one that brought down the father of the primal horde.[10] Conspiracy theory, then, does not need to be based on empirical facts. Its power is drawn from its relationship to a structure of rumormongering and hearsay, from the indelible and unpredictable dissemination of the mark of the conspiratorial *and* the theoretical.

In *Specters of Marx*, Derrida plays with the double meaning of the French term *conjuration*, which can be translated as either "conspiracy" or "exorcism." Marx represented the conspiracy against communism as a conspiracy of ghostbusters aimed at exorcising the specter of revolution, a ghost from the future the threat of which sealed the conspiratorial bond among all the powers of Europe gathered around the séance table:

> All possible alliances are thus forged to conjure away this common adversary, "the specter of communism." The alliance signifies: death to the specter. It is convoked to be revoked. . . . The salon, then, is old Europe which is gathering all its forces [*alle Mächte des alten Europas*]. . . . For the conspirators, communism is a name, the holy alliance is a holy hunt: "All the powers of old Europe have joined [*verbündet*] into a holy hunt [*zu einer heiligen Hetzjagd*] against this specter [*gegen dies Gespenst*]."[11]

A holy hunt could be a witch-hunt: the Red Scare of the McCarthy era was a threat that had to be eradicated through zealous search-and-destroy missions conducted in U.S. government agencies and before government tribunals. The nineteenth-century European salon of antirevolutionary conspirators operated under a less official seal, but its bohemian ambience did not keep away guests from all the ranks of Europe's old powers. Marx's *Eighteenth Brumaire of Louis Bonaparte* depicts a group of corrupt bohemians conspiring to conjure away the threat of an authentic revolution by playing at politics and usurping the place of the proletariat on the political scene by mobilizing a *Lumpenproletariat* with violent inclinations and by crystallizing the narrow-minded interests of small-landowning peasants.[12] The unsavory professional conspirators whose smoke-filled milieu spawned Louis Bonaparte were, according to Marx, simply putschist opportunists in a position of parasitic dependency on the revolutionary class. If Marx was disgusted by such a performance, he was nevertheless capable of acknowledging its success. Benjamin reminds us of the relationship of interdependency between conspirators and revolutionaries evinced by their cooperative building of the Paris barricades; Marx acknowledged that these conspirators built and defended many of the barricades and that Blanqui himself came terrifyingly close to being a putschist who was ready to "anticipate the revolutionary developmental process, to bring it artificially to a head, and improvise a revolution without the conditions for one."[13] If the conspirator-as-putschist anticipates and improvises revolution, he is an impatient actor, not ready to learn his lines and recite them on cue. The revolutionary and the bohemian converged in the ambivalent figure of Blanqui, who gave the professional conspirators a run for their money. The leader of the authentically revolutionary class turned out to be a shady character himself. For Benjamin, Blanqui's literary counterpart is Baudelaire, who conspired with language.

The *Eighteenth Brumaire* amounts to an analysis of failed revolution as successful conspiracy. Marx's critique proceeds as a dramaturgical exegesis of the events leading to victory by a sleazy adventurer who ruthlessly seized the moment. In Marx's "screenplay treatment" of the story of Louis Bonaparte's rise to power, the sequence—a farcical repetition of Napoleon's victories—plots the usurpation of the revolution: "Only when he [Louis] has eliminated his solemn opponent, when he himself takes his imperial role seriously and under the Napoleonic mask imagines he is the real Napoleon, does he become the victim of his own conception of the world, the serious buffoon who no longer takes world history for a comedy but his comedy for world history."[14] Marx critiques the eighteenth Brumaire in re-presenting these events, with his ideological demystification sharpest when describing Louis as a ham actor mouthing sentimental and deferential formulas of flattery to those around him while amassing the kind of terroristic power that has shadowed every twentieth-century despot's uncanny instinct for inspiring the *Lumpenproletariat* and the resentful small-landowning peasantry to acts of exhilarating violence. If there is anything striking about Marx's analysis, it is the elusive presence of that revolutionary urban proletariat—the class whose authentically progressive instincts and intentions are thwarted at every turn and whose presence in this text is elusive insofar as it is strictly virtual, marginal at best and foreshadowed by failure. Such failure might then be the real revolution's fate, Marx's own description of bourgeois revolution as storming swiftly from success to success notwithstanding. If failure is indeed the fate of an authentically progressive class, it can be described as a progressive failure, but one that needs to be acknowledged as such. Failure is dogged by the shadow of the very mourning that Benjamin mobilized to describe the mood of history. While there is no question about the urban proletariat's status as the loser of the eighteenth Brumaire, is it therefore the loser of history?

If bourgeois history is always that of the winners, recent history has been written according to the logic of winners who present themselves as losers, which is not perhaps what Marx had in mind when he described the authentically revolutionary proletariat as the class that rejected facile triumphs in its attempts at revolution. It was in fact Louis Bonaparte who knew how best to mobilize a bunch of real losers, the "adventurous offshoots" of the bourgeoisie: "vagabonds, discharged soldiers, discharged jailbirds, escaped galley slaves, swindlers, mountebanks, lazzaroni, pickpockets, tricksters, gamblers, maquereaus, brothel keepers, porters, literati, organ-grinders, ragpickers, knife-grinders, tinkers, beggars, —in short, the whole indefinite, disintegrated mass, thrown hither and thither, which the French term *la bohème*."[15] Bonaparte, shaping his shadow army, the Society of 10 December, from this unsavory group, is dubbed by Marx "chief of the *Lumpenproletariat*," leading (or catching) the runoff—the scum and refuse of all classes. The Society of 10 December became not only Bonaparte's private army, but also the extras and background crowd in the drama he had scripted for his coup d'état. Bonaparte, observes Marx, conceived "the historical life of the nations and their performances of state as comedy in the most vulgar sense, as a masquerade where the grand costumes, words and postures merely serve to mask the pettiest knavery."[16] The state might always be the *performance of state* and thus at all times capable of being performed as a costume drama played by idiots, but Bonaparte was able to use the theater of nation as a stage where *la bohème* got to play a leading role. And this ragtag group, dangerous because classless—a nomadic amalgamation whose investments and identifications were always purely opportunistic—was always acting. This group understood the performance of state as a *performance*; it was the others—the *classes*—that took themselves seriously. Marx, of course, points to the bourgeoisie as the class that was most deeply self-deceiving in its performance of the rituals of power, and to the bohemian conspirator as the most self-consciously theatrical of actors. But was not Blanqui, the leader of the genuinely revolutionary proletariat—for Marx at least, if not for Benjamin—capable of several grand theatrical gestures himself? Every revolutionary gesture is susceptible to theatrical parody or deformation, but when one group takes its performance seriously the others become all the more capable of taking advantage. The contempt in which Marx held *la bohème* had to do with that group's self-conscious theatricality, its dangerous and parasitic inability to assume a class identity, sustain class interests, or play a properly revolutionary role without exploiting it, but he did not fail to acknowledge that lucidity about the theater of power struggles which enabled the bohemian to triumph over the self-deceiving bourgeoisie: "At a moment when the bourgeoisie itself played the most complete comedy, but in the most serious manner in the world, without infringing any of the pedantic conditions of French dramatic etiquette, and was itself half deceived, half convinced of the solemnity of its own performance of state, the adventurer, who took the comedy as plain comedy, was bound to win."[17]

The bohemian's ability to forgo solemnity for performativity was indeed a dangerous quality—as well as the stuff of which conspiracies could be woven. It was from within precisely this motley group of desperate and sometimes dangerous characters that Benjamin saw a number of key figures emerging to spearhead an allegorical understanding of the conditions of high capitalism. The great powers of Europe may have effectively exorcised the specter of communism through the figure of the professional conspirator (the most successful of whom turned out to be Louis Bonaparte), but conspiracies tend to undermine the legitimacy of revolutionary and counterrevolutionary gestures alike—which is why the specter of conspiracy continues to haunt agencies of power.

Theater is historical, history theatrical, for Benjamin, whose work anticipates the staging of a radically depersonalized psychoanalytic intervention in the genealogy of modernism. This intervention is perhaps not immediately recognizable as such because it occurred via the re-presentation of an allegorical drama on nothing less or more than the mourning after melancholia, an unfinished allegorical ritual of expiation and exorcism implied by the writing of history. Once framed by such a theater of history, that intervention could no longer be readily identified as authentically revolutionary—or not. Fredric Jameson reads the antagonism between Brecht and Kafka (both of whom figure in Benjamin's readings on theater) as seeming "to dramatize some deeper fundamental antinomy in modern cultural thought, if not its reality, namely that which assigns antithetical positions to the political and the subjective or existential, to the didactic and the expressive, to consciousness or agency and to the unconscious."[18] In other words, the antinomy of modern cultural thought—if not modern cultural *reality*—is *dramatized* by the radical incompatibility between political, didactic, conscious agency and the subjective, existential, expressive unconscious. The distance between thought and reality is at once staged and covered up by an apparent contradiction: from a psychoanalytic point of view, the unconscious is not expressive; therefore, "subjective or existential," "expressive," and "unconscious" are unsustainable as terms on one side of an antinomy. The juxtaposition of these terms is possible only within an antipsychoanalytic, commonsense gesture of psychologization. The fundamental antinomy of modern cultural thought (and perhaps reality) becomes pure and unproblematic only when psychoanalytic theory is cut out of the script or cast in an understudy's role. According to Jameson, Kafka's psychology and Brecht's pedagogy are reconciled through the notion of *gestus*, with Kafka in a sense redeemed by Brecht. The opposition between these two forms of modernism remains intact.

Jameson's exclusion of psychoanalysis undergoes a significant transformation in his article on *Specters of Marx*. Here, he takes on the question of the mourning after revolutionary impossibility and even goes so far as to draw the following analogy between psychoanalysis and Marxism:

> Rather than conceiving of materialism as a systematic philosophy, it would seem possible and perhaps more desirable to think of it as a polemic stance, designed to organize various anti-idealist campaigns, a procedure of demystification and de-idealization; or else a permanent linguistic reflexivity. This is, among other things, why Marxism has never been a philosophy as such, but rather a "unity-of-theory-and-practice" very much like psychoanalysis, and for many of the same reasons.[19]

If such a process of de-idealization is to be successful, it would have to start with a reconsideration of the position of the authentically revolutionary proletariat, for if we are to actually forge a kind of psycho-Marxism out of Freud's constitutive aggression and Marx's class struggle, the revolutionary proletariat must be reconstructed against the ground of resentment, group psychology, and the temptations of regression. Mao's totalitarian gesture was built on the mystification and idealization of a worker/peasant/soldier class that would have an authentically progressive insight into every conflict, every struggle.

The proletariat has to be reconceived allegorically in order for the revolutionary gesture to be reframed in a Benjaminian theater of generalized inauthenticity.[20] This is not a simple affirmation of the fact that postmodern subjectivity can be conceived as an inherently and exclusively performative construct. Benjamin's thought experiment of history-as-theater and theater-as-history not only raises a number of difficult questions around the notion of "political gesture," but also poses an implicit challenge to the notions of theater, acting, and performance.[21] From the ruins of traditional theater, it is possible to reassess what the stakes are when one considers the stage, with or without mirrors, as one site of history and politics. Benjamin's theorization of theater changes the conditions of acting (out) itself. As Samuel Weber and Hans Jost Frey have separately demonstrated, Benjamin's *Origin of German Tragic Drama* (or of the "mourning play," as it has been alternatively and perhaps more accurately translated) is a working out—and through—of a conceptualization of history and the historical event which "is incompatible with at least one prominent aspect of Hegelian thought: the dialectical resolution entailed in the notion of 'conciliation': *Versöhnung*."[22] In presenting or representing history as an object of knowledge subject to the radically unpredictable, Benjamin's allegorical arrangement of monadic ideas dramatizes a theatrical space of presentation and representation in which various constellations of props are animated by the gestures of ghostly performers who walk through ever-changing tableaux. These monadic ideas and images conspire to form fleeting associations. As Frey reminds us, Baudelaire and Blanqui are presented together as a couple of performers whose mastery of their respective roles as poet and conspirator leaves no room whatsoever for an extratheatrical evaluation of their ontological consistency. "All presentation is thus theatrical, since it does not say, but performs."[23]

For Benjamin, the stage is inevitably and unhappily implicated as a historical space in which a story of violent and meaningless failures can be told. According to modern genealogy, the Baroque theater was the stage of the despot, who, threatened on all sides by coups, conspiracies, and revolts, had recourse to an absolute force that often brought him to ruin. History is thus the space of highly theatricalized and generalized inauthenticity. In his analysis of the *Trauerspiel*, Benjamin describes the court as the very image of the *Schauplatz* (showplace), with theater then the key to understanding history. The court becomes the setting for nothing less than the "timeless, natural decor of the historical process" itself.[24] Acting in history, or being a historical actor, implies the setup of intrigue or conspiracy. The *courtier* is the third term of a political typology that also includes *tyrant* and *martyr*, action figures of the time–space continuum of absolutism from which the present has received a traumatic and cryptic legacy. The courtier, *der Höfling* as *Intrigant*, is an allegorical figure that renders part of this burdensome inheritance legible. As Weber has demonstrated, "the courtier" (*der Höfling*) inhabits "the court" (*den Hof*) as a showplace or setting.[25] He has no home, no habitat, but rather a stage upon which he can plot and choreograph the intrigues of which he himself can always become the victim. The courtier, as a conspirator, works with and against the tyrant whom he so assiduously serves. Usurpation is the typical historical event that occurs under such a regime, in such a place. History is represented as a series of frozen tableaux that shatter, then fade, only to reassemble as spectral monuments commemorating the ruins of other moments of stasis and consolidation. Benjamin saw the courtier as always doing double duty as a conspirator and a bureaucrat. Indeed, it was in Baroque Spanish theater that this figure's dual role was fully realized: "the intriguer, as the evil genius of their despots, and the faithful servant, as the companion in suffering to innocence enthroned."[26] The courtier is a fascinating combination of intellect, insight, compassion, and absolute dependency. Both mediator and intermediary, the courtier is also a courier—a carrier of messages as well as a currier of favors. He works with and for the tyrant, whose charm derives from both his charismatic personality and the crisis of legitimacy that dogs his rule.

The tyrant is a reminder of the one around whose magical body order can be reinstalled, and as such he bears the mark of the primal father, a figure with whom no one really wants to have much to do anymore. The fraternal conspiracy that brings him down, however, seems to cast a long shadow over the political gesture—the act and acting out that constitutes a historical event. As a violent and absolutely effective power grab, the murder of the primal father produces an almost unmournable loss. The susceptibility of unstable social and political formations to the power of a single despotic individual is only one of the legacies entailed by the primal father's indestructible charisma. Absolute rule must be repeatedly overcome, and, as Marx reminded us, the first time is almost always tragic, the second time farcical. History, then, is the history of repetitions that often pass themselves off as contradictions. For Benjamin, what teaches this lesson is the mourning play because it "is not just opposed to tragedy; it seems to repeat it, as a kind of parody."[27] This parodic repetition takes us right back to the opening lines of the *Eighteenth Brumaire*: "Hegel remarks somewhere that all facts and personages of great importance in world history occur, as it were, twice. He forgot to add: the first time as tragedy, the second as farce."[28] It is the farce, however, that imposes a mood of and for mourning by ushering in the courtier, who comes onto the scene as a lightning rod of ambivalence: as the tyrant's assistant, hatred is his reserve.

Being a revolutionary has increasingly been reduced to *acting* like a revolutionary. A deep skepticism should be cultivated toward all official announcements of revolution in particular, be they cultural or political. Let's not forget that the most recent "successful" revolution to be officially announced and televised in this country was closely associated with Newt Gingrich. We should not, however, leap to the conclusion that all politics and every revolution must be dismissed as *mere* theater. This kind of contempt would be simply giving in to the ideology of commonsensical cynicism. Remaining in a state of disgust with the theatrical setup of political gestures would mean remaining trapped in the most mystifying nostalgia for an arena of *authentic* political action.

Theorizing history and politics as forms of conspiracy and theater enables a greater understanding of the politics of theatricality. It is to engage in a struggle with ideological mystification in order to secure extra-theatrical spaces for authentic gestures. If history is a theater of generalized inauthenticity for the Benjamin of the *Trauerspiel*, politics can be understood as a generalized theater of antagonistic, unstable beings, not unlike, for instance, a negative image of Kafka's Nature Theater of Oklahoma. Benjamin's theater of generalized inauthenticity is saturated with the banality of the struggles of everyday life, while there are no auditions for Kafka's Nature Theater. Perhaps everyone is accepted because, for Kafka as for Benjamin, acting authentically is already *second* nature.

First nature, if we can call it that, is an infinitely deferred origin that has given way to second nature. In second-nature theater, the alienation of the subject is the light that throws an allegory of antagonistic relationships, of inter- and intrapsychic aggressions, into sharp relief. There are no better or worse actors, as each individual is engaged in rendering a copy of him- or herself that must aggressively find its place—its role and strategic position—in relation to other individuals and various social groups and classes. This is perhaps the cue for the signifier's entrance: role-playing, as cipher-like signifiers staged against a changing political backdrop, is engaging in a struggle for the power of representation. Such drama may contain material unsuitable for viewers with an overinvestment in their roles as either guardians of tradition or agents of revolution. This script cannot be adapted for television, cinema, *or* theater, not being transmissible as such, but it can be played as psychodrama. The corridor wars fought in the institutions we inhabit have become as highly ritualized as any sacrificial *corrida*; this is the scene on which we must keep a constant eye. Before we can reach the redemptive space of second-nature theater, we have to cross the hinterlands of mystifying studio-stage sets, where many actors try to pass themselves off as the stars of the only system worthy of our undivided attention.

But let's forget about the authentically revolutionary gesture. Within this forgetting will be encrypted an important reminder: gestures are not the offspring of profound inner experience or lucid revolutionary insight; they are rather the bastards born of couplings between paranoia, necessity, fear, and, occasionally, a pure leap of inexplicable inspiration. The revolution is not of or for our times; it is a contingency for which we must be prepared. If this theory of theatrical gesture defies the temporality of historicism, it is because second-nature theater respects the fact that, in the absolute unpredictability of a convulsive gesture, something appears that looks like hope.

Notes

1 This is one of the reasons why it was so easy for certain intellectuals to take sides in the debate over the Paul de Man scandal. Condemnation and accusation emerged as a particular tone and style; other kinds of writing that urged more reflection were deemed by journalists, and those on their side, irresponsible, evasive, complicit, and so on.

2 The Association's second annual conference, "Psychoanalysis and Social Change," took place in the fall of 1996 in Washington, DC.

3 Sigmund Freud, *Civilization and Its Discontents* (1930), Vol. 21 of *The Standard Edition of the Complete Psychological Works of Sigmund Freud*, 24 vols., ed. and trans. James Strachey (London, 1953–74), 112–13.

4 Ernesto Laclau, "Psychoanalysis and Marxism," trans. Amy G. Reiter-McIntosh, in *New Reflections on the Revolution of Our Time* (London, 1990), 93–96; quotation from 94.

5 See Catherine Liu, "Edible Dad: Psychoanalysis as Conspiracy Theory or One Aspect of the Feminist Fantasy," *Clinical Studies: International Journal of Psychoanalysis* 2 (1996): 87–102.

6 Freud, *Civilization and Its Discontents*, 145.

7 While Freud refused to play the prophet, his work demands a heavy renunciation. When he describes the nonreception of Moses' monotheism by the Israelites, he emphasizes

that this message was delivered as a demand for renunciation—the renunciation of idol worship. According to Freud, it took the murder of Moses and two generations of wandering around in regressed polytheism before the Jews finally identified monotheism as a "precious treasure." What happened to Moses' special delivery of the "message" of monotheism? It got lost in the mail for two generations because it was refused by its addressees and returned to sender. The refusal occurred as a murder—the murder of the messenger, Moses himself. The belated reception of the message as the most precious of missives then demanded that the messenger's murder be assiduously covered up, hence the biblical rewriting of Moses' assassination as a "disappearance." Monotheism was a sort of letter, then, addressed by Akhenaton and carried by Moses to the Jews, who returned it to the sender or perhaps merely forwarded it to the future. The rhythm of this delay in reception was driven by a sequential movement from confusion, violent repudiation, and regression to a subsequent cover-up that facilitated a peculiar acceptance.

8 There is a homologously symptomatic way in which the Left in this country has stopped reading Marx: forgetting about class struggle allows for the management of ethnic, sexual, and racial differences while suppressing class difference.

9 Sigmund Freud, "Review of Reik's *On Ritual*," in Strachey, ed. and trans., *Standard Edition*, 17: 261–62; quotation from 261.

10 According to the Freudian genealogy of groups, the band of brothers, banished from the horde, conspired to take down the primal father because they were no match for him individually.

11 Jacques Derrida, *Specters of Marx: The State of the Debt, the Work of Mourning, and the New International*, trans. Peggy Kamuf (New York and London, 1994 [1993]), 99–100.

12 Karl Marx, *The Eighteenth Brumaire of Louis Bonaparte* (New York, 1984 [1851]).

13 Walter Benjamin, *Charles Baudelaire: A Lyric Poet in the Era of High Capitalism*, trans. Harry Zohn (London, 1985), 16; quoting Karl Marx and Friedrich Engels, review of Adolphe Chenu, *Les conspirateurs* (Paris, 1850) and Lucien de la Hodde, *La naissance de la République en février 1848* (Paris, 1850), *Die Neue Zeit* 4 (1886): 556.

14 Marx, *Eighteenth Brumaire*, 76.

15 Ibid., 75. It is important to include literati in this list of disreputable characters because, like actors, organ-grinders, ragpickers, and knife-grinders, the literati represent an ancient, itinerant, stateless class of artisans whose unstable and nomadic existence put them at the mercy of established, sedentary communities.

16 Ibid., 75–76.

17 Ibid., 76.

18 Fredric Jameson, "Benjamin's Readings," *diacritics* 22 (1992): 19–34; quotation from 21.

19 Fredric Jameson, "Marx's Purloined Letter," *New Left Review*, No. 209 (January/February 1995): 75–109; quotation from 84.

20 For Werner Hamacher, gestures are not so much empty as that they tear into the fabric of meaningfulness; they are also described as sites of opacity that, as such, partake of the particular failures figured by modernity. As read by Benjamin, the nonexpressive gestures in Kafka's writing only become legible as an allegory of a retreat and withdrawal from representation itself; see "The Gesture in the Name: On Benjamin and

Kafka," in Werner Hamacher, *Premises: Essays on Philosophy and Literature from Kant to Celan* (Cambridge, MA, 1997), 293–336.

21 Among the reevaluations of subjectivity as a modality of performance, Judith Butler's take on sexual difference and identity has been highly influential, but seems to neglect the historical conditions of theatricality; see, for example, her *Gender Trouble* (New York, 1990). Samuel Weber's work on Walter Benjamin provides for an understanding of the stage and acts of staging as significant in the historical register; see his "Genealogy of Modernity: History, Myth and Allegory in Benjamin's *Origin of the German Mourning Play*," *MLN* 106 (1991): 465–500.

22 Weber, "Genealogy of Modernity," 467–68.

23 Hans Jost Frey, "On Presentation," in *Walter Benjamin: Theoretical Questions*, ed. David Ferris (Stanford, 1996), 139–64; quotation from 163–64.

This applies to intellectual and academic presentations as well. In the American academy, for example, gestures of self-representation are increasingly hailed as both enfranchising and revolutionary, but in subscribing to such a notion of the political, one must avoid all questions of what might constitute either the "self" or "representation."

24 Walter Benjamin, *The Origin of German Tragic Drama*, trans. John Osborne (London, 1996 [1928]), 93.

25 See Weber, "Genealogy of Modernity," 477.

26 Benjamin, *Origin of German Tragic Drama*, 98.

27 Weber, "Genealogy of Modernity," 489.

28 Marx, *Eighteenth Brumaire*, 15.

Robert Miklitsch

"Going through the Fantasy": Screening Slavoj Žižek

> Far from being the Other of Europe, former Yugoslavia was rather Europe itself in its Otherness, the screen onto which Europe projected its own repressed reverse.
> —Slavoj Žižek, "Caught in Another's Dream in Bosnia"

The Giant of Ljubljana? The Casanova of Slovenia? The Balkan Lacan? Saint Slavoj?

Who, exactly, is Slavoj Žižek, and where does he hail from?

It is all, one might say, in the name. An anecdote: when I first came across this particular proper name—significantly, while reading Terry Eagleton's introduction to *Ideology*—I was struck less by Žižek's remarks on ideology, which offered a slight but crucial revision of Peter Sloterdijk's formula for "enlightened false consciousness" ("they know that, in their activity, they are following an illusion, but still, they are doing it"[1]), than by the sheer strangeness of the name: all those little *v*s and *z*s!

The *South Atlantic Quarterly* 97:2, Spring 1998.

Slovenia as X-Yugoslavia. Žižek hails of course from the East, as in Eastern Europe, or the Balkans, as in "balkanized." More specifically yet, he hails from Ljubljana, Slovenia, which nation–state was once part of Yugoslavia.

Slovenia, then, as X-Yugoslavia.

The *x* here—like the Slavic *v*s and *z*s—indicates the uncanny status of Slovenia for most Americans, where Slovenia might as well be Transylvania, and Dracula the first, insidious emissary of the Sino-Soviet Other. Part of the mysteriousness also derives from Slovenia's being—unlike, say, the United States—the product of an extremely complex geopolitical history. For instance, in 1929, King Alexander I abolished the democratic-constitutional government established in 1921, while, in October of the same year the Serbo-Croat-Slovene Kingdom, which had been proclaimed in December 1918, officially became Yugoslavia ("southern Slavs"). The Balkan Pact's formation in 1934 and, later that year, King Alexander's assassination by a Macedonian revolutionary associated with Croat terrorists centered in Hungary reflect the zeitgeist of the period. In fact, King Alexander's assassination occurred while he was on a diplomatic tour of the European capitals in order to secure alliances against an increasingly bellicose Nazi Germany (hence the Balkan Pact). It is one of those historical ironies that suggests not only the volatility of nationalism in this part of Europe between the world wars (King Alexander's assassination itself almost resulting in a war between Yugoslavia and Hungary) but, rather more to the point of Žižek's work, the near-feudal monarchical character of the nation–state of Yugoslavia (where one could still speak of the assassination of kings, as in *Hamlet*, rather than, as in this country, of presidents).

Although the creation of the sovereign state of Slovenia in 1991 is one terminus to that geopolitical trajectory (bracketing here the whole question of Tito[2]), this inaugural event for Žižek had less to do with Slovenia proper than with the fate of the Balkans in general. The critical moment here—with respect, that is, to the decomposition of "actually existing socialism" in Eastern Europe—is the death of Ceauşescu, a "fall" that situates the "little story" of Slovenia within the metanarrative of macrocommunism even as it recollects Žižek's own Hamletlike meditations on the sublime problematic of the king-thing: "Is this really *him*? . . . Is the thing really with this body? Did it really die with it?"[3]

This double take on the fall of Ceauşescu—the sudden, utter collapse of the Big Other (when the Sleeping Beauty spell of totalitarianism was finally broken) and the post-execution problem of the despot's "two bodies" (which, for Žižek, uncannily reproduces the aporia associated with the Jacobin logic of regicide[4])—is evoked at the very beginning of *Tarrying with the Negative*. There, the sublimity of Ceauşescu's double death—at once imaginary and symbolic, like Madeleine/Judy's in Hitchcock's *Vertigo*—is refigured in the cinematic image of the "rebels waving the national flag with the red star, the Communist symbol, cut out, so that instead of the symbol standing for the organizing principle of the national life, there was nothing but a hole in its center."[5] It is between one death and another—from the assassination of King Alexander to the execution of the king-thing Ceauşescu—or between one nation-state and another—from the Serbo-Croat-Slovene Kingdom to post-Communist Slovenia—within just such a determinate, political-historical space that Žižek's work must be situated.[6] Not to do so is, it seems to me, to radically *ex*-nominate that work.

And yet if Žižek as the voice of X-Yugoslavia offers a partial answer to the question of who he is and where he hails from (i.e., Žižek as nationalist and historical witness), the *x* also signals that it is ultimately impossible to reduce his work to its political and geographical conditions of possibility. As Sartre said famously of Valéry, "Valéry is a petit bourgeois intellectual, . . . [but] not every petit bourgeois intellectual is Valéry."[7] With this in mind, one might argue that the question is not *Who, exactly, is Slavoj Žižek, and where does he hail from?* but *For whom, exactly, does he function as the "sublime" intellectual Other?* To pose the question this way is not only to repose the issue of academic production in all its national and international force; it is also to foreground the issue of reception and consumption, or the problem of desire.

Žižek in America. If "Žižek in America" refers to the English or American, as opposed to the Slovene or even French, Žižek, this Anglo-American figure is, first of all, the Žižek of the *Sublime Object of Ideology*, which was published in 1989 in the Verso series Phronesis, edited by Ernesto Laclau and Chantal Mouffe.[8] While the "French Žižek" is by no means absent from this volume (where he acknowledges Jacques-Alain Miller in the same space that he cites Laclau and Mouffe), the fact that his first book in English appeared in the Phronesis series nevertheless intimates that the American reception of his work is overdetermined by a certain British, post–New Left address.[9] Still, the "American Žižek"—like the Slovene one—exceeds this particular textual-institutional frame as well. It is not simply that he writes in *American* English (which immediately distinguishes him from, say, Lacan), but that Žižek, especially in his later work, has a love affair of sorts with American popular culture, so much so that he appears to know the United States from the inside (as it seems only foreigners can do). This Žižek—the one we love to read because he reflects our own popular-cultural vision of the United States back to us (in reverse, as Lacan would say)—embodies the "whole" problem of subjectivity as envisioned by Lacan and reenvisioned by Žižek himself (e.g., desire as the desire of the Other).

That this Žižek may be a mirror image or even a mirage for American readers is an obvious possibility and one that no doubt accounts, at least in part, for his "popularity" in this country (hence my tactical evocation of the "Slovene Žižek" at the very beginning here, which is intended to forestall any simple, "imaginary" reading of his work). But if his U.S. audience is a restricted, not to say academic, one, his popularity can nevertheless be a useful means of exploring the problematic of popular culture as it intersects with that of postmodernism. Žižek himself has explicitly invoked the dialectical relation between popular culture and postmodernism, but for all the hullabaloo about the postmodernist "deconstruction" of the high-modernist division between elite and mass culture (a project that would appear to be central to Žižek[10]), postmodernism is something of a red herring in his work. That is to say, if Žižek is postmodernist (and it is difficult to imagine a term that better describes his corpus), his postmodernism is—to be crude—more a matter of form than of content. For instance, in the introduction to the *Sublime Object of Ideology*, Žižek observes that the absence of any reference to Althusser in Habermas's *Philosophical Discourse of Modernity* is a "curious accident," adding, in a perfectly Žižekian afterthought, "Of course, we are using the term 'curious accident' in a Sherlock Holmesian sense." A little later, introducing Michel Pêcheux's complicated take on Althusser's notion of interpellation, Žižek—in an abrupt, "bathetic" shift in tonality—recalls a Marx Brothers joke to illustrate the comic short circuit of ideological misrecognition: " 'You remind me of Emanuel Ravelli.' 'But I am Emanuel Ravelli.' 'Then no wonder you look like him!' "[11]

The way Žižek crosses hierarchically differentiated codes here—in particular, those associated with "high theory" and "mass culture,"[12] in the unexpected juxtaposition of Pêcheux with the Marx Brothers—marks his discourse as distinctly postmodernist. In fact, what appeared in the early work to be a strictly ornamental feature—the occasional, illustrative allusion to Coke or Marlboros, Heinlein or Hitchcock, *Alien* or *Invasion of the Body Snatchers*—has, in the later work, taken on a programmatic, even methodological, character, as in *Looking Awry*'s subtitle, *An Introduction to Jacques Lacan through Popular Culture*. This postmodernist tack is confirmed in the book's introduction, where Žižek cites Benjamin, Mozart, and Kant in rapid-fire order (including Kant's archly subversive definition of marriage as "a contract between two adult persons of the opposite sex on the mutual use of their sexual organs") in the course of announcing that *Looking Awry* proposes, apropos of the marriage of opera and philosophy, a "reading of the most sublime theoretical motifs of Jacques Lacan together with and through exemplary cases of contemporary mass culture." Although Žižek's modus operandi here would appear to derive from the Lacan of "Kant avec Sade," the parenthetical cap to the first paragraph of *Looking Awry* is "classic" Žižek: "(If, now and then, the book also mentions 'great' names like Shakespeare and Kafka, the reader need not be uneasy: they are read strictly as kitsch authors, on the same level as McCullough and King)."[13]

Lacan *avec* McCullough—Colleen McCullough, author of *The Thorn Birds*: Could there be any more striking instance of Žižek's postmodernism? And yet, as I have already observed, Žižek—or at least the "early" (Anglo-American) Žižek of the *Sublime Object of Ideology*—took distinct pains to demarcate his critical distance from postmodernism. Thus the introduction to that book concludes with a caveat about "falling prey" to "'post-modernist' traps such as the illusion that we live in a 'post-ideological' condition." Moreover, his later allusion there to "the usual 'post-modernist' anti-Enlightenment *ressentiment*" suggests that the quotation marks are to be understood less in the strict, deconstructive sense than in the more usual pejorative one.[14] The division or separation between popular culture and postmodernism in Žižek's work appears, then, to be a symptom of a certain ambivalence, even a contradiction, whereby the "performative Žižek," who celebrates popular culture, is patently at odds with the other, "constative Žižek," who critiques postmodernism.

That Žižek is a divided subject, that his discourse performs what is ostensibly the effect of postmodernism (i.e., the gradual effacement of the canonic distinction between mass and high culture), comes as no surprise, of course, given his commitment to the Lacanian conception of the subject. However, if there seems little doubt that Žižek's popularity is more a function of his postmodernist style than of his critique of postmodernism (the term itself being virtually absent from the early work),[15] his position on poststructuralism is an altogether different, more material matter. Consider, for instance, his judgment on the absolute difference between Lacan and Derrida. In order to defend Lacan against Derrida, Žižek's dominant gambit from the beginning has been to argue (against the prevailing, received wisdom) that Lacanian psychoanalysis, whatever it is, is *not* a species of poststructuralism.[16] The locus classicus of this brief *against* deconstruction and *for* psychoanalysis is the section headed "There is no metalanguage" that opens the third and final part of the *Sublime Object of Ideology*. Although Žižek contends here that Lacan's work should be carefully distinguished from both hermeneutics (Gadamer) and poststructuralism (Derrida), it readily becomes apparent that the real object of Žižek's critique is not so much hermeneutics or poststructuralism as deconstruction—which is to say, Derrida. Writing in the long wake of deconstruction occasioned by the fall of Paul de Man (among other things), Žižek reasserts the Lacanian "primacy of metaphor over metonymy"—*le point capiton* over "dissemination"—and, consequently, the whole question of "truth." Along these properly *post*-poststructuralist lines, Žižek also declares, in a devastating theoretical flourish, that the "position from which the deconstructivist can always make sure of the fact that 'there is no metalanguage,' that no utterance can say precisely what it intended to say," is in fact "*the position of metalanguage* in its purest . . . form."[17]

Now, the tenor of this critique may remind one of Lacan's elaboration on the position of the "ostrich" critic–detective in his "Seminar on 'The Purloined Letter'"—a symbolic structure of which Derrida himself, to be fair, is clearly aware—but, in its stressing of the real, immanent limits of any metalanguage, Žižek's critique of indeterminacy represents a substantial departure from both Derrida and the intersubjective Lacan of the 1950s.[18] Still, according to Žižek, what is really at stake in the deconstructionist proposition that "there is no metalanguage" is not (*pace* de Man and Derrida) its aporiatic status or structure; rather, the "point" is that the metalinguistic position characteristic of deconstruction is itself predicated on *denial*. Here, Žižek's Freudian emphasis effectively highlights the difference between the rhetoric of deconstruction and what might be called (after Laplanche and Pontalis) the "language of psychoanalysis." This difference—and the invocation of the psychic mechanism of *Verneinung* should not obscure the fact that Žižek's defense of psychoanalysis is a philosophical one—is, in a word, *subjectivity*. Accordingly, when Žižek concludes his *Sublime Object* argument about Lacan's post-poststructuralism, he submits that "the problem with deconstruction" is not its eschewing "a strict theoretical formulation," and thus acceding to "a flabby poeticism" à la Lévi-Strauss (although for Žižek it is obviously guilty of these venalities as well), but rather that its position is in fact "*too* 'theoretical.'" In other words, to claim, as Žižek does, that deconstruction is *too theoretical* is to claim that it "excludes the truth-dimension" and, as such, fails to "*affect* the place from which we speak." Put another way: precisely because it cannot account for affect, deconstruction is—in the final analysis—"affected."[19]

Post-Poststructuralism. If Žižek has carried on a vigorous rearguard battle against deconstruction, most notably, in admonishing Rodolphe Gasché as well as Derrida himself for misreading Hegel,[20] his avant-garde action has been fought on rather different "philosophical" terrain. This terrain is neither postmodernism nor poststructuralism but Marxism. Thus, in the *Sublime Object of Ideology*, he insists that the debate between Foucault and Habermas is a screen of sorts, concealing as it does another, "more far-reaching" opposition between Lacan and Althusser.[21] One way to get at this issue or debate, and its formative effect on Žižek, is to establish the theoretical space of his own work, which is defined, as he himself has noted, by three centers of gravity: dialectics, psychoanalysis, and the critique of ideology—or Hegel, Lacan, and Althusser.

Apropos of Althusser (to take the last "author function" first), Žižek has commented in an interview that the dominant philosophical trends in Slovenia over the last two decades have been Heideggerianism and Frankfurt-school Marxism (as opposed to, say, the Praxis school in Croatia and Hayekian philosophy of science in Serbia). However, neither approach was finally amenable to left Slovene intellectuals like Žižek: Heideggerianism because it was associated with "right-wing populism," Frankfurt-school Marxism because it was, ironically enough, the "official ideology" of the Slovene Communist Party. Consequently, the task for Žižek was "to be a dissident but not a Heideggerian."[22] This theoretically overdetermined political-historical conjuncture also explains the significance of Althusser for Slovene intellectuals, a significance that is dramatized for Žižek in the "big opposition" between Milan Kundera and Václav Havel. While for Kundera what was left of the private sphere and the small subversions one could perform there were the only source of resistance against the Communist regime, for Havel the basis of opposition was not "telling dirty stories" about the regime in private but *doing* some small thing, in public, that would disrupt the ritualistic character of everyday life (in accordance with the Althusserian thesis that state power is effectively reproduced via the public's abject submission to its rituals and practices, routines and ministrations).[23] Žižek elaborates on this aspect of what might be called the publicity of ideology in *Tarrying with the Negative*, where he adds that, for Slovene intellectuals, "the name 'Althusser' triggered an enigmatic uneasiness in all camps." Indeed, for Žižek, the political resistance to Althusser merely confirmed the fact that, although Althusserianism was "defamed as proto-Stalinist," it actually "served as a kind of 'spontaneous' theoretical tool for effectively undermining the Communist totalitarian regimes."[24] In so-called actually existing socialism, then, what counted was not "inner conviction" but "external obedience," not private belief but public practice.[25] In this particular context (which is, of course, the "classic" totalitarian one), the way to be really oppositional, according to Žižek, was to "act naively" à la Havel in order to disturb and subvert the regime's appearance of "ideological consistency."

Yet if Althusser remains one of the theoretical resources for the Slovene critique of ideology, Althusserianism has also always functioned as an object of critique for Žižek, whose lever for this counter-critique is Lacanian psychoanalysis. (Thus "Kafka, critic of Althusser"—a section heading in the *Sublime Object of Ideology*—might be reformulated "Lacan, critic of Althusser.") The key to this Lacanian critique of Althusser is the notion of *jouis-sense* ("enjoyment-in-sense" or "enjoy-meant"), whereby the dimension elided in the Althusserian theory of interpellation is the "dimension beyond interpellation," or what Žižek simply calls "beyond interpellation."[26] So, in the *Metastases of Enjoyment*, he asserts that what remains unthought in Althusser is the "uncanny subject" *prior* to identification and subjectivation.[27]

Now, given Žižek's critique of both Derrida and Althusser, this "uncanny subject" should clearly not be confused with either the Althusserian account of the imaginary dialectic of recognition and misrecognition (interpellation as identification) or the poststructuralist insistence on the irreducible polysemy of the symbolic register (interpellation as dissemination). Unlike Althusserian interpellation, which is the essence of the ideological operation ("all ideology hails . . . concrete individuals as concrete subjects"), Žižek's "beyond interpellation" refers to that "kernel of enjoyment" presupposed by ideology as such ("a *pre*-ideological enjoyment structured in fantasy").[28] The link, then, between Ideological State Apparatuses and interpellation—between, that is, the external "Pascalian machine" (like the one that confronts K. in *The Castle*) and the subject's internalization of this "bureaucratic" structure as belief (K.'s subjectivation)—is *fantasy*. In a nutshell (and it's a hard nut to crack, as Žižek likes to say), "fantasy is on the side of reality."[29]

The Real as Antagonism/Antagonism as the Real. If the drift of Žižek's critique of the Althusserian account of ideology (i.e., fantasy as the ideological support of reality) appears remote from the concerns of Althusser, not to mention Marxism, it is nevertheless, for all its Lacanianism, very much Žižek's own. In fact, I would submit that Žižek's rereading of Althusser's theory of interpellation in terms of the "logic of enjoyment," of *jouissance* as "beyond interpellation," subtly displaces the material-institutional terms of the Althusserian problematic and thereby effects a significant shift in Žižek's corpus from a certain Althusserian Marxism to a certain Hegelian Lacanianism (or Lacanian Hegelianism). This double displacement of Althusserianism and Marxism is announced at the beginning of the *Sublime Object of Ideology*, where, in lieu of the Althusserian and classical Marxist conception of alienation, Žižek proposes the psychoanalytic ethics of separation, as in the "famous Lacanian" maxim "not to give way on one's desire [*ne pas céder sur son désir*]." Like Laclau and Mouffe, Žižek not only understands separation as *antagonism*, but defines antagonism in opposition to the classical Marxist notion of *social antagonism*, which he glosses as follows: (1) "a certain fundamental antagonism" that has "an ontological priority to 'mediate' all other antagonisms, determining their place and their specific weight" (economic determination in the first or last instance, or *economism*); and (2) "historical development [that] brings about . . . an 'objective possibility' of solving this fundamental antagonism" (the revolutionary abolition of class antagonism and economic exploitation, or *revolutionism*).[30]

Now, if post-Marxism arguably represents a break with the global, revolutionary logic of classical Marxism (i.e., "that it is not possible to solve any particular question without solving them all"), psychoanalysis, for Žižek, represents an even more radical break. Where the "usual" post-Marxism affirms "the irreducible plurality of particular struggles" (such that, for instance, racism cannot be reduced to capital), Lacanian psychoanalysis interprets this plurality as so many responses to the "same impossible-real kernel."[31] Indeed, the radicality of Lacanian psychoanalysis—at least from a conventional, post-Marxist perspective—is its emphatic *re*accentuation of a certain "essentialism" or antagonism: "pure" antagonism. Hence, in the context of a discussion of the super-liberality of Laclau and Mouffe's radical-democratic politics, Žižek observes (rightly, I think) that the "condition of being active politically is precisely to *be* unilateral: the structure of the political act as such is 'essentialist.'"[32] But, given the provocative nature of such formulations, a number of critical questions materialize: What is the relation between Laclau and Mouffe's understanding of "social antagonism" and Lacan's concept of "pure antagonism"? What is the relation between the Real and antagonism as such?

The answer to the first question is, as it were, the Same, inasmuch as the "splitting" that traverses social antagonism (or, for Hegel, social Substance) is the same as the splitting that constitutes the subject (for Lacan, the so-called *sujet barré*). As Žižek himself argues with respect to the classic opposition between the individual and society, the subject of social antagonism "is precisely *not* 'in-dividual.'"[33] In other words, the subject as defined by Lacan—that "internal" limit which both subverts and sustains subjectivity—is the same as the social as defined by Laclau and Mouffe. This "paradoxical limit" is encapsulated in their notorious maxim that "society doesn't exist," which (like Lacan's formulation "la Femme n'existe pas"[34]) stresses the paradoxical "nature" of society as at once possible and impossible, or (im)possible. Simply put, societies exist (e.g., "American society"), but no society is identical to itself—to, that is, its founding presuppositions; in fact, to imagine otherwise, to seriously entertain the possibility of a nonantagonistic socius, constitutes—for Žižek as for Claude Lefort—*the* totalitarian temptation.[35] If social antagonism is therefore the same as pure antagonism (which is not to say that they are identical), the answer to the second question above is, again, the Same, since antagonism and the Real refer to the same "thing" (*das Ding*). Thus, commenting on the practico-epistemological "wager" that motivates Adorno's work, Žižek maintains that it is not aimed at " 'resolving' or 'abolishing' . . . contradiction by way of some conceptual clarification"; instead, Adorno's work is aimed at "*conceiving this contradiction as an immediate index of the 'contradiction'—that is, the antagonism—that pertains to social reality itself.*"[36]

Given this definition of the Real as antagonism and (social) antagonism as the Real, it is nevertheless important, it seems to me, to situate Lacan's notion of the antagonistic Real within the microhistorical context of his work. And here one might say that, with respect to the letter of that work, the Real of the 1950s is *not* the same as the Real of the 1960s and 1970s. The Real as a "brute, pre-symbolic reality which always returns to its place" dominates, it is true, the early seminars, as in Lacan's observation (articulated in his own peculiar idiolect) that the Real, "whatever upheaval we subject it to, is always in its place; it carries it glued to its heel, ignorant of what might exile it from it."[37] In the post-1950s seminars, however, the Lacanian Real is understood as a "hard core" that resists symbolization (perhaps its most familiar definition); moreover, in contradistinction to the Lacan of the "Purloined Letter," whether the Real has in fact had a place—if it has "actually occurred" in so-called reality—no longer matters, since, like trauma, it can only be accounted for *after* the fact, *après coup*.

This said, it would no doubt be closer to the spirit of the seminars to read Lacan's various definitions of the Real as different "aspects" of the same problematic, as "both the hard, impenetrable kernel" that resists symbolic integration "*and* a pure chimerical entity" that has "no ontological" substance. Put another way (and there are many ways to put it, as anybody who has read Lacan knows), the Real simultaneously possesses "corporeal contingency" (the Real as *"presupposed"* by the Symbolic) and "logical consistency" (the Real as *"posed"* by the Symbolic).[38] However, lest one think—as it is virtually impossible not to do—that this last, double definition of the Real recollects "some kind of Kantian 'Thing in itself [*das Ding-an-sich*],' " Žižek is quick to assure us that it "is not a transcendent positive entity, persisting somewhere beyond the symbolic order like a hard kernel inaccessible to it"; rather, the Real "is nothing at all, just a void, an emptiness in a symbolic structure marking some central *impossibility*."[39] This reading of the Lacanian Real as, precisely, "no thing" (as opposed to, say, a "positive" limit) usefully points up the radical negativity at the heart of Žižek's project, whereby the Real is in the last instance or final analysis, as in Hegel, a "pure 'Thing-of-Thought [*Gedankending*].'"[40]

Ideology Critique: Going through the Fantasy. Such Hegelian trappings would appear to be the height of idealism (at least from a classical Marxist perspective), but the Lacanian–Hegelian concept of the antagonistic Real has, according to Žižek, a definite purchase on the problem of ideology. So, to formulate a number of the critical terms in circulation here, one might say that *(social) fantasy is to the Real as ideology is to (social) antagonism.*

The most convenient example of this relation, given my earlier construction of the historical-geopolitical preconditions of Žižek's work, is the dissolution of "real socialism," about which Žižek observes, "This disintegration is of course immediately perceived as a 'loss'—loss of the quasi-idyllic stability that characterizes the social fabric of post-Stalinist 'real socialism'"; however, "the idyll was false from the very beginning, society was always-already ridden with fierce antagonisms."[41] Here, in addition to showing how ideology or social fantasy papers over the hole of the Real, Žižek also initiates a critical program. That is to say, if ideology colors in the void of the Real, the critique of ideology necessarily takes the form of a reflexive demonstration of the "logic of fantasy" as, for example, the "loss of loss" (vide *Vertigo*).

This critical-ideological emphasis on lack and negation—on the "analytical" disclosure of the pure, "primordial lie," in other words—hints that if Žižek's program cannot be labeled a "hermeneutics of suspicion" (if only because he has so little use for hermeneutics proper and, more importantly perhaps, because of a certain comic, even Chaplinesque, strain in his work),[42] it is a politics of demystification for all that. And yet, for Žižek as for Lacan, demystification is not all. Thus, contra Althusser, the critique of ideology is not for Žižek simply a metanarrative of misrecognition (and its interpretation) but a "logic of enjoyment" (and the active traversal or coming to terms with this *jouissance*). Indeed, this "double session" represents a psychoanalytic reconfiguration of the abovementioned Lacan–Althusser debate. Whereas the first stage of the critique of ideology is what Žižek calls, after Althusser, the "symptomal reading" or, in the psychoanalytic register, the "interpretation of symptoms," the second stage is the articulation or, more properly, *re*articulation of the deep structure of enjoyment, of the way ideology is predicated on a "pre-ideological enjoyment structured in fantasy." This second stage is what Žižek describes, after Lacan, as "going through the fantasy [*traversée du fantasme*]."[43]

The difference between these two moments or stages—between, that is, interpreting the symptom and going through the fantasy—is crucial. While the symptomatic reading aims to de-totalize the natural, "common-sense" experience of a particular ideological figure (as the Jew, one of Žižek's most privileged tropes, condenses a number of contradictory but socially meaningful mythemes such as "filthy" affluence[44]), "going through the fantasy" exposes the limits of both classic *Ideologiekritik* and psychoanalytic interpretation. Moreover, for Žižek, these limits are not so much those of the Althusserian theory of ideology, for instance, interpellation as imaginary/symbolic (mis)recognition, as those of deconstruction in particular and of poststructuralism in general. In other words, it is not enough simply to interpret a symptom or to deconstruct an ideological configuration; as in the Brechtian theory of alienation (*Entfremdung*), the so-called *E-* or *A-effect*, one must attain some "real" distance from the fantasy by experiencing not only how "ideology" organizes one's sense of enjoyment but, equally or more importantly, how it forms *the* support for one's sense of external reality.[45]

Although Žižek's description of "going through the fantasy" as the performative moment of ideology critique appears definitive, the problem with this procedure—at least within the psychoanalytic scenario—is that it cannot adequately account for the persistence of a symptom beyond both analysis *and* fantasy. The solution to this particular problem, for Žižek as for Lacan, lies in the third and final stage of psychoanalysis, which Žižek christens (dialectically recollecting the first stage of the process) "identification with the symptom," or, rather more allusively, the *sinthome*. This neologism, constellating various associations (e.g., "Saint Thomas," "synthetic-artificial man," "synthesis between symptom and fantasy"), refers to a letter or signifier suffused with idiotic enjoyment, albeit a letter–signifier that constitutes "our only substance, the only positive support of our being."[46]

Žižek summarizes the entire triadic movement in a chapter of *Looking Awry* entitled "The Ideological *Sinthome*":

> First, we had to get rid of the symptoms as compromise formations, then, we had to "traverse" the fantasy as the frame determining the coordinates of our enjoyment: the "desire of the analyst" was thus conceived as a desire purified of enjoyment. . . . In the last stage, however, the whole perspective is reversed: we have to identify precisely with the particular form of our enjoyment.[47]

Here, Lacan's "invention" of the *sinthome* returns us not only to the Real (in this case, the Real of the symptom) but to the drive and, ultimately, as Žižek notes, to the death drive itself.[48] What is at stake in this shift in Žižek's reading of Lacan from the double program of *interpretation of the symptom—going through the fantasy* to that of *going through the fantasy—identification with the symptom*? Rather more to the Marxist point, what is the critical-ideological use-value of the notion of the *sinthome* as well as the "ethical" imperative to identify with the "particular form of our enjoyment"?

Like Brecht's alienation-effect, which relies on what might be called a certain modernist distance, "identification with the symptom," according to Žižek, is "more radical"—because less "defensive"—than "going through the fantasy" (since desire is understood, as in the late Lacan, as a defense against the traumatic symptom that is *jouissance*). In other words, where "going through the fantasy" achieves its effect of distanciation by situating "the phenomenon in its historical totality," "identification with the symptom" makes us "experience the utter nullity of its immediate reality," the "stupid, material presence that escapes 'historical mediation.'" The imperative nature of this aspect of the critique of ideology is reflected in the following collective terms: "What we must do . . . is to *isolate* the *sinthome* from the context by virtue of which it exerts its power of fascination in order to expose the *sinthome*'s utter stupidity."[49]

If Žižek's explanation of "identification with the symptom" hints that it is not without a collective, critical-ideological element, his remarks later in the same chapter of *Looking Awry* on the difference between "acting out" and "passage to act [*passage à l'acte*]" also suggest that his importation of certain late Lacanian concepts into the critique of ideology is not without its problematic aspects. For instance, what is one to make of the assertion that, unlike "acting out," a "'passage to act' entails . . . an exit from the symbolic network, *a dissolution of the social bond*"?[50] This particular formulation (and admittedly, it is only one formulation) italicizes what may well be the irreducible difference between Marxism and psychoanalysis. For whatever Marxism is (political economy, "philosophy of praxis," etc.), it cannot be said to be about the "dissolution of the social bond." Indeed, however utopian Marx's understanding of communism as the solution to the riddle of history ("the dissolution of all classes"), it is in fact predicated on exactly the opposite state of affairs—on, that is, social *association*. What, after all, can it mean to claim that the most *progressive* stage of psychoanalysis—and, one imagines, of ideology critique as well—is identification with the "real of *jouissance*," a state of "being" that Žižek refers to as "subjective destitution"? [51]

Hegel after Marx and Lacan. Although the critical stress in Žižek's work on (over-)identification [52] rather than alienation (or, even more to the political-economic point, *exploitation*) is only one theoretical instance of his turn from Marxism and "return to Lacan," his Lacanian understanding of history also exhibits the very real distance between his project and Marxism. In fact, if post-Marxism represents, as I believe it does, both an affirmation and a negation of classical Marxism, discarding what is not essential (i.e., Hegelian dialectics) while retaining what is most distinctive and valuable (e.g., the analytical valorization of history and economy, if not "historical materialism" per se), then it may be useful to determine the political-theoretical implications of Žižek's problematic relation to Marx(ism). (Not so incidentally, I take it as a given that, in the relativistic wake of poststructuralism, it is imperative to make these sorts of determinations.)

A preliminary critique of Marx and of historical materialism, in particular, is broached near the end of the first chapter of the *Sublime Object of Ideology* ("How Did Marx Invent the Symptom?"). Consider the "common" Marxist–feminist critique of psychoanalysis, according to which the Oedipus complex is a " 'false' eternalization" that misconstrues "a historically conditioned form of patriarchal family" (i.e., the classic bourgeois nuclear family) as a trait "of the universal human condition." The problem with this particular effort at historicization is that it completely ignores "the 'hard kernel' which announces itself through the 'patriarchal family'—the Real of the Law, the rock of castration." [53] In fact, the irony of this position for Žižek is that, not unlike its ideological complement (and ostensible object of critique), " 'false' eternalization," "over-rapid historicization" blinds us "to the real kernel which returns as the same through diverse . . . symbolizations."[54]

As in his post-Althusserian formulation of ideology as "beyond interpellation," Žižek's understanding of the "unhistorical" as the Real of *jouissance* is intended to supplement what he sees as the gross poverty of the Marxist conception of history. However, Žižek's view of the "unhistorical" underscores not only the Lacanian thrust of his theory of history but the ontological repetition on which his work is, as it were, "based": "What the nostalgic image conceals is not the *historical mediation* but on the contrary the unhistorical traumatic kernel which returns as the Same through all historical epochs."[55] If this statement suggests that Žižek's concept of repetition is *un*historical in the pejorative sense, the real irony of his insistent, even monotonous, invocation of "the unhistorical" is that it ultimately leaves his own avowedly post-poststructuralist work open to the same critique he levels against deconstruction in the *Sublime Object of Ideology*. Indeed, it might not be too much to say that Žižek's post-poststructuralism, not to mention his "postmodernist" style, "exists only to embellish some basic theoretical proposition," such as the Real as the return of the (same) "unhistorical" traumatic kernel. One effect of this persistent ontologization of history is that, despite Žižek's theoretic and stylistic ingenuity (and he is nothing if not ingenious), the accent in his work on the unhistoricality of the Real—whether as trauma or the Same, *jouissance* or antagonism—eventuates in just the sort of "bad infinity" that he imputes to deconstruction: "an endless . . . variation which does not *produce* anything new."[56]

Now, if it is in fact the case that Žižek's work revolves around a fundamental Lacanian–Hegelian proposition (call it "the Real as antagonism"), and this proposition bears on his critique of Marxist historicism,[57] what, one wonders, is the relationship between Hegel and Marx in his work? Although there are any number of moments when Žižek reads this much-disputed relationship, the critical instance arguably occurs in *Tarrying with the Negative*, where he claims that the "standard Marxist" (Derridean?) critique of Hegelian dialectics as "a closed economy"—a system whose "every loss is in advance recompensed, 'sublated' into a moment of self-mediation"[58]—should be attributed not to Hegel but to Marx. A paradigmatic example of this *pre*-Hegelianism is Marx's formulation in the *Grundrisse* of the proletarian as "substanceless subjectivity."[59] At stake here is the problem of alienation or, more precisely, *de*- or *dis*alienation, since in classical Marxism the proletariat collectively embodies the reconciliation—structurally blocked in capitalism and only "speculated" about by Hegel—of "subject" and "substance" (or, in the classical Marxist idiom, "labor force" and "mode of production"). But according to Žižek, this revolutionary formulation, which for Marx represented "a 'materialist' version of the Hegelian reconciliation of subject and substance,"[60] must be subjected to a critical *re*reversal.

Žižek's theoretical gambit here is not, it seems to me, particularly scandalous. (Althusser's surmise about the "eternality" of ideology struck, as it were, the first blow against the classical concept of communism as the social figure for absolute de-alienation.[61]) However, Žižek's "apocalyptic tone" *is* scandalous, as when, invoking Marx's materialist critique of Hegel, he proposes that "the time has come to raise the inverse possibility of a Hegelian critique of Marx." In sum, it is now necessary, "after more than a century of polemics on the Marxist 'materialist reversal of Hegel,'" to entertain what for dyed-in-the-wool Marxists is unthinkable—that it is none other than Marx himself who should be stood on his head, that it is Marxism which, under the guise of a combative *anti*philosophy, "retroactively constructs the figure of Hegel" as "*the* philosopher who elevates self-mediating Notion into the Ground and Substance of the universe."[62] That Žižek's target here is Marx rather than Derrida is striking, to say the least, since the conventional reading of Hegel as the philosopher-king of sublation is an aftereffect—at least in the United States—of the influence of deconstruction, which no doubt explains Žižek's chronic antipathy to Derrida.[63] Still, inasmuch as he has also taken Derrida himself to task for his monolithic reading of Hegel, what, precisely, is at stake in Žižek's claim that "'Hegel as absolute idealist' is a *displacement* of Marx's own disavowed ontology"? As Žižek sees it, Marx's ambiguous relationship to Hegel is not merely a "symptom" of that retroactive displacement but an index of the "inherent impossibility of the Marxian project" *as such*.[64] And yet, if it is clear that one of the things at stake in Žižek's return to Hegel is the validity of Marxism as a historical project, what is not clear, what remains unsaid, is the status of Žižek's "desire for Hegel."

I raise here the hydra-headed question of desire because Žižek himself argues, à la Lacan, that what is missing from Marx (and, presumably, from the Marxian project itself) is a sense of subjectivity as "inscribed into the very core of Substance in the guise of an irreducible lack which forever prevents it from achieving full self-identity."[65] If one consequence of this anti-identitarian argument is that the absolute de-alienation associated with communism is a priori impossible, the problem with this critique of Marxism is not so much that it conflates communism with Marxism (arguably very different formations) or that it is predicated on a selective reading of Marx (the sort of critical treatment to which Lacan is rarely submitted by Žižek) as that the Lacan-inspired metalepsis "Hegel after Marx" threatens to *re*install a universal law: the law of desire as the law of castration.[66] Indeed, if, as Butler argues,[67] whatever threatens the invariant "threat" of castration in Žižek's work—Marxism, feminism, or Marxist feminism—is categorically foreclosed, one result of this theoretical foreclosure (and I am thinking here of Žižek's critique of deconstruction) is a certain after*affect*, or "permanent," *pre*political pathos.

However, the question of politics aside, the most surprising thing about Žižek's Hegelian critique of Marxism—given Althusser's influence on his work—is that it is curiously *pre*-Althusserian. Bluntly, Žižek's anti-Marxist defense of the "substantial" subject is arguably a species of humanism and, as such, ideological through and through (since the naturalization of human subjectivity is, *pace* Žižek, the ideological operation par excellence).[68] From this critical perspective, it is not hard to see, as Žižek himself is fond of saying, that his conception of the "substance as subject" (and consequent critique of Marx's understanding of proletarian subjectivity) is intended to *re*inscribe the "ontological" dimension of the historical subject.[69] At the same time, if it is true (as Žižek also claims) that the "ontological" subject radically destabilizes the sort of "historical" subject that Marxism presupposes, the "historical-materialist" nevertheless remains after the subject-as-substance (i.e., the subject subjected to the law of castration) has been subtracted. In other words, if the relation between these two modes of subjectivity—the "ontological" and the "historical-materialist"—is not only irreducible but asymmetrical, the "historical-materialist" subject always already exceeds the "ontological" one—at least *for* Marxism.

Given this asymmetry between history and ontology—what Žižek himself calls the "true critical 'materialist' supplement"[70]—what does it mean to privilege ontology (or, more generally, philosophy) over history? If a Hegelian re-reversal of Marxism is not a species of idealism, what is it? First, whether or not one agrees with Althusser's location of Marx's break with Hegel or, rather more seriously, with the whole notion of an "epistemological break," Althusser, unlike Žižek, maintains the "classic" distinction between Marx and Hegel, namely, that Hegel(ianism), in whatever form, is an analytical and historical regression.[71]

Žižek, of course, thoroughly problematizes this genealogy (i.e., Hegel before Marx). Thus, in *Tarrying with the Negative,* he reverses even as he answers Pierre Macherey's titular question *Hegel ou Spinoza?* so that one might say *as with Marx, so with Althusser.* Or, to rewrite Žižek himself, "[Hegel's] philosophy must be read as a critique of [Althusser]—as if [Hegel] read [Althusser] and was able in advance to answer the latter's critique of ['Hegelianism']."[72] Suffice it to say that if one must choose between Hegel and Althusser (on the analogy of *Hegel ou Spinoza?*), and this is simultaneously a choice between philosophy and antiphilosophy, then Žižek clearly chooses Hegel and philosophy.[73] From a Marxist perspective, though (and this is the theoretical "rub"), to return to Hegel—beyond both Marx and Althusser—is to "engage" in an act of *philosophical* nostalgia, since, as Žižek himself notes, "Marx insists on the inherent limitation of a purely dialectical [i.e., philosophical] presentation."[74] The "inherent limitations" of a strictly Hegelian and/or philosophical approach can be seen in Žižek's inordinately "thin" sense of historicity; hence, whether the specific object of historical analysis is the Gulag or the Holocaust, Hiroshima or Chernobyl, the answer for Žižek is always, somehow, the Same. In this sense at least, Žižek's project, despite its spirited critique of postmodern historicism and its "dialectical" twin, the "logic of nostalgia," is thoroughly historicist—in "spirit."[75]

Still, assuming—for the sake of argument—that Žižek's basic critique of Marx is correct, that Marx's notion of collective subjectivity and therefore of de-alienation are, sensu stricto, an effect of a "perspective-illusion which hinges precisely on the 'closed economy' of the dialectical reversal," why does Žižek "need" to return to Hegel (rather than, say, Baudrillard) in order to effect this critique?[76] In other words, while it is perfectly understandable why Žižek would want to return to Hegel in order to interrogate the received philosophical wisdom about his alleged monism, why is Žižek intent on saving Hegel at the expense of Marx? The answer to this particular question (at least with respect to the "early" Žižek of the *Sublime Object of Ideology*) is that his "reading of Hegel and the Hegelian heritage"—via, of course, the necessary detour of a reading of Lacan—suggests "a new approach to [the problem of] ideology."[77] The historical thrust of this recommendation would appear to be that today (after, presumably, the debacle that was communism) Hegel can teach us something about the critique of ideology that Marx(ism) couldn't or, rather more to the point, can't. And what Hegel can teach us is Subject, where "Subject" is, as it were, a synonym for "Lacan."

Given this psychoanalytic tack, Žižek's brand of Lacanianism is emphatically opposed, it is clear, to that *post*-Hegelian practice which understands itself as antiphilosophy, or "not-anymore-philosophy"—to, that is, Marxism. This *prise de position* is reflected in the oppositional character of Žižek's conclusion to the introduction to *Tarrying with the Negative*, where Marxism is summarily dismissed in favor of "Lacanian philosophy": "One is . . . tempted to risk the hypothesis that what Lacan's 'antiphilosophy' opposes is this very philosophy qua antiphilosophy."[78] Indeed, this "antiphilosophical"-qua-Lacanian Hegelian position is the perspective from which one must read the rhetorico-ecological "demand" that concludes the book as a whole: "Perhaps . . . our very physical survival hinges on our ability to consummate the act of assuming fully the 'nonexistence of the Other,' of *tarrying with the negative*."[79] If this apocalyptic peroration—the concluding emphasis of which echoes Hegel's preface to the *Phenomenology of Spirit*—is plainly hyperbolic, it is also, I think it safe to say, downright gnomic. What does, or can, it mean to "consummate the act of *fully* assuming the 'nonexistence of the Other,'" let alone to consummate the act of "tarrying with the negative"?

Beyond Spinozism. The first thing to understand when trying to decipher the programmatic conclusion to *Tarrying with the Negative* is that the "anxiety of ecology"[80] is tied up, for Žižek, with the "collapse of the big Other" (where the ecological and political referents for this catastrophic event are Chernobyl and the end of communism, respectively). In other words, there is a certain historical, if not strictly logical, relation between the demise of communism and the rise of the ecology movement. Thus, with respect to the "green" issue, Žižek argues that the Lacanian lesson to be applied to the anxiety of ecology (to the unaccountable fear that a natural catastrophe is on the immediate horizon) is that "we must learn to accept the real of the ecological crisis in its senseless actuality, without charging it with some message or meaning."[81] As for communism, the substitution of "green" for "red" politics is staged in the last chapter of *Tarrying with the Negative*, "Enjoy Your Nation as Yourself!" The question here is as simple as it is profound: In the wake of the dissolution of "actually existing socialism" in the Eastern bloc, what is the solution?

If Žižek's long answer to this question is a certain Lacanian ethics, his short, exemplary answer is, as I have already noted, ecology.[82] What is striking about this eco-ethical solution, which cannot of course be divorced from the related issue of ethnonationalism, is that it involves an overt, albeit intricate, critique of Spinozism.[83] The key figure is once again Hegel, where Hegel is understood (as in Althusser and Macherey) as the diametrical opposite of Spinoza.[84] However, the additional Žižekian twist here is that Spinozism is the "ideology of late capitalism." Indeed, in Žižek's account of late capitalism, Spinozism arguably displaces what Fredric Jameson reserves for the culture of postmodernism (i.e., postmodernism as the "cultural logic of late capitalism"). Accordingly, the answer to the ideology of Spinozism for Žižek is not Marxism (as it is for Jameson) but that oxymoronic practice "Lacanian philosophy." Moreover, with the collapse of "actually existing socialism," psychoanalysis itself has acquired a new political urgency, charged as it is—"more than ever," according to Žižek—with the task of defining the "space of possible resistance" to the production and reproduction of capital. Simply put, the political task of psychoanalysis today is to elucidate those decidedly *anti*-Deleuzian forms of subjectivity that contest late (Spinozist) capitalism.[85]

While the so-called ethics of the Real—Lacan's "critique of pure desire" as the "foundation" of Kant's three critiques—can be said to drive Žižek's political philosophy, it must also be said that, his negative invocation of Spinoza notwithstanding, the real object of his critique is not Spinoza per se but a certain reading of him: Deleuze's "affective" interpretation of Spinoza as the premier philosopher of "speeds and slownesses, of frozen catatonias and accelerated movements, unformed elements [and] nonsubjectified affects."[86] What is at stake in this particular reading of Spinoza is the capital-deterritorialized "nature" of postmodern subjectivity, which for Žižek is distinctly Deleuzian in character: "Far from being an autonomous bearer of this process [of 'affective identification'], the subject is rather a place, a passive ground for the network of partial lateral links." The postmodern subject described here—plural, affective, dispersed—may sound subversive, but, according to Žižek, this *form* of subjectivity is not only *not* subversive, it is in fact the subject of late capitalism, prone as it is to those "particular, inconsistent modes of enjoyment" that are the hallmark of post-Fordist, consumer-driven capital. For Žižek, the critical question is therefore: Is there a "way out of this vicious circle of late-capitalist Spinozism"?[87]

In order to mount a really effective critique of contemporary ideological phenomena it is necessary, according to Žižek, to "go through the fantasy" of postmodern capitalism. But perhaps it would be more accurate to say that the aim of Žižek's "return to philosophy" is to root out what might be called the *double fantasy* of the contemporary (left) "universal intellectual." This fantasy is premised on two, equally untenable propositions: (1) that the decentered, libidinal subject of postmodernism is the liberatory subject of capitalism (affirmative position); and (2) that the "cure" for this pathological symptom is Marxism (negative position). The problem with this argument for Žižek is that neither Marxism nor Spinozism can be said to represent a genuinely radical critique of late capitalism, since Marxism is merely the negative and "universal" Other of the "new Spinozism," while the latter discourse is reflexively—and, therefore, uncritically—predicated not on negation (as in Marxism) but on affirmation, not on lack or loss (as in psychoanalysis) but on affect and desire. In other words, Marxism and Spinozism are simply two sides of the same coin: the coin of late capitalism.

Still, if neither Marxism nor Spinozism is the answer to late capitalism, liberalism is no solution either. As Žižek sees it, the "fundamental" political opposition today (at least in Eastern Europe) is not the apparent, "external" one between different regimes of social-political regulation—between nationalism and liberalism, for example, or even socialism and liberalism—but a strictly "internal," economic one. That is to say, the real opposition should be located *within* capitalism itself, between those who will be permitted "inside"—integrated into the New (liberal-democratic) World Order—and those who will be condemned to the "outside" or periphery.[88] In this context, it is worth noting that if, or precisely because, ethnonationalist fundamentalism is the Other or hidden presupposition of Western-style capitalism (as the epigraph to this essay suggests), the emerging nation-states of what was once Yugoslavia will be especially subject to the draconian diktats of this global political-economic logic—in a phrase: play or pay.

Consequently, the only way out of the "vicious circle" of late Spinozist capitalism—the reactive inverse of which economic universalism is ethnonationalism—"is not to fight the 'irrational' nationalist particularism but to invent forms of political practice."[89] Moreover, it is in just this combative, democratic-inventive sense that our "physical survival" as a species can be said to depend on the "coming ecological crisis," since only such a planetary crisis will allow us to completely come to terms with the "nonexistence of the big Other." Put another way, the "real" value of ecology and its apocalyptic death drive is that, in forcing us to seriously entertain the "idea" of the nonexistence of the planet, it simultaneously compels us to consummate the act of "going through the fantasy" of nationalism as well as of Nature itself. In fact, with that last grand ideologeme in mind, one might say that on the other side of the fantasy of (super-)natural apocalypse or catastrophe is the terrible intuition that Nature, like God, doesn't exist. Or, to cite Spinoza himself, not God or Nature (*Deus sive Natura*), but neither God nor Nature. Of course, if even capital is a "chimeric apparition,"[90] and Marxism merely a fantasy, what is left for the Left to do?

The "New" New Left (Marxism without Marxism/"Capitalism without Capitalism"). As the foregoing speculations about the ecology movement intimate (and such speculations are the stuff of Žižek's project), there is a significant theoretical difference between his project—founded as it is on the Hegelian notion of *Gedankending*—and Marxism. For if capital is a monster (*Ungeheuer*) and, strictly speaking, "no thing," it is also always *something* for Marx, and that something is surplus-value.[91] But if Žižek does not credit Marxism with any liberatory force (and, it sometimes seems, with only a residual explanatory one), his repeated affirmation of "new social movements" such as ecology indicates that he has by no means abandoned the Left in general. However, Žižek's considered recommendation is that while the politics of "the New" and its various forms of refusal (e.g., ecological "hysteria") signify a "dimension beyond capital" as well as a necessary utopian sense of futurity, they must also actively engage the recent, catastrophic past. Accordingly, the current task for the Left—a rather formidable one, given the abrupt collapse of communism—is to imagine a viable future without completely forsaking the past, "to keep alive the memory of all lost causes, of all shattered . . . dreams and hopes attached to leftist projects." This, for Žižek, is the "real" ethics of the drive, the "compulsion" to "mark," insistently, the "site" of the trauma, the "Cause *qua* thing"—with the crucial proviso that this "lost Cause" or "Thing" (and one cannot, perhaps, emphasize this point enough) is not "actually existing socialism" or even communism but that traumatic impossibility which communism sought, tragically, to suture.[92]

Žižek's politics for the present juncture are predicated, then, on a dialectical refusal of both the current incarnation of contemporary capitalism (i.e., late Spinozism) and that nostalgia for the past-as-simulacrum which is postmodernism (e.g., the "back to the future" Reagan 1980s). In fact, for Žižek, the ethics of the drive—"far from confining the Left within a nostalgic infatuation with the past" (e.g., with the historical failure of revolutionary socialism)—is the only option left for getting some real "distance on the present," whether understood as the New (post-Communist) World Order or the inhuman, fascist face of ethnonationalism associated with Bosnia.[93]

Still, if Žižek's exhortation of "an ethics of the Real"—especially in its utopian, repetitive-compulsive aspect (Freud's *Zwang*)—obviously speaks to some real tactical concerns currently facing the post-Marxist Left, the limits of this very "same" recommendation are equally obvious in the conclusion to "Beyond Discourse-Analysis," where he presents the "practical" end point of his politics of the (death) drive: "The fact that the signifying field is always structured around a certain fundamental deadlock . . . doesn't entail any kind of resignation—or, if there is a resignation, it is a paradox of the *enthusiastic resignation.*"[94] I suppose one can understand this properly Kantian imperative as a version of Gramsci's memorable precept "pessimism of the intellect, optimism of the will," but the sort of historical tension between theory and practice embodied in Gramsci's work is, it seems to me, all but lost in Žižek's "sublime" formulation. The "willful," "intellectual" character of Žižek's petition for "enthusiastic resignation" is even more manifest in the *Sublime Object of Ideology*, where, addressing the crucial question of the efficacy of "at first sight purely speculative [read: Kantian–Hegelian] ruminations" for a psychoanalytic theory of ideology, he introduces a moment synonymous with that of "enthusiastic resignation," which he labels, after Freud, *die Versagung*, or "subjective destitution."[95]

From a psycho-Marxist perspective, the theoretical interest of this moment—of, that is to say, the "sacrifice of the sacrifice"—is substantial, since *die Versagung* is allegedly beyond both castration *and* alienation. Indeed, with the prototypically Marxist concept of alienation in mind, Žižek has argued that the sort of utopianism associated with the ethics of the Real "is possible only on the basis of a certain fundamental 'alienation.'"[96] Drawing out the necessary political implications of this ethics of separation in *Tarrying with the Negative*, he even adds, "What Eastern Europe needs most now is *more alienation*."[97]

Žižek's application here of the logic of separation to the former Yugoslavia makes real political sense, especially given the relative scarcity of civil-social institutions vis-à-vis the State in Eastern Europe; but it seems to me that alienation cannot be understood simply (and however profoundly) as separation, but must ultimately be thought together with the concept and the reality of exploitation. Perhaps (post-)Marxism needs to come to terms, as Žižek's work so ably attests, with the question of "castration" and even "separation." Certainly, if it is ever going to speak persuasively to the problems of capitalism and ethnonationalism, among other things, it needs to be able to better articulate the way subjectivity is inscribed into the very heart of the discourse of political economy. However, while it may well be true that separation is *the* ethical-political answer to the problem of castration, *die Versagung* is not, and cannot be, *the* answer to the problem of exploitation. And, to the question of exploitation in its most "base," even banal sense, Žižek has—in the final analysis—no real answer.

"Dialectical Punctuation." While preparing an abridged version of this essay for a conference, I composed the following provisional conclusion: "If the critique of ideology ends, for Žižek, with the death drive, it may well be that his Lacanianism—at least for those of us still committed to the project of Marxism—represents a dreadful, if fascinating, dead end." The point of my "dialectical punctuation" was to propose that, for all its force and interest, Žižek's project is decisively bereft of the sort of *theoretical* use-values that contemporary Marxism needs most today.[98] In the time between writing the conclusion and delivering the paper, though, it struck me that American academic Marxism seems to be dominated more and more by a kind of political neo-pragmatism, the simplistic version of which attitude is "Žižek isn't Marxist enough!"[99] Forget that Žižek—unlike most, if not all, of his American critics—has actually lived most of his life under a Communist regime and thus may have something important, even urgent, to say to those of us who have never really experienced life in a putatively

Socialist country. Forget that Žižek's critique may have something to teach us about the practical *and* theoretical limits of Marxism.

Given the fall of communism and the so-called triumph of transnational capitalism—not to mention the local but by no means insignificant issue of the impact of these events on American academic Marxism (a student recently asked me at the beginning of a course on Marxism and psychoanalysis, "How can one justify teaching Marxism today?")—given, that is, this unprecedented conjuncture, Žižek's work, to tarry with the negative, cannot *not* be found wanting. While his political philosophy sometimes appears to be a very real defense against desire and historicity, the *historicity of desire* (and a defense, therefore, against political despair),[100] he can hardly be expected to produce a completely satisfying set of answers to the extraordinarily complex issues that confront the post-Marxist Left at this particular moment.

In any event, it was with these sorts of unorthodox thoughts in mind (to return to my anecdote) that I began to rethink the polemical conclusion to my conference paper, so much so that when I finally read it I immediately put it "under erasure." My ex tempore argument was that, precisely because of the current conjuncture, it is imperative for post-Marxists and left intellectuals in general not to foreclose on theoretical work whose political efficacy is not immediately apparent. In order to illustrate this point and underscore the performative contradiction of my conclusion, I also mentioned a slip of the pen that I had "suppressed" in the final version of my paper. Instead of writing "Žižek's Lacanianism represents a *dreadful*, if fascinating, dead end," I had written "Žižek's Lacanianism represents a *deeply troubling*, if fascinating, dead end."

The meaning of this slip ("deeply troubling" when I had no doubt meant to say something like "deeply troubled") is, I take it, that Žižek's work is *deeply troubling for Marxists*, not least because, as a left East European intellectual, he does not reflect back the "naive," fascinated gaze of his not-so-sublime other: the gaze, that is, of the North American Marxist. In this sense (a profound one, it seems to me), Žižek refuses to give us what "we" want, refuses to satisfy "our" desire. Therein, one might say, lies our dread and our fascination, our dreadful fascination.

Notes

1 Quoted in Terry Eagleton, *Ideology: An Introduction* (London, 1991), 40.

2 In *The Destruction of Yugoslavia: Tracing the Break-Up, 1980–92* (London, 1993), Branka Magas writes that "Tito's death in 1980 marked a point of no return for Yugoslavia" (xii); see also "Tito's Deluge" (79–83).

3 Slavoj Žižek, *For They Know Not What They Do: Enjoyment as a Political Factor* (London and New York, 1991 [1990]), 256; and, on the death of Ceauşescu, see *Enjoy Your Symptom! Jacques Lacan in Hollywood and Out* (New York, 1992), 40–41.

4 See Žižek, *For They Know Not What They Do*, 253–54 and 256–60.

5 Slavoj Žižek, *Tarrying with the Negative: Kant, Hegel, and the Critique of Ideology* (Durham, 1993), 1.

6 For some sense of the context of Žižek's work, see Peter Osborne's interviews with him and Renata Salecl, "Lacan in Slovenia" and "Postscript," in *A Critical Sense: Interviews with Intellectuals*, ed. Peter Osborne (New York, 1996), 21–35 and 36–44.

7 Jean-Paul Sartre, *Search for a Method*, trans. Hazel E. Barnes (New York, 1968 [1960]), 56.

8 Slavoj Žižek, *The Sublime Object of Ideology* (London and New York, 1989). Laclau's preface (xi) includes a partial bibliography of Žižek's works in French and in Slovene. Laclau and Mouffe's statement about the theoretical program of the Phronesis series ("We believe that an anti-essentialist theoretical stand is the sine qua non of a new vision for the Left conceived in terms of a radical and plural democracy") can also be found in the front matter of this volume.

9 Part of this address or context is, as Laclau notes, so-called screen theory and, in particular, the notion of "suture" (on suture and the gaze, see also Osborne, "Lacan in Slovenia," 27). As Laclau observes, the "younger" generation of Lacanians "attempted to formalize Lacanian theory, pointing out the distinctions between the different stages of his teaching, and placing an accent on the theoretical importance of the last stage, in which a central role is granted to the notion of the *Real* as that which resists symbolization" (*Sublime Object of Ideology*, ix–x). The influence of this particular reading of Lacan on Žižek is obvious in the latter's own reaccentuation of the Lacanian Real.

10 Of course, one could also argue that the distinction between popular culture and "high theory" remains intact in Žižek's work, since "low" or mass culture is used simply to illustrate "high" theory (e.g., Lacanian psychoanalysis). See Slavoj Žižek, "Taking Sides: A Self-Interview," in *The Metastases of Enjoyment: Six Essays on Woman and Causality* (London and New York, 1994), 167–217, where he says that he is "convinced of [his] proper grasp of some Lacanian concept only when [he] can translate it successfully into the inherent imbecility of popular culture" (175). In this context, I might reiterate that what he calls Lacan's "most sublime theoretical motifs" are thought "*together with* and *through* exemplary cases of contemporary mass culture"; Slavoj Žižek, *Looking Awry: An Introduction to Jacques Lacan through Popular Culture* (Cambridge, MA, 1991), vii; my emphases. In other words, mass- or popular-cultural objects retain a certain specificity in Žižek's work.

11 Žižek, *Sublime Object of Ideology*, 1, 3.

12 Žižek, *Enjoy Your Symptom*, 113.

13 Žižek, *Looking Awry*, vii.
14 Žižek, *Sublime Object of Ideology*, 7, 79.
15 Žižek's engagement with postmodernism does not really commence until *Looking Awry* (see esp. 141–53). See also *Enjoy Your Symptom*, 80–83 and 122–24, as well as (and most importantly) Žižek's reading of the difference between Lacan and Foucault with respect to the question of Kant and the Enlightenment (179–84). For Žižek's own restricted definition of himself as a postmodernist, see Osborne, "Lacan in Slovenia," 34.
16 In *Looking Awry* (142–43), Žižek asserts—against all odds, as it were—that "it is only with Lacan that the 'postmodernist' break occurs. . . . In this sense we could even say that deconstructionists are basically still 'structuralists' and that the only 'poststructuralist' is Lacan." Cf. what Žižek says about the "unexpected connections" between Lacan and Derrida in *The Indivisible Remainder: An Essay on Schelling and Related Matters* (London and New York, 1996), 189–236, esp. 193–96.
17 Žižek, *Sublime Object of Ideology*, 154, 154–55.
18 Jacques Lacan, "Seminar on 'The Purloined Letter'" (1955–56), trans. Jeffrey Mehlman, in *The Purloined Poe: Lacan, Derrida, and Psychoanalytic Reading*, ed. John P. Muller and William Richardson (Baltimore, 1988), 28–54. With respect to Derrida, I am thinking of not only the historico-philosophic metalepsis "Socrates *after* Plato," but also the "homosexual" structure (*a tergo*): "Socrates is in front of Plato, no, Plato is behind him"; see Jacques Derrida, *The Post Card: From Socrates to Freud and Beyond*, ed. and trans. Alan Bass (Chicago, 1987 [1980]), 9.
19 Žižek, *Sublime Object of Ideology*, 155.
20 See Žižek, *For They Know Not What They Do*, 72–80. On Gasché's alleged misreading of Hegel, see also *Indivisible Remainder*, 92–186, esp. 180 n. 45. For a more balanced appraisal of the dispute between Žižek and Gasché, see Peter Dews, "Tremor of Reflection: Slavoj Žižek's Lacanian Dialectics," in *The Limits of Disenchantment* (London, 1995), 256–57 n. 37.
21 Žižek, *Sublime Object of Ideology*, 1. Judith Butler argues that the Žižekian Real "stands theoretically as a counter both to Foucauldian linguisticism . . . and Habermasian rationalism," in *Bodies that Matter: On the Discursive Limits of "Sex"* (New York, 1993), 192. Butler's real point, though, is that Foucault (like feminism and poststructuralism) represents a radical "challenge" to Žižek's construction of the Real as the law or "threat" of castration. Needless to say, Butler is also arguing pointedly, if implicitly, about "homosexuality" here.
22 Quoted in Osborne, "Lacan in Slovenia," 22; see also 22–25 (on the history of theory in Yugoslavia).
23 See Žižek, "Superego by Default," in *Metastases of Enjoyment*, 54–85, esp. 62–65.
24 Žižek, *Tarrying with the Negative*, 229.
25 On the Pascalian aspect of Althusser's theory of Ideological State Apparatuses, see Žižek, "Superego by Default," 59.
26 Žižek, *Sublime Object of Ideology*, 44, 124.
27 Žižek, "Superego by Default," 60–61.
28 Louis Althusser, "Ideology and Ideological State Apparatuses," in *Lenin and Philosophy*,

trans. Ben Brewster (New York, 1971 [1969]), 127–86; quotation from 173; Žižek, *Sublime Object of Ideology*, 125; my emphasis.

29 Žižek, *Sublime Object of Ideology*, 44.

30 Ibid., 3. On Žižek and Laclau and Mouffe, see Butler, *Bodies that Matter*, 191–94 and 209–11; Rey Chow, "Ethics after Idealism," *diacritics* 23 (1993): 3–22, esp. 14–15; Elizabeth J. Bellamy, "Discourses of Impossibility: Can Psychoanalysis Be Political?," *diacritics* 23 (1993): 24–38, esp. 30–35; Anthony Elliott, "Psychoanalysis, Ideology, and Modern Societies," in *Social Theory and Psychoanalysis in Transition: Self and Society from Freud to Kristeva* (Oxford, 1992), 162–200, esp. 177–99; and Robert Miklitsch, "The Rhetoric of Post-Marxism: Discourse and Institutionality in Laclau and Mouffe, Resnick and Wolff," *Social Text*, No. 45 (Winter 1995): 167–96.

31 Žižek, *Sublime Object of Ideology*, 4.

32 Quoted in Osborne, "Lacan in Slovenia," 34.

33 Žižek, *Tarrying with the Negative*, 30.

34 For a feminist critique of Žižek's recapitulation of Lacan's "la Femme n'existe pas" (which critique I presuppose throughout), see Butler's *Bodies that Matter*. For his response to Butler's critique, see Žižek, "Taking Sides," 202–3; and Osborne, "Postscript," 40–43.

35 For Žižek's recourse to Lefort, see *For They Know Not What They Do*, 253–70. See also Robert Miklitsch, "News from Nowhere: Reading Raymond Williams's Readers," in *Cultural Materialism: On Raymond Williams*, ed. Christopher Prendergast (Minneapolis, 1995), 71–90.

36 Žižek, "The Deadlock of 'Repressive Desublimation,'" in *Metastases of Enjoyment*, 2–28; quotation from 13.

37 Lacan, "Seminar on 'The Purloined Letter,'" 40. For Žižek's take on Poe's "Purloined Letter," see "Superego by Default," 74.

38 Žižek, *Sublime Object of Ideology*, 169. On the two aspects of the Lacanian Real, see also "Does the Subject Have a Cause?," in *Metastases of Enjoyment*, 29–53, esp. 51 n. 11.

39 Žižek, *Sublime Object of Ideology*, 173; my emphasis.

40 Ibid., 172. See also Žižek's comments on his disagreement with Laclau (in Osborne, "Postscript," 42–43): "The element that *limits* [the] boundless parade of symbolic reinscriptions is the level of phantasy enjoyment. These are not just symbolic differentials, they exist as historical traumas, registered by the *real*" (my emphasis). Moreover, says Žižek elsewhere (*Indivisible Remainder*, 97), "for Lacan the 'Real' is *not*, in the Kantian mode, a purely negative category, a designation of a limit without any specification of what lies beyond—the Real *qua* drive is, on the contrary, the *agens*, the 'driving force,' of desiring."

41 Žižek, *For They Know Not What They Do*, 168.

42 On the "primordial lie," see Žižek's introduction to *Indivisible Remainder*, 1; and for his reading of *City Lights*, among other things, see *Enjoy Your Symptom*, 1–9. See also Lacan's by no means incidental remarks on the "comic" in *The Four Fundamental Concepts of Psycho-Analysis*, ed. Jacques-Alain Miller, trans. Alan Sheridan (New York, 1978 [1973]), 4–5.

43 Žižek, *Sublime Object of Ideology*, 74.
44 Ibid., 201–7.
45 See Žižek, "Superego by Default," 80–82; and Osborne, "Postscript," 38.
46 Žižek, *Sublime Object of Ideology*, 75.
47 Žižek, *Looking Awry*, 138.
48 In an interview by Peter Canning, Žižek says of the moment of "identification with the symptom," which he situates between Lacan's *Ethics of Psychoanalysis* (1959–60) and "Kant avec Sade" (1962): "In this other logic, [the question] is no longer one of pure desire, where every identification with *jouissance* means betraying desire. Now, it is the opposite: the only authentic thing to do is to identify with your symptom. . . . In other words, the only true desire is the death drive"; Peter Canning, "The Sublime Theorist of Slovenia," *Artforum* 31 (1993): 84–89; quotation from 88.
49 Žižek, *Looking Awry*, 129.
50 Ibid., 139; my emphasis.
51 Ibid., 139–40.
52 On "identification with the symptom" as overidentification, see, for example, Osborne, "Postscript," 39. Butler, of course, views *dis*identification as "itself the point of departure for a more democratizing affirmation of internal difference" (*Bodies that Matter*, 219).
53 Žižek, *Sublime Object of Ideology*, 49, 50. For a counter-Žižekian critique of the Marxist–feminist critique of psychoanalysis, see Butler, *Bodies that Matter*, 200–203. See also, more generally, Robert Miklitsch, "Troping Prostitution: Two or Three Things about (Post-)Marxism/Feminism," *Genders* 12 (1991): 120–39.
54 Žižek, *Sublime Object of Ideology*, 50. Žižek also contends that "what all epochs have in common is not some universal positive feature, some transcendental content; what they all share, rather, is the same deadlock, the same antinomy" (*Indivisible Remainder*, 217).
55 Žižek, *Enjoy Your Symptom*, 81; my emphasis.
56 Žižek, *Sublime Object of Ideology*, 155.
57 For Žižek's critique of Marxist and Lukácscian historicism in particular, see "Taking Sides," 200.
58 Žižek, *Tarrying with the Negative*, 25.
59 For Žižek's formulation of "the point at which the Hegelian identity of subject and substance begins to break up," see *Enjoy Your Symptom*, 180 n. 24.
60 Žižek, *Tarrying with the Negative*, 26.
61 The problem of history in Althusser is "directly related" to his uncritical appropriation of the Freudian unconscious as *the* analogue of ideology (i.e., "ideology *in general*"). As Althusser puts it ("Ideology and Ideological State Apparatuses," 161), the thesis that "ideology has no history can and must . . . be directly related to Freud's proposition that the *unconscious is eternal*." For his explicit position on historicism, see Louis Althusser and Etienne Balibar, *Reading "Capital,"* trans. Ben Brewster (London and New York, 1970 [1968]), 199–244.
62 Žižek, *Tarrying with the Negative*, 26.
63 For the articulation of Marxism and deconstruction in the United States, which was largely a function of Derrida's prior reception (*Of Grammatology* having appeared in 1976), see Michael Ryan, *Marxism and Deconstruction* (Baltimore, 1982); and Gayatri

Chakravorty Spivak, *In Other Worlds: Essays in Cultural Politics* (New York and London, 1987).

64 Žižek, *Tarrying with the Negative*, 26.

65 Ibid.

66 On the communism/Marxism distinction, see Robert Miklitsch, "From Adorno to The Clash," in *From Hegel to Madonna: Towards a General Economy of "Commodity Fetishism"* (Albany, 1998), 9–36. For one instance of Žižek's *critical* attention to Lacan, see "Taking Sides," where Žižek claims that the "only way to approach Lacan . . . is to read 'Lacan contre Lacan'" (173). On the "rock of castration," Butler observes: "The figure of substance . . . appears misplaced . . . unless we take it as a figure for incontrovertibility, specifically, the unquestionable status of the law, where that law is understood as the law of castration" (*Bodies that Matter*, 201).

67 See Butler, *Bodies that Matter*, 207. As forceful as Butler's reading is (and I have obviously found it of particular interest), its force also appears almost directly proportional to its reduction of the Žižekian text—that is, to its *rhetoric*. To rewrite Butler on Žižek on Lacan: "[Žižek's] own textuality is not considered in the often brilliant appropriations to be found in [Butler's] work" (197). The irony of Butler's reading, then, is that for all its deconstructive zest it privileges the "declarative mode" itself, as if Žižek's text were without performative effects. Bluntly, part of the interest of Žižek's work on, say, the Real as that which exceeds the Imaginary/Symbolic is the way it *specifically* embodies this "rhetorical" remainder. Accordingly, Butler's reading of the Žižekian text would be *more* persuasive if her critique recognized the "real" rhetoricity at *work* there. Another, interrogative way to put this would be to ask and endeavor to answer the following question: Why do "we"—including Butler—(want to) *read* Žižek?

68 If Žižek's "humanism" puts him at odds with Althusser's antihumanism, his understanding of the Real of *jouissance* as the "kernel" of ideology also aligns his work with the Althusserian notion of "permanent ideology," as Butler suggests (ibid., 278 n. 5). See also Louis Althusser, *For Marx*, trans. Ben Brewster (London, 1977 [1965]), 219–47.

69 Although what Teresa Brennan calls "the concept of a transhistorical psychical fantasy as such" (or what I here call "the ontological") "gives the psychical some autonomy in history," allowing "for a tension between psychical factors and sociohistorical ones," to term *any* fantasy "transhistorical"—no matter how "ubiquitous" it may appear to be—is "to impute" to it an immutable status "when we simply do not know if it is immutable, and exempt from historical scrutiny"; *History After Lacan* (London and New York, 1993), 22.

70 Žižek, *Indivisible Remainder*, 13–91; quotation from 46.

71 See, for example, Althusser, *For Marx*, 32–34; and Althusser and Balibar, *Reading "Capital,"* 30–31.

72 Žižek, *Tarrying with the Negative*, 140.

73 In his "Errors of Classical Economics," Althusser declares that "Spinoza's philosophy introduced an unprecedented theoretical revolution in the history of philosophy, probably the greatest philosophical revolution of all time, insofar as we can regard Spinoza as Marx's *only* direct ancestor" (Althusser and Balibar, *Reading "Capital,"* 91–118; quotation from 102; my emphasis). More to the point, in his 1975 *soutenance* for his *doctorat d'état* from the University of Picardy, he noted that he had "turned the weapon of Spi-

noza against Hegel"; Louis Althusser, *Philosophy and the Spontaneous Philosophy of the Scientists and Other Essays*, ed. Gregory Elliott, trans. Ben Brewster et al. (London and New York, 1990), xviii. As for Lacan's relation to Spinoza/Kant, see *Four Fundamental Concepts of Psycho-Analysis*, where Lacan suggests that "Kant avec Sade" and, more generally, the turn in his work to the concept of *die Versagung* ("desire in its pure state") is a direct refusal of Spinoza's position: "This position is not tenable for us" (275–76).

74 Žižek, *For They Know Not What They Do*, 211.

75 See Žižek, *Looking Awry*, 111–16. On his problematic relation to historicism, see also Robert Miklitsch, "'Out of the Past': Psycho-Historicism" (forthcoming).

76 Žižek, *Tarrying with the Negative*, 26. On the "restricted" use-value of Baudrillard for (post-)Marxism, see Robert Miklitsch, "The Commodity–Body–Sign: Toward a General Economy of 'Commodity Fetishism,'" *Cultural Critique*, No. 33 (Spring 1996): 5–40.

77 Žižek, *Sublime Object of Ideology*, 7 ("the only way to 'save Hegel' is through Lacan").

78 Žižek, *Tarrying with the Negative*, 3–4.

79 Ibid., 237.

80 See Robert Miklitsch, "*Total Recall*: Production, Revolution, Simulation, Alienation-Effect," *Camera Obscura* 32 (1995 [1993–94]): 5–39.

81 Žižek, *Looking Awry*, 35.

82 For Žižek's more recent remarks on ecology, see *Indivisible Remainder*, 128, 131.

83 I am using "ethnonationalism" in Walker Connor's sense of a nation as "a group of people who believe they are ancestrally related"; see his *Ethnonationalism* (Princeton, 1994).

Spinoza has, of course, been a resource for the radical environmental movement; see, for example, Robert Hurley's preface to Gilles Deleuze, *Spinoza: Practical Philosophy*, trans. Robert Hurley (San Francisco, 1988 [1981]), 11. In "Seeing Green," Stanley Aronowitz observes that for the Greens (and, in some sense, for Žižek as well), ecology is an "alternative 'system' to Marxism and liberalism, the dominant frameworks for working-class and middle-class politics in Western societies," in *Dead Artists, Live Theories* (New York, 1994), 286–95; quotation from 287. For an original reconceptualization of Marxism and ecology, see Brennan, *History After Lacan*, 166–96.

84 See, in particular, Christopher Norris, "Spinoza *versus* Hegel: The Althusserian Moment," in *Spinoza and the Origins of Modern Critical Theory* (Oxford, 1991), 21–53.

85 See Žižek, *Tarrying with the Negative*, 216–19.

86 Deleuze, *Spinoza*, 129.

87 Žižek, *Tarrying with the Negative*, 218, 219.

88 Osborne ("Postscript," 37) quotes Žižek as saying that although "Marxism is still valid in its belief in a fundamental antagonism pertaining to today's liberal democracy," the antagonism "has assumed a new form": "It is no longer capitalists versus proletariats, but those who are inside the system versus those who aren't."

89 Žižek, *Tarrying with the Negative*, 220.

90 Žižek, *Enjoy Your Symptom*, 123.

91 On the "monstrous nature of the commodity," see Thomas Keenan, "The Point Is to (Ex) Change It," in *Fetishism as Cultural Discourse*, ed. Emily Apter and William Pietz

(Ithaca, 1993), 152–85, esp. 152–61. See also Brennan's gloss of *Capital*: "The transformation of labour-power into labour is none the less, and oddly, a transformation from something immaterial to something material" (*History After Lacan*, 203). Accordingly, to think surplus-value is to think this "something."

92 Žižek, *For They Know Not What They Do*, 271, 272.

93 Ibid., 273. For an especially illuminating example of Žižek's understanding of the Bosnian war, see "Taking Sides," 210–17.

94 Slavoj Žižek, "Beyond Discourse-Analysis" (1987), appendix to Ernesto Laclau, *New Reflections on the Revolution of Our Time* (London, 1990), 249–60; quotation from 259. See also "In His Bold Gaze My Ruin Is Writ Large," in *Everything You Always Wanted to Know about Lacan (But Were Afraid to Ask Hitchcock)*, ed. Slavoj Žižek (London, 1992), 211–72, esp. 252–55, as well as 262–63, where he mobilizes the moment of *die Versagung* in his reading of *The Silence of the Lambs*: " 'Eat your being-there!' " For Žižek's reading of the Kantian distinction between "fanaticism" (*Schwärmerei*) and "enthusiasm" proper, see *Sublime Object of Ideology*, 204.

95 Žižek, *Sublime Object of Ideology*, 230. Elsewhere (*Enjoy Your Symptom*, 176), Žižek observes that "what Freud called *Todestrieb* [death drive] . . . ultimately equals *die Versagung*"; see also *Indivisible Remainder*, 92–95 and 115–22.

96 Žižek, *Looking Awry*, 142. Elsewhere, Žižek comments, "When you want to actualize your non-alienated project and you are confronted with some limit, disalienation does not consist in annihilating the limit, but in seeing how this limit is the positive condition of your very activity" (Osborne, "Lacan in Slovenia," 25).

97 Žižek, *Tarrying with the Negative*, 211. See also his observations on the Slovene punk band Laibach, whose fundamental cry was "We want more alienation" (Osborne, "Lacan in Slovenia," 24).

98 "Dialectical punctuation" is an allusion to Lacan's theory and practice of the short session (*séance scandée*); see Jacques Lacan, "The Function and Field of Speech and Language" (1953), in *Ecrits: A Selection*, trans. Alan Sheridan (New York and London, 1977 [1966]), 30–113, esp. 95.

99 Cf. Žižek's comments on his relations with the Slovenia Green Party, "which threw [him] out for not being enough of a Marxist" (Osborne, "Lacan in Slovenia," 29).

100 With respect to the question of the transhistorical, Victor Wolfenstein has argued—convincingly, I believe—that transhistorical "theories of human nature" such as Žižek's "function as defenses against the unremitting historicity of human existence," in *Psychoanalytic-Marxism: Groundwork* (New York, 1993), 164. Moreover, philosophies of transhistoricization—again, such as Žižek's—constitute not only a "resistance to or defense against the analysis of desire," but, most importantly (given the geopolitical conditions of possibility of Žižek's work), a "defense against political despair" (ibid.). This last defense is most obvious, it seems to me, in Žižek's recourse to the concept of *die Versagung*.

Notes on Contributors

ELIZABETH JANE BELLAMY is Associate Professor of English at the University of New Hampshire. She is the author of *Translations of Power: Narcissism and the Unconscious in Epic History* (1992) and *Affective Genealogies: Psychoanalysis, Postmodernism, and the "Jewish Question" After Auschwitz* (1997).

TERESA BRENNAN, Schmidt Distinguished Professor of Philosophy and Sociology at Florida Atlantic University, is the author of *History After Lacan* (1993) and the coeditor (with Martin Jay) of *Vision in Context: Historical and Contemporary Perspectives on Sight* (1996). *The Transmission of Affect* is forthcoming this year.

ROSARIA CHAMPAGNE is Associate Professor of English and Women's Studies at Syracuse University. A political activist in Syracuse, she is the author of *The Politics of Survivorship: Incest, Women's Literature, and Feminist Theory* (1996), as well as essays on queer theory, the religious right, and psychoanalysis. Her current projects include a book on humanities citizenship and civic pedagogy.

STATHIS GOURGOURIS, Assistant Professor of Comparative Literature at Princeton, is the author of *Dream Nation: Enlightenment, Colonization, and the Institution of Modern Greece* (1996), as well as articles on modernist literature, psychoanalysis, political theory, and music. *Literature as Theory (for an Antimythical Era)* is forthcoming from Stanford University Press.

CATHERINE LIU is Assistant Professor of Cultural Studies and Comparative Literature at the University of Minnesota–Twin Cities. She has recently completed a book, *Copying Machines: Taking Notes for the Automaton*.

KATHLEEN MCHUGH is Associate Professor of Comparative Literature at the University of California–Riverside. *American Domesticity's Invisible Style: Pedagogy, Hollywood Melodrama, Avant-Garde* is forthcoming from Oxford University Press, and she is currently writing a book on experimental autobiographies.

ROBERT MIKLITSCH, Associate Professor of English at Ohio University, is the author of *From Hegel to Madonna: Towards a General Economy of "Commodity Fetishism"* (1998).

ABDUL-KARIM MUSTAPHA, a member of the Latin American Subaltern Studies Group, is writing a novel on fascism and the Cold War in West Africa.

LAURENCE A. RICKELS is a Professor in the Art Studio, Film Studies, and German Studies departments, University of California–Santa Barbara, and a theorist/therapist affiliated with the Santa Barbara Westside Neighborhood Medical Clinic. The author of *The Case of California* (1991) and editor of *Acting Out in Groups* (forthcoming from University of Minnesota Press), his *Nazi Psychoanalysis* and *Vampire Lectures* are also coming soon (to a bookstore near you).

EUGENE VICTOR WOLFENSTEIN is Professor of Political Science, University of California–Los Angeles, and Member of the Faculty, Southern California Psychoanalytic Institute. The author of *The Victims of Democracy: Malcolm X and the Black Revolution* (1993 [1981]) and *Psychoanalytic-Marxism: Groundwork* (1993), he is currently writing a book on Nietzsche, psychoanalysis, and gender.

SLAVOJ ŽIŽEK is Senior Researcher at the Institute for Social Sciences, University of Ljubljana, Slovenia. Among his many works on Lacanian psychoanalysis and the critique of ideology are, most recently, *The Indivisible Remainder: An Essay on Schelling and Related Matters* (1996), *The Plague of Fantasies* (1997), and *Cogito and the Unconscious* (1998).